Spiritual Growth Through the Gospel

Until He Comes

Exploring The Call and Means to Perseverance
in Faith and Fidelity
in Matthew's Gospel

Fr. David M. Knight

Cover design by Dottie Petrilak

copyright ® 2001 by David M. Knight
All rights reserved. First American edition 2001
ISBN 0-942971-28-0

His Way Communications
1310 Dellwood Ave   Memphis, Tennessee, 38127
901 357 6662   www.hisway.com

DEDICATION

This book was officially finished on October 1, 2001, the feast of Saint Thérèse of Lisieux, popularly known as "the Little Flower." I had always thought of her as a sweet, pious nun, spoiled by God and by her parents, for whom religion was a path of light strewn with roses and leading to a heaven full of stars. I pictured her as being always "turned on" by the things of God.

How wrong I was!

As I finished this book I was re-reading her autobiography and realizing that, although I had read it many years before, I was really reading it for the first time. Thérèse may have grown up as God's "little flower," in a garden of spiritual delights cultivated by the deep faith and devotion of her family. But as she climbed up the mountain of God, the meadows and flowers gave way to rocks and crags, and she entered into the numbing obscurity of the "dark night of the soul." As she describes it to the prioress who had commanded her to continue writing her autobiography:

> My Beloved Mother, it might seem to you that I am exaggerating my trial. And as a matter of fact, if you judge by the feelings I express in the little bits of verse I composed this year, I must seem to you to be a soul filled with consolations — one for whom the veil of faith is almost torn apart. The truth is, it is no longer a veil for me; it is a wall that reaches to the heavens and blocks out the sky and the stars. When I sing of the blessedness of Heaven, the eternal possession of God, I feel no joy at all in it, because I am only singing about what I WANT TO BELIEVE. Sometimes, it is true, a tiny ray of sunshine comes down to enlighten my darkness. Then the trial ceases for *a moment*. But afterwards, the memory of that ray of light, instead of giving me joy, makes my darkness even more impenetrable....
>
> ....This trial took away everything that might have given me any natural satisfaction in the desire that I had for Heaven.

But she just kept climbing — feeling all the while, of

course, that she wasn't getting anywhere. She did what the saints and spiritual masters down the ages have told us we should do when we "feel nothing":

Ah! May Jesus forgive me if I have offended him, but he knows very well that even though I am without the enjoyment of the Faith, I try at least to keep doing the works of faith. I think I have made more acts of faith in the past year than throughout my whole life. (For references, see chapter three, note seven below).

This is the key to perseverance: the best way to persevere is to just keep persevering. John of the Cross said, "Where you don't find love, put love and you will find it." A Jesuit novice master, Fr. Anthony Mangiaracina, said, "If you don't have faith, act as if you did and you will have it."

I hope little *big* Thérèse will accept it if I dedicate this book to her and to all who are having to do just that.

Acknowledgements

The Scripture quotations are from the New Revised Standard Version Bible, © 1989 by the Division of Christian Education of the National Council of Churches of Christ in the U.S.A. Used by permission. All rights reserved.

TABLE OF CONTENTS

Chapter One
The Unlikely Lord
"Son of David" — Read Matthew 21:1-11

Jesus is approaching Jerusalem. It has been a long hike
from Caesarea Philippi, but now Jesus and his disciples are
only about two miles from the city. They have left Jericho
behind and are climbing Mount Olivet toward Bethphage,
close to its summit, after passing through Bethany, a village
on its eastern slopes. Olivet was also called the "Mount of
Olives," and further down, on the western slope, facing Jerusalem, there is an olive grove and a garden named Geth-
semane, which means "olive press." Popular belief associated Mount Olivet with the Day of the Lord and the coming
of the Anointed One. It was "the hill of oil, of anointing"
— an appropriate starting point for what Jesus is about to
do.

On the peak of this mountain Jesus prepares for the high
point of his public self-revelation — his triumphal entry
into Jerusalem. Just a few days from now, at the bottom of
this same mountain, he will undergo his "agony in the garden," revealing himself to a few chosen disciples at the
lowest point of his earthly experience, crushed in anguish
and terror at the prospect of the fate that awaits him,
sweating blood and begging the Father for relief. With this
contrast of triumph and terror the final revelation of Jesus
as Lord begins.

Jesus sends two of his disciples into the village of Bethphage with instructions to untie and bring to him a donkey
and her colt which they will find there. "If anyone says
anything to you," he tells them, "just say that the Lord has
need of them and he will send them right away."

The disciples do as Jesus ordered. They bring the ass and
the colt and lay their cloaks over them, and Jesus mounts.
Then some of the crowd spread their cloaks in front of him
and others cut branches from the trees and spread them on

the road. Those marching in front of him and behind him start crying out, "Hosanna to the Son of David; blessed is he who comes in the name of the Lord; hosanna in the highest."

"Son of David" (Matthew 21:1-11)

This is a climactic moment in Matthew's Gospel. From beginning to end he has presented Jesus as the promised "Son of David," the Anointed One who fulfills all the prophecies and promises made about the Messiah. He has used the title "Son of David," which he gives to Jesus only three times in direct address (Mt. 9:27; 15:22; 20:30), to mark the major transitions in his Gospel from one theme to another. And now this title is being shouted in acclamation by the crowd — "Hosanna to the Son of David" — as Jesus enters Jerusalem to begin the final act in the drama of his redemption of the world.

The key to understanding this whole scene is to recognize that Jesus is indeed the promised "Son of David," but in a way very different from what he was expected to be. He is entering Jerusalem in triumph, but as a prelude to being handed over to his enemies. He is entering the "city of David" as the promised successor to King David, but the only throne he will mount there is the cross. He is entering acclaimed as a conquering hero, but he will refuse to conquer anyone except through free conversion of heart. He enters as the champion of peace and justice, but there will be no universal peace or justice for centuries to come, because Jesus will not use force to impose them. He will use no weapons except the witness of truth and love. He is entering Jerusalem to establish the Reign of God, but it will be a reign marked by powerlessness and poverty of human resources until the end of time.

As might be expected, given the means he intends to use, the Kingdom Jesus enters Jerusalem to inaugurate will be a long time coming! It will not be fully established, in fact, until Jesus comes in glory at the end of the world. All those who believe in him, therefore, as Messiah, Lord and King will have to *persevere in faith and fidelity*, believing in his kingship and working to establish it until he comes again. This is the challenge in the chapters that follow.

Review and preview: Can you accept Jesus?

In the first nine chapters of his Gospel Matthew invites us to accept Jesus as the promised Messiah and Savior of the world. To really accept him as Savior — and only Savior — of the world means we have come to realize with a "life-giving despair" of all other saviors that no area or activity of our lives can ultimately be "saved" from veering off into destructiveness or distortion, mediocrity or meaningless-ness unless in some way Jesus is involved in it. When we also believe that he *can save* whatever we involve him in — our family and social life, business and politics — and determine to give him an active role in everything we do, we have made the basic act of faith in Jesus as *Savior* which makes us *Christians*.

But in these first nine chapters Matthew invites us to more: he calls us to convert to being, not only Christians but *disciples*; that is, *students* of the mind and heart of Jesus, be-lievers whose lives are characterized by reflection on his teaching and example. We have not accepted Jesus as the Savior he really is until we have also accepted him as our own mentor and Teacher of life.

Can you accept the Church?

Beginning with chapter ten, Matthew raises the ante; he challenges us to accept Jesus in the *Church*. This is a more difficult challenge, because in the Church we have to ac-cept Jesus in the flesh; that is, with the limitations that any particular, concrete, physical way of being necessarily en-tails. This is a consequence of the Incarnation itself: the infinite perfection of God cannot take physical form without choosing to leave something out. God cannot take flesh in one and the same body, for example, as both man and woman, as a retarded child and as a genius, as a member of every race and nationality simultaneously. The Gentiles who met Jesus in Galilee had to accept God as a Jew. The rich had to accept him as poor. The sick had to accept him as healthy. And we who meet him in his Church today must accept him in whatever body we find him, with all its particularities and limitations.

This is made more difficult by the fact that the Church, which is the actual body of Christ on earth, is a sinful body. In the Church the risen Jesus lives but is still growing "to full stature" (see Eph. 4:13). In the Church, which is sanctified by his presence, Jesus nevertheless comes to us marked by the woundedness of his incompletely purified members. The Jesus people met in Galilee was at least free of all sin. But the Jesus we meet today in the Church asks us to accept him in his ugliness as well as in his beauty. This is a much more difficult challenge to faith and love.

It is an even more difficult challenge to accept to *be Church*; that is, to take on in an active way our baptismal commitment to continue the mission of Jesus as *Prophet, Priest* and *King*. These three ministries constitute the "job description" of a Christian. At Baptism we were solemnly and explicitly consecrated to perform them. Like the prophets, priests and kings of Old Testament times, we were anointed on the head with chrism "as Christ was anointed Priest, Prophet and King" and exhorted to "live always as members of his body, sharing everlasting life" (Rite of Baptism for Children). To share Christ's life is to share his mission. And so, when Matthew, in chapter ten, starts challenging us to accept Christ in his Church, he begins with the "mission discourse," which describes how the disciples (and therefore we as his body on earth) are to continue to carry out the mission of Jesus. Chapter ten teaches us to be Christ's embodied presence in the world, sent to "live always as members of his body," sharing in everlasting life ourselves and sharing his life with others. We make him present everywhere, in "all the cities and villages," teaching, proclaiming the good news, and healing the woundedness of the world (see Mt. 4:23 and 9:35).

Can you accept the cross?

But Matthew takes us farther. Beginning with chapter sixteen, he shows us Jesus revealing to his disciples the doctrine of the *cross*. All who follow him must be willing to *die to themselves* and to everything this world has to offer, in order to live entirely for God and other people in love. They must unite themselves to Jesus, Victim and Priest, and accept to be offered as "living sacrifices" in Christ for the redemption of the world (see Rom. 12:1-2).

This is a commitment to *ministry*; that is, to fulfilling our baptismal consecration as *priests* by dedicating ourselves to the work of mediating the life of God to others. We do this by *giving expression* to the grace that is within us. We let our invisible faith, hope and love take flesh, become visible, in physical, human actions. Our bodies become the medium through which the divine light and love and life of God are communicated to others.

This is also a commitment to "take up the cross;" that is, to *endure evil with love* as Jesus did; to accept whatever suffering and injustice the sin of the world lays on our shoulders and to "love back." This is the call to renounce power and violence in order to unite ourselves with Jesus, "Lamb of God," who takes away the sins of the world by enduring them and offering love in return. To accept this call is to accept the new commandment, the new morality, the new way of life taught by Jesus the Way, the Truth and the Life:

"I give you a new commandment.... that you love one another *as I have loved you*" (John 13:34; 15:12).

Can you accept to wait?

And now, beginning with chapter twenty-one, Matthew offers us his fourth and final challenge: "Can you *persevere in faith and fidelity until Jesus comes again*?" Can you persevere in the faith you felt when, because you thought the Kingdom had come, you joined the jubilation of the crowd and marched into Jerusalem with Jesus, shouting "Hosanna to the Son of David!"? Can you continue to believe in him as Messiah and King when, two thousand years later, the crowds are apathetic, Jesus isn't visible, and the world is still a mess? When Christianity appears helpless and defeated, can you still proclaim with conviction, "Jesus is Lord!"

In other words, are we willing to wait? In the Communion Rite of every Eucharistic celebration we who believe Jesus has come as Savior still describe ourselves as "waiting in joyful hope for the coming of our Savior Jesus Christ." Jesus is the "once and future king," *rex olim, rexque futurus*, not as the fabled King Arthur was, about whom this phrase was coined, but as the King who was, who is, and who will be; who died and was glorified, and is now "seated at the right hand of the Father." From there he "will come again in glory to judge the living and the dead."

The theme of waiting for Christ to come again in glory is a major theme in Christian spirituality. It is a challenge, not just to keep believing in his victory, but to *express* our belief and our unshakable hope by continuing to work, as *stewards of his kingship*, for the *transformation of society*, for the establishment of his reign over every area and activity of human life until he comes again in triumph.

As Matthew enters into the final phase of his Gospel, his theme is encouragement: he exhorts us to persevere in faith, laboring as faithful stewards to establish the reign of God on earth until Jesus comes again. But this perseverance is made difficult by the fact that at any given moment of history Jesus seems to be winning by losing!

For those who have eyes to see, however, the Gospels reveal a pattern of victory through defeat, of Christ triumphing, not only through vulnerability and powerlessness, but through the very events which seem to defeat him. When Herod tries to kill Jesus at his birth, it brings about the fulfillment of the prophecy, "Out of Egypt I have called my son" (see Mt. 2:15). And Jesus' return from exile at the end of that story is a preview of his return from the grave at the Resurrection and of his coming in triumph at the end of time. Matthew is showing that God repeatedly realizes his own plans through the very efforts of his enemies to defeat them.

This is the pattern which reaches its climax on Calvary, when Jesus triumphs in the act of being defeated by his enemies. And it is the recurring history of the Church, continually rising renewed and purified out of the ashes of apathy and corruption. Because discouragement is the great temptation of those who give themselves to the work of God, we need to take an explicit, conscious stance toward this pattern of victory through defeat. This is what Matthew is calling us to do in this final, "eschatological" portion of his Gospel. [1]

The paradox of Jesus' entry into Jerusalem

When Jesus enters Jerusalem, this is the triumph of a king taking possession of his kingdom without any display of power or force. He enters into the City of David as the prophet foretold he would: "Tell the daughter of Zion, 'Look, your king is coming to you, humble, and mounted on a donkey, and on a colt, the foal of a donkey.'" Jesus is actually entering Jerusalem to be defeated and to die. But his enemies' victory over him is the very thing that will bring about the defeat of all evil in the triumph of the cross and Resurrection.

Two entries, one theme

There is a parallel to this story in the account of Jesus'
birth. In both events Jesus is entering a city to begin something. He enters Bethlehem in the womb of his mother to be
born; he enters Jerusalem surrounded by the crowd to be
crucified and to rise again, "the firstborn from the dead"
(Col. 1:15-18; Rom. 8:29; Heb. 1:6, 12:23; Rev. 1:15). In
both cases he enters in unassuming humility and powerlessness.

In both stories he is acclaimed and recognized, but not by
the ruling class or authorities. When Jesus enters Jerusalem
he is acclaimed by the crowd and recognized by little children. At his birth he is announced by a star and recognized
by foreigners: the Magi. In Luke's account of his birth he is
announced by angels and acknowledged by Israel's outcast
class: the shepherds. In none of these stories did the
authorities of the people recognize or accept him.

In Luke's Gospel, when Jesus was born in Bethlehem the
angels sang "peace" and "glory in the highest heaven."
When he enters Jerusalem the crowd echoes their song,
shouting "Blessed is the king who comes in the name of the
Lord! Peace in heaven, and glory in the highest heaven!"
(see Luke 2:14 and 19:38). In Matthew's Gospel both ar-
rivals of Jesus throw people into turmoil: King Herod "and
all Jerusalem with him" when the Magi announced his
birth; and now "the whole city" is in turmoil when Jesus
enters Jerusalem to die. [2]

There is another parallel: not in the Gospels, but created by
Christian devotion. In the Gospels Jesus is only placed on a
donkey one time: when he enters Jerusalem as King. But
Christian imagination places him on a donkey once before
this: when he enters Bethlehem in his mother's womb to be
born as Savior. This invites us to take a second look at the
donkey. [3]

The donkey and "Son of David"

In Matthew's scene of Christ's triumphal entry into Jerusalem the donkey is a key player. First of all, the donkey shows that Jesus is entering Jerusalem as the promised "Son of David." In Matthew's account Jesus claims the donkey with that *authority* which is associated with the title "Son of David." When he sends his disciples to get the donkey and the colt he tell them, "If anyone says anything to you, just say this, 'The Lord (*Kyrios*) needs them,' And he will send them immediately." But it is an authority which appeals only to the freedom and good will of those to whom he speaks; it is not an authority backed up by threat of force. This man who is about to enter Jerusalem surrounded by symbols of kingship — the people spreading cloaks and branches before him — is dependent on the good will of a villager for a donkey to ride on!

The title *Kyrios* can be translated as "Master," "owner" or "Lord" and Matthew may be suggesting that in this case it means all three. In his Gospel Jesus is frequently called *Kyrios* in the sense of "Master" or just "Sir." But in the claiming of the donkey Matthew may be making a parallel with David's instructions about the anointing of his son Solomon as king (see 1 Kings 1:32- 45). In that story it is stressed three times that Solomon was mounted on David's "own mule." Matthew may be making the point that Jesus was the "owner" of the donkey in the sense that as the promised "Son of David" he had right to claim David's "own mule," and this donkey was designated to play that part in his triumphal procession.

Matthew might also be suggesting that it is the "Lord" in the sense of Yahweh, God the Father, who is designating the donkey for Jesus, as David did for Solomon, precisely to make the point that Jesus is his chosen one, the rightful heir to the Kingdom of God. Or Jesus may be calling himself "Lord" in a sense to be revealed only after his resurrection.[4]

A peaceful David

There was another reason for the donkey. Kings and con-
querors entered cities on horses or in chariots. The Lord
promised the people through Jeremiah: "If you obey me
wholeheartedly... then, through the gates of this city, kings
who sit upon the throne of David will continue to enter,
riding in their chariots or upon their horses... This city will
remain inhabited forever" (see Jeremiah 17:24-25).

But Matthew wants to show that Jesus entered Jerusalem as
a king very different from the kind the people expected. He
came, not on a horse, but on a donkey, which was the
mount of a prince who entered a town in peace: "This took
place to fulfill what had been spoken through the prophet,
saying, 'Tell the daughter of Zion, Look, your king is coming to you, humble and mounted on a donkey, and on a
colt, the foal of a donkey.'"

To show that this was the fulfillment of God's prophecy
Matthew combines two texts here: Isaiah 62:11: "Say to
daughter Zion..."; and Zechariah 9:9: "Lo, your king comes
to you; triumphant and victorious is he, humble and riding
on a donkey, on a colt, the foal of a donkey."

This explains why Matthew alone mentions the colt: it is
included in the text he adds from Zechariah. Zechariah's
text puts the king among the "lowly" or "meek," who are
the same class of people as the *anawim*, the "poor in spirit"
of the first Beatitude. They are the ones who are powerless
and non-aggressive, and to them the Beatitude promises
that "they will possess the eschatological land of Israel, re-
stored by the saving deeds of God." The parallel with Jesus
is obvious. He enters Jerusalem as king only to accept
death like a "lamb led to the slaughter." And this is how he
comes into possession of his Kingdom. But his reign on
earth will continue to appear as powerlessness and defeat
until the eschatological or "end" times when his victory
over sin and its consequences will be complete. The only
kingdom Jesus enters Jerusalem to inaugurate is the King-

dom promised to the powerless and poor in spirit.[5]

A world-shaking event

Matthew tells us that when Jesus enters Jerusalem, "the whole city was in turmoil" (or in a more literal translation, "shaken") asking, 'Who is this?'" He is reminding us of the day when Joab asked, "Why is the city in an uproar?" because Solomon, the first "son of David," had entered Gihon and the people were shouting with joy "so that the earth quaked at their noise."

The verb Matthew uses here for "shaken" is *seio*, from which our word "seismology" comes. He is saying that Jesus' entry caused something like an emotional earthquake. But he is saying more than this. "For Matthew, the whole Christ-event is earthshaking. He presents it under the metaphor of an earthquake, into which we must all follow Jesus... When Matthew says that Jerusalem was shaken as if by an earthquake as Jesus entered the city, he is proclaiming that 'the age to come' has arrived! Jesus is coming to assert his messianic authority in the temple. Thus the prophecy of Haggai is fulfilled, 'I will fill this house with glory.'"[6]

Matthew uses the same verb two other times in his Gospel: first, when Jesus dies and the earth quakes (Mt. 27:51); and secondly when he rises and there is "a great earthquake" and the guards "quake" [same verb] and fall down like dead men (see Mt. 28:2-4).

Clearly Matthew is giving us the message that Jesus' entry into Jerusalem was a world-shaking event. But on the surface and visibly, what was it? It was not even recorded as history at that time except in the Christian Scriptures. Jesus was a small-town itinerant Jewish preacher and healer who rode a donkey into a provincial city of the Roman Empire surrounded by a tiny mob of enthusiasts, most of whom lost faith in him a few days later. He came into an occupied city

without money, military power or other human means of
establishing his kingship. And he was arrested, summarily
tried and executed. End of story — or so it appeared to everyone at that time. And so it continued to appear for years
to come, except to those who accepted to interpret the
events through the eyes of faith.

Appearances deceive

And so it is today. What clear and visible signs do we see
that Jesus is, in fact, the promised "Son of David" for us?
As Son of David or Messiah, Jesus was the "Anointed
One" sent to bring all of God's promises to fulfillment. Do
we see those promises fulfilled? Is there peace on earth? Is
there justice? Is there unity between the nations and na-
tionalities of the world? Has the lion lain down with the
lamb? Are all nations streaming into the Church, saying,
"Come, let us climb the Lord's mountain, to the house of
the God of Jacob, that he may instruct us in his ways, and
we may walk in his paths" (see Isaiah 2:3)?

On the individual level, do all the people on earth wake up
every morning bent on pursuing that fulfillment which
comes from growing in knowledge and love of God as the
highest value on earth? Do people really relate to Jesus as
Savior, looking first and foremost to deep, personal, interactive relationship with him in everything they do as the
only means to the solution of the world's problems? How
many real Christian *disciples* are there — that is, people
who live lives *characterized* by reflection on the message
of Jesus? Are his teachings the source to which everyone
automatically turns for guidance in family and social life, in
business and politics? How many give themselves to living
lives of prophetic *witness*, asking in every decision of their
lives, not just whether this action is right or wrong, but how
it expresses and embodies the ideals, the attitudes and values Jesus taught? Wherever Christians are, do they minister
to those around them as a "royal priesthood" (1Peter 2:9), a

community of priests giving expression to their faith and to their love in a way that is life-giving for all? And how effectively are believers *transforming society* — not only family and social life, but business and politics —as faithful stewards of Christ's kingship? How many are taking personal and communal responsibility as Christians for establishing the reign of God on earth: that Kingdom in which Jesus brings "everything in heaven and on earth together into unity under his headship" (Eph. 1:9-10; Col. 1:13-27)? Do we see evidence that Jesus is winning?

On the surface, the entry of Jesus into Jerusalem as king was ridiculous. Imagine it taking place in Los Angeles or New York! How much impact would it have had? The military governor, if anyone even bothered to report it to him, didn't see enough threat in this mob of fanatics proclaiming a prophet on a donkey as king of Israel even to send a police patrol to keep an eye on it. So much for appearances!

Jesus' triumphal entry into Jerusalem really was ridiculous if we understand "kingship" to mean what it normally means on earth. In spite of the — literally — deadly seriousness of what he was doing, Jesus must have been smiling. Whether the people understood it yet or not, he was laying to rest forever their dream of a kingdom based on worldly power and prestige.

A challenge to faith: Is Jesus "Son of David"?

Seen with the benefit of hindsight, Jesus' triumphal entry into Jerusalem was then and still is now a challenge to faith. The people who marched with him rejoicing saw his entry as the start of his final campaign to take over the government of Israel. They thought this was the beginning of a series of steps which would put him, first at the head of an army to cast out the occupying Romans, and then on the throne. After that would come the real triumph, his definitive entry into Jerusalem as conquering hero and king.

What we know now is that this entry was it. This was the only triumphal entry into his kingship that Jesus would make upon earth, the only public triumph he would have. The next step for Jesus would be arrest, crucifixion and death. And when he rose from the dead, it would not be to establish his reign in Jerusalem as an earthly king. Contrary to all expectations — and it took the Apostles and the Church decades to revise their expectations — the Kingdom Jesus aimed at was a reign over human hearts which would be brought about only by free and loving conversion, not by power and force. His Kingdom would be established in the measure that believing human beings, individually and in community, would surrender their minds to his truth, their hearts to his love, and their actions to the inspirations of his Spirit dwelling within them.

Through Jesus' followers — but only in the measure that they can do it lovingly and without violence — all the structures, institutions and customs of human society will gradually be reformed. The goal of Jesus' mission will be accomplished — everything in heaven and on earth will be "brought together into unity under his headship" (see Eph. 1:10) — but it will only be accomplished by divine power working through the human weakness of the members of his Body on earth: through their efforts, their witness, and their deaths in continuation of his. The real triumphs of his campaign, continued in his Church, will be triumphs of peace and gentleness, of forgiveness, patient endurance and love. Anyone who looks for a triumph which relies on any power other than that which Jesus expressed by riding a donkey into Jerusalem to die will be failing in understanding and in faith.

Jesus' "triumphal" entry into Jerusalem says it all: he entered in poverty, powerlessness and peace. Can we accept this as setting the tone for every authentic celebration of Christ's kingship on earth until he comes again?

And in the light of this, can we accept Jesus as the rightful

"Son of David," the one God anointed and sent into this world to fulfill all God's promises to the human race? Can we accept him in all his disappointing, apparent powerlessness? Or shall we "look for another" (see Mt. 11:3)?

CHAPTER ONE:
THE UNLIKELY LORD
"Son of David" — *Matthew 21:1-11*
Summary

Jesus entered Jerusalem in triumph, but as a prelude to being handed over to his enemies. He entered to establish the Reign of God, but it will be a reign marked by powerlessness and poverty of human resources until the end of time.

The Kingdom Jesus entered Jerusalem to inaugurate will not be fully established until Jesus comes in glory at the end of the world. All those who believe in him, therefore, will have to *persevere in faith and fidelity*, believing in his kingship and working, as *stewards of his kingship*, to establish his reign over every area and activity of human life until he comes again.

This perseverance is made difficult by the fact that at any given moment of history Jesus seems to be losing. However, the Gospels reveal a pattern of victory through defeat, of Christ triumphing through the very events which seem to defeat him.

Because *discouragement* is the great temptation of those who give themselves to the work of God, we need to take an explicit, conscious stance toward this pattern of victory through defeat. This is what Matthew is calling us to do in this final, "eschatological" portion of his Gospel.

The goal of Jesus' mission will only be accomplished by divine power working through the human weakness of the members of his Body on earth.. Anyone who looks for a triumph which relies on any power other than that which Jesus expressed by riding a donkey into Jerusalem to die — the power of peace and gentleness, of patient endurance and love — will be failing in understanding and in faith.

The response to which Matthew calls us in this final, "eschatological" part of his Gospel is to persevere in the belief that Jesus is the "Son of David," sent to bring all of God's promises to fulfillment, and to keep laboring to establish the reign of God on earth, even when everything around us seems to say that Jesus has failed and is failing. This is what it means to be "faithful stewards" of his kingship.

Have you understood?

What Gospel stories can you remember that show God turning the apparent success of Jesus' enemies into success for him?

How does Jesus appear to be losing today? In what ways? In what areas of life (business, politics, social life, family)?

What signs of power did Jesus show in his "triumphal" entry into Jerusalem? What made him appear weak or powerless?

What signs or evidence do we see today that tell us Jesus is the promised "Son of David," Savior, Messiah and King? What are the signs that his reign is being established in individual human hearts?

What does the "reign of God" really consist in?

What is the only authentic way to bring about God's reign on earth? What way is inauthentic?

What is the challenge of this chapter? To our faith? To our hope? To our love?

Making it your own

What are the key thoughts in this chapter? (Jot them down and give the page number where each is found).

What questions do I have about this chapter? (Bring them up in discussion or ask someone who should know the answers).

What struck me the most in this chapter? After reading this chapter, what do I understand better than I did before? What do I appreciate more?

What do I think is the point of the whole chapter? What response does Matthew want to evoke from those who read or hear this part of his Gospel?

What can I use as a visible reminder (a symbol) to keep me aware of the challenge of this chapter? Where will I put it?

Questions for prayer

Do I really believe Christ wants to reign over business and politics, social life, family life? What does this mean?

If he did reign in these areas, what would I see that would be different?

What have I done to establish his reign where I work, where I live, recreate?

What could I do in these areas?

What discourages me the most from working to change things in these areas?

What encourages me the most?

How can I apply to my life what I have come to see by reflecting on this chapter? What concrete action do I choose to perform to express my belief in what I have seen?

FOOTNOTES

[1] The word "eschatological" refers to the "end times" — Christ's final victory and his coming in glory, the fulfillment of all God's promises and plans. The last part of Matthew's Gospel (chapters 21-28) urges us to wait for this, persevering in faith and fidelity until Christ comes again.

[2] See Mt. 2:3 and 21:10 and Paul Hinnebusch, O.P., *St. Matthew's Earthquake*, Servant Books, 1980, chapter five: "The Earthquake at the Magi's Coming."

[3] The donkey at the manger in Bethlehem is not just an imaginative decoration. Fr. Raymond Brown quotes an opinion which "relates the symbolism of the Lucan manger to God's complaint in the LXX [Septuagint version] of Isaiah 1:3: 'The ox knows its owner; and the donkey knows the manger [*phatne*] of its lord; but Israel has not known me; my people has not understood me.'" *The Birth of the Messiah*, Doubleday, 1977, on Luke 2:6-7, p. 419. See also p. 399, note 7 to his commentary on Luke 2:5-7.

[4] See the *Jerome Biblical Commentary*, (Prentice-Hall, 1990) on this passage. Fr. John McKenzie says that this is the only time in the Synoptic Gospels when Jesus is called *Kyrios* in the sense that it has here, which is "the sense in which it is used of Jesus in the Pauline epistles

[where] this title was understood to belong to Jesus after His resurrection."

⁵ See John McKenzie in *The Jerome Biblical Commentary* on Mt. 21:1-9 and 5:3-12. See also McKenzie's commentary on 5:38-42, where he explains what this ideal of meekness means when lived out in practical life. According to McKenzie, our Lord's development of His command, "Do not resist evil people" calls us to *endure with love*: 1. *physical violence* without retaliating ("turn the other cheek"); 2. *lawsuits* without entering into contention ("give your cloak as well"); 3. *forced labor* or service by doing more than required ("go two miles"); and *requests for gifts or loans* without refusal ("give to whoever..."). McKenzie is aware of how radical his interpretation is, but he argues that it is not an interpretation; just the clear and obvious meaning of Jesus' words. He says, "It is difficult to see how the principle of non-resistance and yielding could be more clearly stated. The rationalizations of the words of Jesus do not show that his words are impractical or exaggerated, but simply that the Christian world has never been ready and is not ready now to live according to this ethic. The passage is echoed in Romans 12:17-21."

⁶ See 1Kings 1:32-45 and Hinnebusch, *op. cit.*, pp. 1-3. The text from Haggai is: "I will shake the heavens and the earth and the sea and the dry land; and I will shake all the nations, so that the treasure of all nations shall come, and I will fill this house with splendor, says the LORD of hosts" (Haggai 2:6-7).

Chapter Two
"In joyful hope…"
Jesus as Savior — Read Matthew 21:9- 14

In the Communion Rite of the Eucharistic celebration, we say that we are "waiting in joyful hope for the coming of our Savior, Jesus Christ" (literally "awaiting the blessed hope and coming of…").

The problem is, our Savior has already come. What more are we waiting for? Is it the same thing his people were waiting for?

When Jesus entered Jerusalem in triumph, Matthew tells us the people were shouting "Hosanna to the Son of David! Blessed is the one who comes in the name of the Lord! Hosanna…!" (Mt. 21:9).

The literal meaning of the word "hosanna" is, "Save, we pray." It was originally a cry for help in distress (see 2 Samuel 14:4). By using it, the people were acclaiming Jesus as the Messiah God had sent to save them.

It is true that this acclamation, in the minds of those who were shouting it, did not express a recognition of Jesus as the kind of Savior we now know him to be. As a matter of fact, the shouts of the crowd are a citation of Psalm 118:25-26, which seems to identify salvation with the good life on this earth!

> O Lord, grant salvation! O Lord, grant prosperity!
> Blessed is he who comes in the name of the Lord.

Most Jews understood "Messiah" (Anointed One) to mean nothing but the earthly king who would bring Israel to its destiny. We know now this is not the kind of savior Jesus came to be.[1]

But when Matthew recorded the acclamation of the crowd, he knew the kind of Savior Jesus really came to be, and he undoubtedly saw in their use of "Hosanna" God's affirmation of Jesus as the Savior the angel told Joseph he would be:

> Joseph, son of David, do not be afraid to take Mary as your wife,
> for the child conceived in her is from the Holy Spirit. She will bear
> a son, and you are to name him Jesus, for he will save his people
> from their sins (Mt. 1:21).

And after Jesus drove the merchants out of the temple,
Matthew says that "the blind and the lame approached him
in the temple area, and he cured them." The sign of the
Savior is here (Mt. 21:14).

So what do we mean when we say we are "awaiting the
blessed hope and coming of our Savior, Jesus Christ"?
What do we expect of Jesus as Savior? Is it something he
has already done? Something he is still doing? Or is it
something that remains to be done?

The answer, of course, is "all of the above." Jesus saved the
world, essentially, by becoming flesh, dying on the cross
and rising. But he came to this moment through a whole
lifetime of human actions and responses. And he began the
specific mission of establishing the kingdom by joining
other human beings to himself and engaging with them in
human acts of ministry for several years. If Jesus had just
come down from heaven, died on Calvary and risen, then
our redemption would not have been a fully human process.
It would have been a single act of God made flesh in Jesus,
offering himself once and for all on the cross, without prelude or follow-up, and going back up to heaven, "mission
accomplished." That is not the way it was.

"Jesus"— "God saves" (Matthew 21:9, 14)

Matthew focuses on four activities of Jesus to describe his
saving ministry:
- *being present* (touring the towns and villages),
- *teaching*,
- *proclaiming* the good news, and
- *healing* (see Mt. 4:23 and 9:35).

Jesus seems to have valued proclaiming and teaching over healing (see Mt. 8:18; Mark 1:37-38). Still, in terms of sign value he appears most obviously as Savior in his acts of healing the sick and casting out demons (see Mt. 8:1-17). Matthew explicitly makes a connection between Jesus' healing miracles and his sacrificial death, which healed the human race at its core (see 8:16-17; see also 1Peter 2:24 and Isaiah 53:5). And when Jesus sends his disciples out as Church, it is in virtue of their identification with him through the mystery of his death and resurrection that he can give them the power to do what he does (see "authority" in Mt. 10:1, 20; 28:18).

The healing miracles worked on the body were signs of the healing Jesus came to bring to the soul: giving light to the spiritually blind, enabling the morally crippled to walk in the way of virtue, cleansing all flesh of the "leprosy" of sin, opening the ears of those deaf to the word and voice of God, restoring the life of grace to those spiritually dead through sin (compare with Mt. 11:4-5). That is why all of Jesus' healing miracles were rooted in his passion and death, through which he brought ultimate healing to the world. And it is the power of his death and resurrection that continues to work and show itself in the saving ministry of the Church, his risen body on earth.

When we proclaim that we are still "waiting in joyful hope for the coming of our Savior," this does not mean we believe that Jesus has come and gone and left us alone again. We are not abandoned, deprived of his saving presence on earth, just looking and longing for him to return. His salvation is not something we don't really begin to enjoy until we get to heaven. If it were, it would be hard to see how our hope can be "joyful" here on earth. It would be more like a teeth-gritting endurance, "mourning and weeping in this valley of tears" until we are delivered by death or the end of the world.

The truth is, we believe, not only that Jesus has come as

Savior, but that he is still present with us here on earth today, still saving us. But if he is still saving us today, we
have to ask, "From what?" If the crowd who welcomed Jesus to Jerusalem had known that two thousand years later
crime, poverty, violence, oppression, sickness and suffering
would still be rampant on earth, would they have been
singing "Hosanna!" with the same enthusiasm? With how
much enthusiasm do we sing it during Mass? We need to
come to terms with this.

Romans, chapters 7 and 8: saved in hope
(Scripture citations below are from Romans 7:15 to 8:39)

Jesus does not want people to suffer physical or emotional
pain, violence or oppression, injustice or poverty, indignity
or loneliness, failure or betrayal. But in a world where human beings are free, people are going to sin, and their sins
are going to affect the whole human environment. Then
others are going to suffer. God doesn't want this, but he
cannot keep it from happening without taking away human
freedom. And Jesus didn't come to do that.

There is more. When we say this is a "sinful world," we
don't just mean that people do things that cause pain to
other people; we mean that the sins people commit have an
effect, not only on themselves, but on what other people are
interiorly. Sins are human actions; they change the environment, and the environment provokes interior changes in
other humans. By transforming society, sins distort people's cultural perception of truth and values. They encourage bad attitudes, priorities and patterns of behavior to
evolve within peer groups, produce fears and artificial desires that constitute social pressure; in short, produce all of
those effects inside of us which we call "cultural conditioning."

When we feel the weight of the attitudes, values and priorities which have been programmed into us by our society,
we cry out with St. Paul:

For I do not do what I want, but I do the very thing I hate…. Who will rescue me from this body of death?

St. Paul's answer, of course, is "Jesus Christ our Lord!" He is the Savior. But he rescues us, not by taking all cultural conditioning out of our psychological make-up, but by uniting us to himself, sharing his Spirit with us, making us his own body. Now we are not just members of our society immersed in our culture. Now we are also "in Christ," and members of his body. "There is therefore now no condemnation for those who are *in Christ Jesus*." This, essentially, is what it means to be "saved." To be saved means to be freed from slavery to this world, its darkness and its sin, through union with Jesus Christ, by sharing in his life, in his mind and will and heart. We are freed in fact, though not immediately free in every act, because now we know we have other options in addition to the choices held out to us by our culture. Light has come into the world and it is available to us.

We owe no conformity to our culture: "we are debtors, not to the flesh, to live according to the flesh…" We don't "owe it" to our culture to live according to our programming. We have an alternative. Our cultural conditioning remains part of our human make-up because we are still physical members of the human race, in bodily contact with all the conditioning influences of our culture. But we are also a "new creation"(2Cor. 5:17). Because we are "in Christ" we are true sons and daughters of God in Jesus the Son: "For all who are led by the Spirit of God are children of God." The programming that is in us has not been totally replaced, but its power has been broken by the indwelling presence of the Holy Spirit, by the guiding light and empowering love within us which are of God himself. This is our salvation: Jesus "saves" us by sending us his Spirit, empowering us to live by the Spirit instead of by the "flesh" which is permeated by the attitudes and values of this world.[2]

An apparent contradiction

How do we experience this salvation? St. Paul makes two apparently contradictory statements in almost the same breath. On the one hand, he says that we

> *have received a spirit of adoption.* When we cry, 'Abba! Father!' it is that very Spirit bearing witness with our spirit that we are children of God....

On the other hand, he says that we, along with the rest of creation,

> groan inwardly *while we wait for adoption*, the redemption of our bodies.

Are we adopted or not? Are we redeemed or not?

St. Paul is saying that in each one of us salvation is not a completely accomplished fact. It is a fact, yes. It is real, yes. But it is not yet all that it should be, and we should not expect to experience ourselves as totally enlightened by the Spirit, totally surrendered to God in love, totally free from the desires and temptations which come from the world, the flesh and the devil.

Here again we see the theme of waiting, of persevering in faith and fidelity until the saving work of Jesus is complete:

> For in hope we were saved. Now hope that is seen is not hope. For who hopes for what is seen? But if we hope for what we do not see, we wait for it with patience.

We can only accept Jesus as the Savior he really is if we are willing to live with the experience of incomplete redemption. Our Savior brings us to the fullness of life and salvation gradually, little by little, through countless invitations and inspirations which respect our human pace. He does this with individuals, with any given society and with the human race as a whole. The reign of God is always at hand but never just handed to us; always coming and never established. We have to live with this. But to live with it doesn't mean we just passively settle for it. It means that we labor with all our strength, in unwavering hope, to bring redemption to completeness in ourselves and in the world — in society, in everything that is human. It means perseverance in efforts to transform the world, its attitudes, values, structures, customs, practices and laws — and our own hearts as well. To do this shows that we believe Jesus has triumphed and that he is in fact the Savior of the world. This belief gives us joy and encouragement even while we groan under the weight of society's programming and pressures.

This is the "waiting in joyful hope" which St. Paul recommends to us:

> Who will separate us from the love of Christ? Will hardship, or distress, or persecution…? No, in all these things we are more than conquerors through him who loved us.
>
> For I am convinced that neither death, nor life, nor angels, nor rulers, nor things present, nor things to come, nor powers, nor height, nor depth, nor anything else in all creation, will be able to separate us from the love of God in Christ Jesus our Lord. (This is the end of the citations from Rom. 7:15 to 8:39).

Nothing can separate us from Christ our Savior or prevent him from bringing our salvation to completeness, provided we are willing to persevere in cooperating with him and to "wait in joyful hope" for Christ to grow to full stature in us. But there are times when we are tempted to doubt that this is happening at all.

The experience of abandonment

No matter how much we accept in theory everything said above, when it comes to day-by-day living, we all tend to fall into some very natural but damaging errors about what we should expect from Jesus. The first error — and perhaps the root of all the others — is the assumption that living the life of grace should give us felt comfort and peace of soul.

"If I am really doing what I should; if I am united to Christ and living the divine life of grace, shouldn't I be at peace?

Shouldn't I have some sense of intimacy with God?
Shouldn't I feel joy?"

The answer is, "Yes — and no." "Yes" if you mean that
sometimes you should feel these. And "Yes" if you mean
that this peace and joy should be a constant reality somewhere deep in your soul — perhaps too deep for you to be
always aware of it. But "No" if you are identifying the experience of grace with the feeling of being graced; the experience of believing and hoping and loving with the feeling that you are believing and hoping and loving. And very
definitely "No" if you are identifying being loved by God
with the feeling that you are loved by God.

It would be easier to accept Jesus as the kind of Savior he is
if he always gave us the gift of enduring our sufferings with
joy, or at least with felt peace of soul. But that is not the
Christian experience. It was not the experience of Jesus
himself during his agony in the Garden when he prayed,
"Abba, Father, for you all things are possible; remove this
cup from me..." (Mark 14:36); nor later on the cross when
he cried out, "My God, my God, why have you forsaken
me?" (Mt. 27:46). It was not the experience of the modern
martyr, Father Walter Ciszek, S.J., who learned in Russia's
Lubianka prison what to expect and not to expect from
prayer:

> Being human, I made the same mistakes in prayer every human
> being makes. I prayed for the conversion of my interrogators for
> example, but none of them ever showed the slightest sign of con-
> version. I prayed hard for more food... Nevertheless, pray as I
> might, I never received an extra portion of food or cup of hot wa-
> ter.... And I learned soon enough that prayer does not take away
> bodily pain or mental anguish. Nevertheless, it does provide a cer-
> tain moral strength to bear the burden patiently. [3]

We want Jesus to be a Savior who takes away our cross;
but instead he gives us strength to carry it. Jesus promises
to give us the strength to carry our cross, but he doesn't
promise us the consolation of feeling — or even of always

knowing — that we are doing it well. He tells us salvation
is found in carrying our cross with faith, with hope and
with love — but the grace he gives us to do this may not be
perceptible to us on the feeling level. When we feel most
desperately our need for faith he may give it in the form of
the "dark night of the soul." When we are in fact making
our greatest act of hope, it may seem to us nothing but a
futile "hoping against hope" (Rom. 4:18). And when we are
loving God more deeply than we ever have in our lives we
may feel nothing but distance from him. It is this that
makes the cross so difficult to bear. [4]

Not a matter of feelings

One of the hardest lessons to learn in the spiritual life is
that feelings have no moral value at all: that loving God or
other people does not require us to feel any affection for
them; that forgiving our enemies is perfectly compatible
with emotional rage and resentment, or with being obsessed
by fantasies of violent revenge. St. John of the Cross
teaches that we experience pure faith in the measure that
we continue to believe when we have no natural feeling of
conviction; that hope is more purely hope in God when we
continue to make the choices that express hope although we
feel no trust in God whatsoever; that we give love to God
more purely and more freely when we choose to do the acts
of love while feeling that we have no relationship with him
at all. [5]

The fact is that our feelings are not under our direct control.
Feelings are the effects of causes, and where the causes
exist the effects will exist, whether we choose to have those
feelings or not. To feel anger when we are treated unjustly
is as natural as feeling cold when a winter wind is blowing.
We don't condemn ourselves for feeling cold, so why
should we flog ourselves with guilt when we feel anger?
We cannot make cold go away by choosing not to feel it,
and we cannot make desires go away by choosing not to

have them. This is true of all desires: anger, avarice, lust, laziness, envy, or anything else that is a spontaneous, unchosen inclination. We are no better or worse for having any of them, and we should never blame ourselves or accept any guilt at all for feelings.

The same is true of fear and repulsion: we cannot just will them away. Whether or not we feel desire or revulsion, courage or fear, this has nothing to say about how holy we are. Jesus in his agony in the garden felt so much fear and revulsion that he was ready — on the feeling level — to back out of redeeming the whole human race! "Abba, Father... remove this cup from me..." And yet, on the deepest level of his soul, where there is no human cause except free, deliberate choice, he never wavered. It was the pure essence and core of his love — and of his own free will — that he experienced when he added: "yet, not my will but yours be done" (Luke 22:42).

It is in experiences like these — "dark night" experiences — that we also experience *grace* most clearly and unambiguously. When we feel dead to every human motive for believing but still choose to believe, we know we are acting by the divine gift of faith. The same is true of hope and love.

There is always the possibility, of course, that our lack of devotion is due to some bad choice, some wrong direction we are taking. When we get off course in our spiritual life, it is natural that we should feel cold toward God, alienated from the Church and judgmental about other Christians. When this happens, we need to take an honest look at what we have changed in the way we are living, what attitudes and values we are freely choosing to accept, what religious practices we may be neglecting (for example, prayer, Mass, Confession, reading Scripture, discussing our faith with others). It can be helpful to read our feelings as signals, as long as we stay aware that the feelings themselves are just effects; it is their causes we need to examine. Our response to God consists in choices, not in feelings. If we refuse to accept guilt for our feelings, it will give us more energy to deal with our real sins, which are our bad choices.

Deliverance from sin

That is another source of discouragement: our sins and the sins of others. It would be immeasurably easier to believe in Jesus as Savior if he gave us instant deliverance from sin and from the consequences sin has caused in our world. If Jesus would just manage, whether by force, genius or manipulation, to purge our cities of crime, our children of drugs and every other addiction; to purge business and politics of dishonesty; the Church of apathy; and society in general of every kind of visible sin, he would really stand out as the Savior of the world. And people would believe in him.

In fact, we would find it easier to believe in him as Savior if he would just deliver us once and for all from our own individual, personal temptations and sins. But both individually and as a society, we seem, at times at least, to be helpless and hopeless against the power of sin still strong and active in our hearts and in the world.

The hype of instant healing

Some pastors and preachers apparently achieve impressive results in turning people away from sin on the level of simplistic morality. And they gain credibility by that very fact — even though their methods and their results may both be questionable. Some changes in behavior can be prodded and propped by social pressure. Some are made appealing through over-simplification: by making all moral issues seem black-and-white. And some preachers use the stick-and-carrot technique of threatening people with damnation for certain obvious sins which already afflict them with guilt — those which have made the fundamentalist short list — while assuring them they will be "saved" if they just turn to Jesus.

A religion focused on avoiding obvious sins and performing obviously good acts can make Jesus look effective as Savior. However, this kind of religion slides very easily into the hypocritical legalism of the Pharisees, making clean the "outside of the cup," while the inside is full of filth (see Mt. 23:25). And the fundamentalist preachers are in danger of making the same showcase display of those they have dramatically "saved from a life of sin" that the TV evangelicals make of those they have "healed" of physical infirmities. In both cases the overall results are questionable, but the promise, or even the appearance, of widespread instant healing has a strong appeal. Authentic Christianity cannot — in conscience must not — capitalize on the hype of instant healing, whether physical or moral. This is not a faithful representation of the kind of Savior Jesus came to be.

The level of grace

The healing Jesus gives is slow because it aims at more than just healing. He came to do more than restore conventional morality. St. Paul tells us what will be expected of us when we accept Jesus as teacher:

> Do not be conformed to this world, but be transformed by the renewing of your minds, so that you may discern what is the will of God — what is good and acceptable and perfect" (Rom. 12:2).

Jesus calls us to a whole new understanding of ourselves, of God's desire for us, of what religion is and how it should affect our relationship with this world. And we resist even hearing about it. We do not want to hear him when he calls us to more than what we already accept as decent human behavior.

It is not hard to hear someone condemning the sins we already feel guilty about. There is even a release of sorts, a catharsis, in listening to a preacher describe how foul and ugly the people are who commit these sins, if that is the way we already feel about ourselves. What makes us uncomfortable is preaching that summons us to rethink the behavior we take for granted. We all want a Savior who lifts us out of our recognized mire and enables us to live good, satisfying human lives. But we resist a Savior who calls us to live on the level of God. That is why fundamentalist preaching is strong on personal morality but weak on social justice; strong on love of family but weak on love of enemies — especially criminals and enemies of our country who threaten our established way of life; strong on love of acceptable neighbors but weak on the universal love that reaches out to other races and to the politically oppressed.

A case in point

The Memphis *Commercial Appeal* for April 19, 1998, ran an article attempting to explain why Hispanics are leaving the Catholic Church to join the more fundamentalist "evangelical" churches. Jose Zepeda of El Salvador, who once was Catholic, is now a Baptist minister. The article explains:

> His move to the Baptist faith is inextricably linked to the politics of his native country: civil war-torn El Salvador.
>
> "The Catholic Church ... was getting involved in the movement against the government ... and supporting the labor unions," said Zepeda, who moved to Memphis in 1980 after watching opposing forces battle in front of his home and having one son temporarily kidnapped.
>
> "There was violence," Zepeda said, "So people were trying to look for a church (where) they could worship in peace. That movement made the Catholic church lose thousands and thousands and thousands of people."

El Salvador is the country where, on March 24, 1980, Archbishop Oscar Romero was shot to death at the altar during Mass for protesting from the pulpit and on the radio the tortures, assassinations and massacres carried out by the Salvadoran military and para-military death squads. On December 2, 1980, Salvadoran national guardsmen, acting on orders from superior officers, kidnapped, raped and murdered three Maryknoll Sisters and a lay volunteer whose only crime was helping the poor. On December 11, 1981, troops of the elite, U.S.-trained Atlacatl Battalion entered the Salvadoran town of El Mozote and massacred nine hundred men, women and children. More than half the townspeople were born-again evangelicals who were determined to remain neutral in the civil war. On November 16, 1989, a unit of the same Atlacatl Battalion broke into the Jesuit residence at the University of Central America in San Salvador, dragged outside and machine-gunned to death six Jesuit priests, their housekeeper, Elba Ramos, and her sixteen-year-old daughter, Celina. Robert Ellsberg's account of this atrocity explains why so many Catholic priests, nuns and catechists were targeted by the government death squads.

> For years the Jesuits of the university had been a thorn in the side of the military and ruling elite. This was not because they supported the rebels, but because they had consistently denounced the injustice and repression that fed the bitter war, and because they had sought to promote a negotiated settlement to the conflict.... Ellacuria and his fellow priests were no communists. They were priests who had struggled hard to live out the church's proclaimed 'option for the poor' .....As intellectuals, as well as priests, they had committed the university itself to this mission, believing that in a world of conflict a Christian university must stand for truth and with the victims of violence. Because of this stand, the university had become a frequent target of bombs and right-wing terror.

If Jose Zepeda abandoned his Catholic religion in search of a church which would allow him to worship in peace by ignoring the violence being inflicted on the poor and the powerless, his defection is a credit to the Catholic Church in El Salvador and its martyrs rather than something we need to be concerned about. Would that all who left the Church had no better reason than this! [6]

Christians may find it comforting to enfold themselves with Jesus in a salvation cocoon that embraces only their personal sins and virtues; but this is to misunderstand Jesus as Savior. He came to save, not just sinners, but the society they live in. He came to establish his reign on earth, "a kingdom of justice, love and peace." As soon as we focus only on being saved and not on saving others, we have distanced ourselves from Christ. And "saving others" does not mean enclosing them in the same little cocoon of personal justification we have folded around ourselves; it means launching them into the world as stewards of the kingship of Christ, faithful stewards intent on establishing his reign of love in every area and activity of human life. If our "Christian morality" does not include this commitment, it is not the morality of Christ. When Jose Zepeda says that the violence in his country moved people to "look for a church (where) they could worship in peace," the peace they were looking for was not the peace of Christ.

New wineskins: redefining ourselves

The reform Jesus calls for is a reform that places the ax at the root of the tree. It calls us to change, not just our behavior, but the very definition of what we are. This is a *metanoia* that takes time. For individuals it takes a lifetime. For the human race as a whole it takes millennia.

A banker once told me his bank had decided that tellers should begin making some decisions that formerly only officers of the bank could make. "We expect it to take three to five years for the tellers to accept this," he said. In response to my astonishment he explained that this was not just a simple policy decision; it was one which called for a "cultural change." It required the tellers to redefine their jobs. Management knew it would take time for the tellers to do that.

We see this same thing happening in the Church year after

year, century after century. The call to "change our minds" is constantly repeated. Every new age has its challenge. For example, forty years after Vatican II, how many Catholics have accepted the changes the Council called for? Some changes are no problem: the ones that just call for a slightly different way of acting on the level of behavior. But if the change of behavior also requires people to accept a whole new image of the Church and of themselves and to redefine their role in the Church, it will take, as it already has taken, years for most people to accept it.

Liturgical reform is a glaring example. The bishops can change particular procedures at Mass by decree; but they cannot bring about "full, active, conscious *participation*" in the Mass until the laity redefine the Mass and their own role in it. The concept of the Mass as a *communal prayer* must replace the concept of the Mass as a ceremony performed by a priest which others are free to attend, and in which each member of the congregation participates privately according to personal devotion. The laity cannot accept the Mass as a group production and their authentic role in it until they understand and accept the meaning of their baptismal consecration as *priests*. Until the people in the pews realize that they are at Mass to *minister* as actively as those in the sanctuary are, we will keep seeing the scandal of people sitting as separated from each other as they can get, not singing, and barely muttering the responses. The same people who would be astounded if half the singers in a musical walked off the stage before the end of the closing number will themselves walk out of church before the end of the recessional hymn in order to be first out of the parking lot. This kind of behavior shows that they still think of themselves as spectators at Mass, not players; as customers who are there to be served, not as members of the work force who come to actively celebrate the redemption of the world.

Another example: Vatican II wrote eloquently about the

"apostolate of the laity," and as an application of this
teaching the United States bishops have declared as a body
that Catholics should be actively involved in bringing about
peace on earth:

> Peacemaking is not an optional commitment. It is a requirement of
> our faith. We are called to be peacemakers, not by some movement
> of the moment, but by the Lord Jesus.... We believe work to de-
> velop non-violent means of fending off aggression and resolving
> conflict best reflects the call of Jesus both to love and justice. [7]

But Catholics are not actually going to do what the bishops
are asking here, or even listen to speakers invited by their
parish to tell them how they might, until they redefine their
"job description" as Christians and accept their baptismal
consecration as *kings* or stewards of the kingship of Christ.
We are not interested in hearing about what we ought to do
until we are convinced this follows from what we are. If we
think that being a "good Catholic" just means keeping out
of sin and showing up for Mass every Sunday, we will look
upon everything else as an "extra," no matter what the
bishops say. The "mission of the Church" is not anything
we see ourselves committed to embrace until we realize
and accept that the Church is us.

Jesus prepared us for this:

> No one sews a piece of unshrunk cloth on an old cloak.... Neither
> is new wine put into old wineskins.... but new wine is put into
> fresh wineskins" (Mt. 9:16).

It takes time to produce "new wineskins." And if Christ
seems to be taking a long time to overcome sin in the
world, it is because his work of redemption is a work of
transforming the attitudes and values of the whole human
race, reversing the immeasurable damage — in the form of
cultural conditioning — that has been caused in society by
the free choices of innumerable individuals to commit sins.
Every sin has an impact on other people's attitudes and
values. Enough sins will distort the attitudes and lower the
values of a whole society. Human beings, by freely choos-

ing to sin, have nudged the human race into darkness and destructive patterns of behavior for centuries upon centuries. God, instead of just repairing all this damage himself by some instantaneous miracle, will use human beings to do it. And that will take more centuries.

The "glory of God" — God working in us

Jesus is a slow-working Savior because he won't save us just by divine power; he requires our human cooperation. He refuses to just write off the human nature God created, accepting it as a hopelessly flawed product and expecting nothing from it. He won't save us like inert matter. We may be lying paralyzed in sin, but Jesus won't carry us limp and helpless into heaven. He says to us what he said to the paralyzed man on earth: "Stand up and walk" (Mt. 9:5). Jesus will get us home, and we need his grace and guidance to get there. But he will not instantly transport us; we have to walk. This sets redemption at a human pace.

But this is the "glory of God" that Jesus as Savior came to re-establish: not just the magnificence God has in himself, but his greatness, power and mercy displayed through his creation. Human beings are the glory of God — because when they live by the life received through Jesus Christ, the life of God shines in them and through them. Jesus "saved" God's glory as Creator by saving human nature. He healed human beings and empowered them by grace to live and act on the level of God. He lifted up his followers to become men and women freely accepting the fullness of light and truth; freely and personally embracing the ideals and values of God; freely living and acting by grace on the level of God himself. And for those who have eyes to see, this life still shines, no matter how feebly, even in members of Christ who are wounded and crippled by sin.[8]

Jesus saves people by making people saviors. Through Christ, with Christ, and in Christ as members of his body, human beings are cooperators and co-workers with Jesus in the work of their own redemption. The Church celebrates this:

> We recognize that it is typical of your immense glory that you would come to the rescue of our humanity by your divinity, and even use our humanity itself to provide the remedy for us, and save us who were lost by the very thing [human nature] which destroyed us, through Christ our Lord.[9]

Because God wants to do it this way, the "hard way," redemption takes time. For God, "to save" means to change people, not just their performance. If the people don't change interiorly, the performance is not really theirs. Authentic salvation means sharing in God's divine life and living on the level of God; becoming "new wineskins" filled with the new wine of grace. It is not just the wine that is new; the wineskins themselves have to be renewed, "and so both are preserved." Jesus came, not just to throw away the old wineskins and replace them with new ones straight out of the factory. He came to make new the wineskins already created, and to do it with the wineskins' free cooperation.

Meanwhile, during the long process of renewing the wineskins, sin continues to play out the power left to it. And all who live on earth will suffer from the consequences of "humans' inhumanity to humans" until "all of us come to the unity of the faith and of the knowledge of the Son of God, to maturity, to the measure of the full stature of Christ" (Eph. 4:13).

A delayed-action Savior

Obviously, giving human beings responsibility for making decisions allows for a lot of human error, and the errors can make the Church Jesus founded look bad. This can call into question the whole power of grace and the effectiveness of Christ's redemption. We want a fix-it God, and Jesus was

not sent to be one. God sent Jesus to initiate the transformation of the human race through a slow process of free,
personal conversions. He insists that human beings play a
part in their own redemption, so that the end result will be
their work as well as God's. This is not the way to achieve
instantly impressive results. And it is a challenge to the
faith of those who want to believe in Jesus as Savior.

The challenge to our faith is the challenge to accept a Savior who does not save us immediately from the common
suffering of all humanity: the pains of sickness and death,
and the suffering imposed on us by our own sins and by the
woundedness and sins of others. There are still drunken
drivers who kill, manufacturers who pollute, drug addicts
who rob, greedy speculators who wreck the economy,
"profits only" executives who eliminate jobs irresponsibly,
abusive and powerful people who oppress and exploit, and
people in positions of trust who conceal and distort the
truth. Can we believe in a Savior who does not protect us
from the suffering caused by sin, but waits instead on human beings to convert freely and waits on us to bring others
to conversion? Can we accept a Savior who, while redemption is slowly diffusing itself through all creation,
uses his divine power, not to neutralize our enemies, but to
give us the spiritual strength to endure evil with love, to
accept whatever cross the sins of others lay on our shoulders and to carry it patiently while "loving back"?

And can we find joy in this, in the salvation Jesus is actually giving us right now by empowering us to "endure evil
with love"? Can we see in our own carrying of the cross the
power God shares with us? Can we find in our experience
of loving our enemies the sign and assurance that Jesus is
indeed "overcoming the world" in us? And in his victory
over the violence in our own hearts, can we see the sign
that his reign is being established over every area and activity of human life? Because of this, can we find joy in the
coming of our Savior, Jesus Christ, even when that joy is

not on the level of our feelings? Because we know he has come and believe we are experiencing his action in our hearts right now, can we continue to "wait in joyful hope for the coming of our Savior" until his glory is complete?

When Jesus entered Jerusalem in anticipated triumph, the people were shouting, "Hosanna! Save us, we pray." They were acclaiming Jesus as the Messiah God had sent to save them. We know now that this acclamation, in the minds of those who were shouting it, at least, did not express a recognition of Jesus as the kind of Savior he was actually sent to be. But have we ourselves accepted Jesus deeply and personally as the Savior whose saving action waits on our response? Do we accept him as the God-made-flesh who has chosen to let his divine power be limited, or at least delayed, by human beings' refusal to cooperate? Are we determined to *persevere* in faith and fidelity (faith lived out in action), cooperating with his saving work on earth, no matter how weak and futile it seems, and no matter how long it takes, until he comes again?

We know that Jesus has come, died, and risen in triumph. And yet we still proclaim in every Eucharistic celebration that we are joyfully awaiting "the blessed hope and coming of our Savior, Jesus Christ." Can we pledge ourselves to this with absolute determination? In spite of all we suffer and struggle against in this period of the world's purification, can we still acclaim Jesus as Savior every day from hearts that cry out unreservedly, "Blessed is he who comes in the name of the Lord; we bless you from the house of the Lord!"

CHAPTER TWO:
"IN JOYFUL HOPE..."
"Jesus" — Matthew 21:9-14

Summary

We can only accept Jesus as the Savior he really is if we are willing to live with the experience of incomplete redemption while laboring in unwavering hope, to bring redemption to completeness in ourselves and in the world. Waiting means persevering in efforts to transform the world, its attitudes, values and structures — and our own hearts as well. This is what shows that we really believe Jesus has triumphed as Savior.

It would be easier to accept Jesus as Savior if he always gave us the gift of enduring our sufferings with joy, or at least with felt peace of soul. But that is not something we can count on. One of the hardest lessons to learn in the spiritual life is that feelings have no moral value at all, good or bad. Only free choices have moral or spiritual value.

It is in "dark night" experiences — when we feel dead to every human motive for believing, hoping or loving but still choose to *do what expresses* faith, hope and love — that we experience grace most clearly and unambiguously.

Two thousand years after Christ's coming crime, poverty and violence are still rampant on earth. Why is it taking Jesus so long to establish his reign?

1. Freedom: The first reason is that God made people free. In a world where people are free, people are going to sin, and their sins are going to make others suffer. Jesus did not come to take away human freedom.

2. Cultural conditioning: Sins produce all of those effects inside of us which we call "cultural conditioning." Individuals' sins transform society by distorting people's perception of truth and value. Jesus does not just erase this by an act of divine power. He frees and converts us gradually, through human ministry. In the measure more and more believers accept his attitudes and values and embody them in their lives, the light and love of Christ spread throughout the world and heal society itself.

3. The height of our call: Jesus came to do more than restore conventional morality. He calls us to live on the divine level of God, to change, not just our behavior, but the very definition of what we are.

This is a *metanoia* that takes time. For individuals it takes a lifetime. For the human race as a whole it takes millennia.

4. The role of human nature: Jesus refuses to just write off the human nature God created as hopelessly flawed and save us like inert matter. He insists that human beings play a part in their own redemption, so that the end result will be their work as well as God's. He is saving human nature itself and bringing about the transformation of the human race through a slow process of free, personal conversions. This sets redemption at a human pace.

Have you understood?

What does it mean to say that Jesus has saved the world, is still saving it, and will not finish until he comes again?

What should we think when we find no devotion in prayer, when religious things "turn us off"? What should we do?

Give four reasons why it has taken and is taking so long for Jesus to heal individuals and society from bad attitudes, values and ways of acting.

What does it mean to "wait" in joyful hope for the "blessed hope and coming of our Savior, Jesus Christ"? Why does it show more faith and hope to actively work to bring about what we are waiting for than just to sit around waiting for it to happen?

What is the challenge of this chapter? To our faith? To our hope? To our love?

Making it your own

What are the key thoughts in this chapter? (Jot them down and give the page number where each is found).

What questions do I have about this chapter? (Bring them up in discussion or ask someone who should know the answers).

What struck me the most in this chapter? After reading this chapter, what do I understand better than I did before? What do I appreciate more?

What do I think is the point of the whole chapter? What response does Matthew want to evoke from those who read or hear this part of his Gospel?

What can I use as a visible reminder (a symbol) to keep me aware of the challenge of this chapter? Where will I put it?

Questions for prayer

Do I ever feel that Jesus is not able or willing to purify my heart of the attitudes and desires that lead me to do destructive things? Do I recognize the power of cultural conditioning in me? Have I settled down to just live with this?

How much use am I making of the human means Jesus gives me to change my attitudes and values? Do I reflect on his words? Spend time admiring his example? Use the sacrament of Reconciliation for regular support and advice? Participate in a discussion group?

Do I ever give up on prayer, Mass or other religious practices because they "just don't mean anything" to me? What should I do?

Do I ever blame God for the free choices of others that have brought me suffering? Have I come to terms with God's choice to create people free? Do I really accept it?

Have I accepted the slow pace of human conversion? Am I willing to keep working at changing my heart, without getting discouraged when progress is slow? What are the remedies I use consistently and perseveringly?

Am I determined to keep trying to transform the world, beginning with the people around me, regardless of visible results?

How can I apply to my life what I have come to see by reflecting on this chapter? What concrete action do I choose to perform to express my belief in what I have seen?

FOOTNOTES

[1] John McKenzie, *The Power and the Wisdom*, Bruce, 1965, pp. 73,76.

[2] Our deliverance from the power of cultural conditioning and all the destructive, distorted attitudes and values of this world is ritualized in the anointing with the oil of catechumens and in the "prayer of exorcism" that precedes infant baptism:

Almighty God, you sent your only Son to rescue us from the slavery of sin, and to give us the freedom only your sons and daughters

enjoy. We pray now for these children who will have to face the
world and its temptations, and fight the devil in all his cunning.
Your Son died and rose again to save us. By his victory over sin
and death, bring these children out of the power of darkness.
Strengthen them with the grace of Christ, and watch over them at
every step in life's journey. ...Through Christ our Lord.

And the minister continues:

We anoint you with the oil of salvation in the name of Christ our
Savior; may he strengthen you with his power, who lives and
reigns for ever and ever... (Rite of Baptism for Children).

[3] *He Leadeth Me*, Doubleday/Image Books 1975, chapter 5, page 64.
Ciszek was released after serving fourteen years in Siberia and later
repatriated to the United States, where he died a natural death. He is a
"martyr" in the sense in which the early Church used the word: a witness made credible by enduring persecution for the faith.

[4] See St. John of the Cross, *The Dark Night*, chapter 7, no. 7, in *The
Collected Works of St. John of the Cross*, tr. Kieran Kavanaugh, O. C.
D., and Otilio Rodriguez, O. C. D., ICS Publications, 1991, p.409.

[5] *The Ascent of Mount Carmel*, Bk. 2, ch. 6, no. 1; *Ibid.* p. 166.

[6] See the Memphis *Commercial Appeal* for April 19, 1998, (pages E-1,
8) and Robert Ellsberg, *All Saints*, Crossroad, 1997: "November 16,"
"December 2," and "December 11." See also: *New York Times*, April 3,
1998; *National Catholic Reporter*, April 17, 1998, p. 13; and also Oct.
27, 2000, p.3 ff. for the trial of Salvadoran generals charged in a civil
lawsuit with responsibility for the massacre of the nuns. The generals
had been given asylum in the United States. They were acquitted on the
questionable grounds that they did not have control over the behavior
of their troops.

[7] See *The Challenge of Peace*, United States Catholic Conference,
1983, pp. vii and 25.

[8] See St. Irenaeus' famous saying in his treatise *Against Heresies*,
quoted in the Office of Readings for his feastday, June 28: "Life in humans is the glory of God; the life of humans is the vision of God."

[9] This is my own translation of the third Preface for Sundays in Ordinary time.

Chapter Three
God Present *In Absentia*
Jesus is "Son of God" — Read Matthew 21:12-16

Matthew tells us that Jesus entered Jerusalem "humble, and mounted on a donkey," and on a borrowed one at that! Then he "entered the temple and drove out all who were selling and buying," after which the "blind and the lame came to him in the temple, and he cured them."

There is a double swing of contrasts here. Jesus enters the city on a donkey, the picture of meekness and humility. Then he swings into action, overturns the tables of the moneychangers and the seats of the people who are selling doves, and drives out the merchants in a prophetic gesture of anger and authority. But immediately afterwards the blind and the lame gather around him with no fear at all and he cures them: the picture again of the gentle, non-intimidating Savior. Meanwhile the children begin chanting again, "Hosanna to the Son of David!"

The chief priests and the scribes don't know what to make of the double signals. Jesus is obviously not claiming the earthly power of the Messiah-King they expected. But the people are acclaiming him as the long-awaited "Son of David" and he is accepting the title. It is their turn to be angry. "Don't you hear what these people are saying," they ask him. And Jesus answers:

> Yes; have you never read, "Out of the mouths of infants and nursing babies you have prepared praise for yourself"?

A hint of divinity

Jesus' answer to the shocked objections of the priests and scribes shows that he is claiming more for himself than just prophetic inspiration and zeal. When the crowd marched into Jerusalem with him shouting, "Hosanna to the Son of David," Matthew tells us, "the whole city was in turmoil, asking, 'Who is this?'" But all the crowd was answering at that time was, "This is the prophet Jesus from Nazareth in Galilee."

Now, however, Jesus justifies the children's acclaim of him as "Son of David" by hinting that he is much more than a prophet. He asks if the priests have never read a verse from Psalm 8 which clearly refers to the praise of God Himself:

> O LORD, our Sovereign, how majestic is your name in all the earth! You have set your glory above the heavens.
>
> Out of the mouths of babes and infants you have founded a bulwark because of your foes, to silence the enemy and the avenger.
>
> When I look at your heavens, the work of your fingers, the moon and the stars that you have established;
>
> what are human beings that you are mindful of them, mortals that you care for them? (Psalm 8:1-4)

By applying these words to himself, Jesus is claiming to be something more than just a human being who is concerned about due reverence for the temple — even one especially chosen and favored by God. Behind the lowliness of his unassuming entrance into Jerusalem there is the veiled mystery of the majesty of God.[1]

Jesus' first act upon entering the temple precincts already suggests this. He drives out all who are using the place for business purposes, saying, "It is written in Scripture, 'My house shall be called a house of prayer,' but you are making it a den of robbers."

Theoretically, any prophet could have done this, and the act itself expresses nothing more than zeal that the worship of Yahweh should be what it ought to be in the temple dedicated to him. But in the context it says more than this. Jesus has just entered Jerusalem as Messiah and King, and his first act is to assert his authority over the temple, which, together with the Law, was considered at that time to be the "second great institution of Judaism." He has already claimed authority over the Law by his reinterpretation of the Commandments in the Sermon on the Mount, and over the Sabbath by his claim to be "Lord of the Sabbath" in defiance of the Pharisees' restrictions against healing on that day (see Mt. 5:17-42 and 12:1-14). Now he is claiming authority over the temple as well. This makes him more than a prophet. In John's Gospel Jesus claims this authority explicitly as Son, saying, "You must not make *my Father's* house a place of business!" (see John 2:16).[2]

If Jesus is more than a prophet, more than an inspired, human teacher of religious truth, then the religion he gives us, the way of living to which he calls us, must also be more than just a good, human way of honoring God. The religion of Jesus the "Son of God" must be as far above every humanly imaginable way of living as Jesus himself is above the son of every human father and mother. That gives us something to think about.

Two principles

To understand the presentation of Jesus as "Son of God" in this passage, it will help to keep two principles in mind. The first is a guideline St. Ignatius of Loyola gives for those contemplating the passion and death of Jesus: "Consider how the divinity hides itself." In this prelude to the passion narrative, Jesus enters Jerusalem "humble, and mounted on a donkey," without any display of power, human or divine. From this point until Jesus rises from the dead Matthew will report Jesus working miracles only twice. The first time is the short comment, "he cured them," when the blind and the lame approach him in the temple, and Matthew's focus here is not on Jesus' power to heal, but on his accessibility and outreach to the poor and marginal. The second instance is the withering of the fig tree (Mt. 21: 19), which is certainly presented as miraculous, but with focus, not on Jesus' act of power, but on the failure of Israel to bear fruit, and on the power of any prayer made with faith.[3]

In this section of his Gospel Matthew is downplaying anything that would make Jesus appear divine or powerful. And yet, paradoxically, his intention here is precisely to teach us how to believe in Jesus as divine.

The explanation of this is in a second principle: one that we've seen operative before in Matthew's Gospel. To put it briefly, and in a way that requires some qualifications, it is: *the absence of the human reveals the presence of the divine.*

This is not an absolute statement, and should not be applied indiscriminately to everything. It is not a rejection of what is human or a refusal to use human resources. That would be against our whole understanding of the Incarnation. But it does affirm that in some situations it is precisely the absence of human resources which reveals the presence and action of divine power.

For example, when the angel told Mary that she was to conceive as a virgin, without any human act of intercourse, the purpose of this was precisely to make it clear that the fruit of her womb was divine. There was no great show of divine power, but in the absence of any human father or means of conception, the Father of Jesus could only be God himself (see Mt. 1:18-25).

For the same reason, when Jesus first sent his apostles out as a preview of his Church, giving them his own authority to cast out unclean spirits and to "cure every disease and every sickness," he told them to go without the resources of this world: "Take no gold, or silver, or copper in your belts, no bag for your journey, or two tunics, or sandals, or a staff" (Mt. 10:1-10).

One reason for this instruction was to make it obvious that the life-giving power active in the words of the disciples was a power that came from God. Jesus did not send them out accredited by theological degrees and human eloquence. (All human knowledge and gifts are helpful, of course, but as servants of the message, not as validating it). Nor was there any showy display of divine power; just some low-key acts of healing which the Gospel narrative hardly mentions. It was first and foremost the absence of reliance on human resources which showed that the disciples were relying on the action of God for any fruit their ministry would bear.

Another example: when Peter recognized Jesus as Messiah and "Son of the living God," there was no obvious show of divine revelation: he wasn't a visionary reporting some divine apparition. What Jesus called attention to was the absence of human evidence: Peter could not have known who Jesus was by his natural human powers: "Blessed are you, Simon son of Jonah! For flesh and blood has not revealed this to you...." Jesus was not acting like the kind of Messiah Israel (and Peter) expected; he had neither money nor power, and showed no interest in acquiring either of these or in establishing the kind of Kingdom Israel expected. If, in the absence of all human reasons for believing that Jesus was the Messiah, Peter did believe and recognize him, it followed that the real source of his understanding was divine; namely, "my Father in heaven" (see Mt. 16:17).

Jesus: "Son of God" (Matthew 21:4-8. 12-16)

And now, as Jesus enters Jerusalem, the same principle is at work. Jesus enters Jerusalem as king, but without any show of divine power and no human resources at all: on a borrowed donkey, sitting on cloaks his followers laid on its back for a saddle, identified in his unassuming gentleness with the *anawim*, the poor in body and spirit. He enters Jerusalem with the same obvious dependence on divine rather than on human power that he required of his disciples when he sent them out on mission. And yet that divine power is not visible except through the absence of human power. This should make it clear, to those who have eyes to see, that Jesus is entering Jerusalem, not as a human conqueror, politician or strategist, but as the Anointed One, the Son of David who is also the Son of God. In the absence of all the means which would have enabled him to establish his reign as a human being, it must be that he is entering Jerusalem to establish it as the Son of God. [4]

Divine goal, human pace

This gives us further insight into two questions that are the background of this whole book: why is the establishment of God's reign on earth taking so long? And why don't we find more satisfaction in our religion? Why is it so hard to persevere in waiting, in faith and fidelity, for Christ to come again?

Why, after two thousand years of Christianity, is there still so much blindness, ignorance, hatred and division on earth? Why are there still wars, oppression and poverty? Why does the pain of living in our society drive so many people to the imprisoning escapism of alcohol and drugs?

And why do those who try to live by Christ's teachings have to go through such long periods of finding no satisfaction in their religion: being bored or disgusted by the very things that should give them enthusiasm: prayer, the Mass, homilies and spiritual readings; feeling no faith, no hope, no love — all the trials the spiritual writers describe as "desolation," dryness or "aridity," "abandonment," the "dark night of the soul"? Why don't those who embrace the "breadth and length and height and depth" of Christ's way (see Eph. 3:18) feel that instantaneous "joy, joy, joy, joy deep in their hearts" that the fundamentalists and the followers of the "quick fix" devotions claim to have? Or, if they do experience this, as most serious beginners do at some time, why doesn't it last as they draw closer to Christ in intimacy and love?

Part of the answer to this has been given in the previous chapter: God has chosen to redeem the world through the cooperation of human beings; therefore the pace of re-demption is no faster than the pace of human conversion. But another clear, precise and basic element of the answer is this: Jesus calls us to a level of life that is divine, not just human. The height to which we are called is beyond the level to which human acts of conversion — human deci-sions and choices based on reason — can take us. To sur-render fully to God we have to go beyond our natural guid-ance system, beyond our natural way of perceiving, decid-ing and choosing, and accept to live by that pure faith, pure hope, pure love, which come from God alone and are a sharing in his own act of knowing and loving. It is not easy to make the transition from responding to God in a way that is mostly natural, although empowered by grace, to a way of responding that is so dependent on the power of grace that it doesn't feel natural at all.

Any choice to live according to the way our human natures were designed to act is aided by nature itself. Our natures cry out for healthy living, for reasonable behavior that re-spects all human values. Jesus, however, does not save us just by raising us out of the mire of sin so that we can bask in the healthy, ordered reasonableness of good, decent hu-man behavior. He saves us by calling and empowering us to live on the level of God; to be perfect as our heavenly Father is perfect (see Mt. 5:48); to love one another as Je-sus himself has loved us (see John 15:2); to live by the Spirit of God, guided by the Holy Spirit (see Gal. 5:25). And whereas there is always pleasure and satisfaction in living according to our human natures — everything works best when we follow the manufacturer's instructions — the same is not always true when we go beyond them to live on the level of God. When we do this it is precisely in the ab-sence of human satisfaction that we experience our surren-der to the divine.

The dark night of the senses

What usually happens is this: Once we seriously choose to begin living for God, God seduces us to pursue deeper relationship with him by letting us find our pleasure in spiritual things. St. John of the Cross calls this phase of our growth the "active dark night of the senses."

It is "active" because we are actively making the choice not to use pleasure or pain as our guidance system when we decide whether to gratify or not gratify our sense appetites. Instead, we use a guidance system our sense appetites do not understand; that is, whatever we perceive to be pleasing to God.

But it is a "dark night" for the senses, because this choice, lived out, puts our sense appetites "in the dark." By their nature, our sense appetites have no way of perceiving the objects of their desire except under the light of pleasure and pain, and these have been ruled irrelevant. Hence they do not understand why we sometimes say "yes" to things that are pleasant and sometimes "no." We have switched to a different guidance system: the will and pleasure of God, which our sense appetites cannot relate to at all. This leaves them completely in the dark. However, because we have determined not to seek sense pleasures for their own sake any more, God in turn lets us find delight in the pleasures of the spirit: in prayer, in reading and discussing the Scriptures or other spiritual books, in the Eucharistic celebration, in living out the teachings of Jesus in daily life.[5]

The passive dark night

But we can become attached to these spiritual delights in a selfish way. So after a while God takes away the pleasure ("consolation") we find in spiritual things and leaves us in "desolation" and spiritual dryness or "aridity." Nothing religious turns us on as it used to. We hit a blank wall when we try to pray or think about God. God does this so that we can learn to love him unselfishly, seeking God himself, not just the pleasure he gives us when we deal with him. St. John of the Cross calls this phase of our growth the "passive dark night of the senses." It is passive because we don't choose this condition; it just happens to us. And while our sense appetites are still in the dark as before, now there are no compensating spiritual pleasures to make up for the human satisfactions that have been ruled irrelevant. In their absence we are learning to distinguish between seeking the "God of all consolation" or just seeking the consolations of God. [6]

The spiritual life can seem unrewarding at this point, because we have given up seeking satisfaction in life from physical pleasures (and only a fool would go back to that), but we no longer find satisfaction in the things we turn to instead. To keep growing we just have to keep going by what seems to be sheer will power and commitment. But it is in fact the power of grace, unaided by human feelings, working through faith, hope and love. We feel like we are standing still, if not going backwards. But we are actually growing spiritually, moving into purer, stronger, more committed faith, hope and love. Our perseverance in spite of the absence of human motivation is our experience of these divine gifts active within us.

The dark night of the spirit

There is still some human motivation at work, though, from our intellect if not from our feelings. Aristotle defines pleasure as that which we experience in any proper exercise of our human powers. So even when we don't feel devotion in our religious acts, we still find pleasure and satisfaction in using our human powers. We are getting insights with our intellects, making good choices with our wills, focusing our attention on good and beautiful things, gazing at truth, experiencing love, recognizing the goodness, the rightness of our own responses. The will can peacefully choose physically painful or laborious activities if it sees them as necessary for survival or helpful for a happier life, because by nature the will chooses what the intellect presents to it as good for our overall well-being. So even though the special pleasure ("consolation") God gave us in spiritual activities is taken away, there is still the human satisfaction of knowing that we are choosing what we know to be good. Our sense appetites may be in the dark, but our "spiritual" powers of intellect and will are functioning in a satisfying way. We can find satisfaction in just being strong, rational human beings.

So in order to purify us, not only of all selfishness, but also of all dependence on our limited, human way of knowing and loving, God takes us farther: into the active and then into the passive "dark night of the spirit" (For brevity we will combine these).

Now it is our "spirit" (intellect and will) which is left in the dark. By nature the will sees its objects under the light of what the intellect presents to it as good. But in the "dark night of the spirit," God takes us beyond any motivation our intellects are able to appreciate and leaves us with no other light to steer by than faith in his word. We are asked to make choices that go beyond what the intellect presents to us as beneficial to human nature and existence. We are asked to choose what faith alone holds up to us as good. This deprives the will of its natural guidance system — the assurance reason gives that what we are doing is beneficial to us — and leaves it "in the dark." This is not a comfortable condition to be in.

Now, not only do we not seek or find gratification on the level of our physical appetites (active dark night of the senses); or feel the emotional delight of the spiritual consolations God used to give us in our religious practices (passive dark night of the senses); but even our minds are of no help to us. We no longer find reassurance in the conviction we are acting rationally. In this stage of purification, it isn't that our intellects don't work anymore, or that we understand any less; it is just that what we understand intellectually doesn't mean anything to us; it doesn't give assurance to our spirit or motivation to our will. We are left feeling doubt even about the existence of God, not to mention a sense of despair about the authenticity of our own response to him. We are "in the dark" because we are guiding our lives by a light which is darkness to intellect alone, the "dark light of faith," which is in fact the clearest, most certain light there is, but which is beyond and higher than our natural way of knowing. This way of choosing doesn't feel natural to us, because it isn't; and that is why we are uncomfortable with it until our surrender to living purely by divine faith, hope and love is complete.[7]

Beyond human wisdom

This is where we experience the difference between Jesus' Way and any way of living based on homey wisdom or even the profound insights of human seers and gurus. It is easier to accept the ancient "natural religions" than it is to accept Christianity, because these are based, not on faith in God's own word in Scripture, but on the philosophy or spiritual wisdom, the insightful sayings, directions, practices, rites and ceremonies of an enlightened teacher or people. We would not deny that the creators of Buddhism, Hinduism, Islam and the Native American religions were "inspired" in the sense of being aided and enlightened by God in much of what they have given to the world. At the Second Vatican Council the bishops affirmed that "the Catholic Church rejects nothing which is true and holy in these religions. She looks with sincere respect upon those ways of conduct and of life, those rules and teachings which, though differing in many particulars from what she holds and sets forth, nevertheless often reflect a ray of that Truth which enlightens all people."[8] Nevertheless, much of the appeal these religions have is in the acceptable response they give to felt human questions and needs, their human reasonableness, or in the sense they give of being in harmony with nature and the cosmos. The laws God gave to Israel had this appeal, and Moses told the people to "observe them diligently, for this will show your wisdom and discernment to the peoples, who, when they hear all these statutes, will say, 'Surely this great nation is a wise and discerning people!'" (see Deut. 4:5-8).

When Jesus came, however, the revelation of God was brought to its fullness.[9] The same Vatican II document goes on to say that the Church "proclaims and must ever proclaim Christ, 'the way, the truth and the life' (John 14:6), in whom people find the fullness of religious life, and in whom God has reconciled all things to himself" (see 2Cor. 5:18-19).

This fullness of truth goes beyond what appeals to human reason. St. Paul bore witness to this:

> But we proclaim Christ crucified, a stumbling block to Jews and foolishness to Gentiles, but to those who are the called, both Jews and Greeks, Christ the power of God and the wisdom of God.
>
> For God's foolishness is wiser than human wisdom, and God's weakness is stronger than human strength (1Cor. 1:18-25).

A touch of this at Mass

A flight attendant on an airplane once told me, after noticing that I was a priest, that as a Protestant she found the Mass confusing. The Liturgy of the Word she could follow; "but after the preaching, you go into all that ritual mumbo-jumbo and you lose me."

Many Catholics might say the same thing. The Liturgy of the Word — the hymns, prayers, readings, responses and homily — are human activities which, if they are well done, can be quite meaningful and enjoyable even to a person with no faith; and all the more so to any Christian. But once we get into the Liturgy of the Eucharist, when the celebration focuses explicitly on the mystery of Christ's self-offering on the cross, there is no way anyone can participate in what is going on without faith. The ritual is empty except to those who actively and consciously believe that Jesus on the cross is present to us now, offering himself for us and calling us to offer ourselves with him and in him for the life of the world.

That is why this part of the Mass, the "Liturgy of the Eucharist," is our most unambiguous experience of worship. Given the mystery of what is taking place and the fact that our participation in it is mostly silent, this cannot be just a superficial, external participation in a pleasing group activity. We might enjoy being with others, meeting our friends, singing hymns and saying prayers together. We might find the Scripture readings interesting and the preacher's explanation of them inspiring. And because of our human enjoyment of these activities, we may not get to the level of experiencing either our own deep faith or the action of God. But during the Liturgy of the Eucharist there is very little we can meaningfully do except unite ourselves in faith and love to the action taking place on the altar. This is where, if we were not there already, the Mass takes us into another dimension.

The spiritual stratosphere

In an airplane flying at a low altitude we are able to breathe the oxygen mixed into the surrounding air; our bodies are still in their natural environment. But as the plane climbs toward the stratosphere and pressure decreases, we become unable to breathe without the artificial life support of supplied oxygen. In the same way, on the lower levels of our ascent to God we can breathe the Spirit through human activities and experiences, because God is truly found in them. But there comes a time when we need to "breathe the Spirit pure." Then nothing human can help us very much; we need faith, hope and love supplied by God in a relatively pure state, not bonded with human elements in mixed divine-human composites. This is when we experience divine life most purely.

A religion which offers nothing but a way to live as wise, enlightened human beings on earth can give human satisfaction through the human resources it activates to do this. Human means are effective for producing human results. If a teaching is good, we can understand it. If a moral exhortation is persuasive, we can decide to reform our behavior. If ceremonies are appealing, we can be moved by them. If a congregation is warm and embracing, we can feel loved. When all of these work together, we can believe we have found God — and on a beginner's level God may in fact be revealing his truth and love to us through all of these. This is what makes emotionally-charged experiences like Search weekends, Cursillo and charismatic prayer meetings so powerful. But if we do not make a clear distinction between the human feelings and the divine reality underlying them, then later on, when these events are no longer humanly satisfying, we run the risk of turning away from them in anger and disillusionment. And if we are to grow to spiritual maturity, the day must come when they are no longer humanly satisfying; otherwise we will never know what it is to persevere purely by committed faith, hope and love.

Here again the principle is operative: "the absence of the human reveals the presence of the divine." When our religion does not focus on, and does not give, a great deal of human satisfaction drawn from having clear and simple ideas about truth, clear and simple laws to follow, a strong human support system for some clear and simple patterns of behavior, and a warm community of fellowship and affirmation, the very lack of emphasis on these human supports can alert us to the Church's focus on something else: life on the level of God. This is the goal of our religion: not human wisdom, but putting on the mind of Christ; not good, moral behavior, but loving on the level of God; not good, moral behavior, but loving on the level of God; not feeling loved by God and good about ourselves, but experiencing that deep union and identification with Christ which St. Paul asks God to grant us:

> I pray that, according to the riches of his glory, he may grant that you may be strengthened in your inner being with power through his Spirit, and that Christ may dwell in your hearts through faith, as you are being rooted and grounded in love.

> I pray that you may have the power to comprehend, with all the saints, what is the breadth and length and height and depth and to know the love of Christ that surpasses knowledge, so that you may be filled with all the fullness of God (Eph. 3:16-19).

A goal like this is not easily attained and cannot be attained at all as the effect of human causes. And even when God does bring us to this, it is not within our power to experience it consciously at will. The practical conclusion to draw from all this is that, when we do not find human satisfaction or gratification in our religion, we should use this absence of the human as a reminder to set our sights on what is divine: responding to God in everything we do with pure faith, pure hope and pure love "until he comes again" with his gifts of consolation, light and peace.

Experience vs. experiences

In the light of all this we can understand a common phenomenon in the spiritual life, which is that sometimes the closer we get to union with God, the more distant God seems to be. To a child walking about in a garden, the moon appears comfortingly close — a big, beautiful light in the sky, just a little higher than the housetops. But an astronaut knows that the moon is in fact a cold, dead body from which we are separated by an almost unimaginable expanse of outer space. Yet astronauts will risk their lives to get there.

This is something like the mystics' knowledge of God: not that God is cold and dead, just the opposite! But the mystics are so aware that the true fire and life of God's own, authentic Being are beyond anything that can be experienced in this life that when God does give them felt consolations and feelings of devotion, something deep within their heart rejects these. Their experiences are real; they are from God; but they are just too pitifully inadequate.

As St. John of the Cross put it in a bold poem of protest to God:

> Ay!, who can ever heal me?
> Finish giving who you are:
> Stop sending from afar!
> From this day on
> Let no messengers come near
> Who don't know how to tell me
> What alone I long to hear.

In his explanation of this stanza John says it is as if the soul were saying to God, "Among all the delights of the world and satisfactions of the senses and consolations and sweetness of soul, I know for sure that nothing will be able to heal the wound of my desire, nothing will be able to satisfy me." This is why the soul says, "Finish it! Give yourself to me as you really are."

He continues: "We should take notice here that no soul which truly loves can find satisfaction or be content until she possesses God wholly. This is because all other things not only do not satisfy her, but rather make the hunger and the longing to see him as he is increase in her... And so she says, 'From now on, don't send me any more messengers...'" The soul tells God to stop giving her consolations and visions and ecstasies which promise and do not deliver. Until God is ready to give his whole Self entirely, everything else is just tantalization which increases her torment of desire.[10]

Moonstruck: those "instant conversions"

Sometimes, listening to fundamentalists who have "found Jesus," or to people newly "baptized in the Spirit" in charismatic prayer groups, one gets the image of children dancing around a garden in the moonlight, snatching at the moonbeams. What they have found is real; it is just not the deeper reality of God. They think they have arrived, and one hesitates to burst their bubble by telling them of the long, cold journey ahead.

One hesitates because bubble-bursting can be destructive. It may be that the strength of the fundamentalist religions and of the spiritualities of enthusiasm is dependent on their shallowness. People who have just discovered Jesus are able to sing, "I've got that joy, joy, joy, joy, deep in my heart!" (although it isn't as deep as they think it is), because of the euphoria of believing they have enrolled as disciples of Jesus, passed all the courses and been graduated with honors, all in the same day! Take that away from them and they might lose it all.[11]

When the enthusiastic speak glowingly of the joy of being "saved," we can presume they have had some good experience of responding to God. But we often get the impression they have no idea of the kind of Savior Jesus really is, or of what it really means to love him. They are like newlyweds on a honeymoon — and certainly no one should envy them their romance or try to take it from them. But the proof of their love for God, like that of the newlyweds for each other, will be found in their perseverance.

They have indeed "turned their lives over to Jesus," and the conscious act of doing this is a very important step in the spiritual journey, as the wedding is in a marriage. It is a step too many people fail to make. But it is only the first step into the vestibule of the training school in which they will be laboriously prepared for what they will experience when they finally make it to the launching pad to begin the long journey toward perfect love of God.[12]

This is not to say we shouldn't rejoice in good feelings and felt joy ("consolations") when God gives them to us. On the contrary, we should make the most of them, strengthening ourselves for those moments when our only experience of God will be abandonment. We should rejoice and sing and dance in the joy of the Lord. We just should not think these feelings will endure, or that they are the essential reality of faith, hope and love.[13]

It is not our feelings that determine who and what we are as persons; it is the responses we make freely with our wills. God's grace is given to help us choose, because choosing is loving, and love is that "fullness of life" which is the salvation Jesus came to give. And because love is sometimes most pure and most free when we give it without, or even contrary to, our feelings, God lets us lose our good feelings about him for longer or shorter periods of time ("desolation"). When he does this, it is not that Jesus has stopped saving us; he is just continuing to save us by an advanced strategy which we may not understand.

"Ordinary mysticism"

The Second Vatican Council proclaimed that "all the faithful of Christ of whatever rank or status are called to the fullness of the Christian life and to the perfection of charity."[14] St. Paul said earlier what this means:

> I pray that you may have the power to comprehend, with all the saints, what is the breadth and length and height and depth, and to know the love of Christ that surpasses knowledge, so that you may be filled with all the fullness of God (Eph. 3:18-19).

What Paul is describing here is "ordinary mysticism" — not the visions and ecstasies described by the saints, but the experience every Christian should have who is living out, consciously and seriously, the mystery of the life of grace that is within us all.

Every human being has a "spiritual life," because every human being has a spirit. And every person who is sharing in the life of God by grace is living a "mystical life," consciously or not, because the mystery of God's life is a reality within each one. But in ordinary language we don't say that people are really "living a spiritual life" until they *realize that something is going on between themselves and God and decide to get involved in it.* And we don't say they are living a "mystical life" unless they have some conscious experience of life on a level that is divine. This experience, which we are calling "ordinary mysticism," is open and available to all, but not everyone seeks it or experiences it. That depends on each one's deep, personal choice. And that choice is to enter into the four dimensions of love to which St. Paul invites us: love in depth and length and breadth and height.

We begin to experience the *depth* of love when we start making everything we do in response to God a *personal choice.* This means that in all our actions we consciously and personally embrace the goal God holds out to us, and do what we are doing as a deliberately-chosen means to arrive at that goal.

For example, we don't just go to Mass on Sunday because it is an obligation or a practice of our religion. We go because we have reflected on the goal, the purpose of our presence at Mass, and we have chosen to participate in the Mass in a way that will help us achieve that goal. Participating in Mass then becomes for us a personal activity, a means we have personally adopted to achieve a goal we have personally embraced. The first step into "ordinary mysticism" is to strive to make personal in this same way every act and practice of our religion; in fact, of our lives.

We reflect on who Christ is for us personally, what we want him to be, how we will make him this for ourselves in fact and act. We take a deep, conscious, personal stance toward him as Savior and Lord. This is to enter into the *depth* of love. It makes us personally and consciously *Christians*.

We accept the *length* of love when we decide and choose to go "all the way" in responding to Christ's teachings, his invitations, his desires. We no longer ask what we "have to do" in our religion or settle for minimum participation; we seek with desire and determination to do everything for God that he allows, invites and empowers us to do. We want our response to be *total*. We don't measure out our morality until the scales tip just enough to get us into heaven; rather we study the Scriptures to see how far Christ invites us to go, to find more and more ways of responding generously to his love. We look for chances to learn more and to be challenged to more. We read books and go to talks on the spiritual life; we make retreats, we participate in adult religious education classes and formation sessions. We become more than followers of Jesus; we become *disciples*, students of his mind and heart. As disciples we accept as the working principle of our lives Christ's exhortation:

> Give, and it will be given to you. A good measure, pressed down, shaken together, running over, will be put into your lap; for the measure you give will be the measure you get back (Luke 6:38).

This doesn't mean that we are able overnight to respond to God totally, with unlimited generosity. Again, there is a parallel with marriage: married couples don't love each other perfectly the day they pronounce their vows; but from that moment they are committed to try to grow to perfect love with each other. This makes a fundamental difference in their lives. In the same way, as soon as we commit ourselves to go all the way with Jesus and to seek the "perfection of love" we are already launched into the *length* of love. We are committed to total response as *disciples*.

We embrace the *breadth* of love when we extend the dimensions of depth and length to embrace the whole breadth of our activity. We try to make our response to God personal and total in everything we do: in family and social life, in business and politics, in all our personal and professional decisions. This is *integral* response to God, living out the mystery of our divine life in everything we do, "right across the board."

By trying to make every detail of our life and lifestyle bear witness to the truth and values of Christ, we are living out our baptismal consecration as *prophets*. By ministering constantly to others, making it our preoccupation to communicate the divine life of God to everyone we deal with by giving physical expression to the invisible faith, hope and love in our hearts, we are living out our baptismal consecration as *priests*. By taking responsibility for establishing the reign of God in every area and activity of our lives — family and social life, business and politics — we are living out our baptismal consecration as *stewards of the kingship* of Christ. This is the *breadth* of love.[15]

But in this chapter it is above all the *height* of love that we are talking about. All the dimensions above are human dimensions. Even though they are extensions of the divine mystery of the life of grace, and even though we depend on grace to make the choices they call for, nevertheless, the effort itself to live out our response to Christ personally, totally and integrally — to embrace the depth and length and breadth of love — is an effort that is quite consistent with our natural, human way of doing things. There is human satisfaction in making all our choices personal, in deciding to be total and to go all the way in love, in knowing that we are living an integral rather than a fragmented response to God, that we are being whole and entire in living out our baptismal consecration.

But even people who are glad to respond to God in depth and length and breadth may hesitate when asked to let God take them to the heights of "transcendent" response; that is, to a level of responding to God that transcends, goes beyond, rises above the natural level of human activity.

Obviously, any graced action transcends our natural, human level of operation. But as we have seen above, a graced response to God can make more or less use of our natural, human powers. God can enlighten our intellects to understand and rejoice in divine truth, or he can take us beyond anything intellect can understand and call us to respond by the "dark light of faith" alone. He can seduce our wills with sweetness and reassure them with reason; or he can call us to love him in the agony of a garden that has lost its flowers and a light that has turned to darkness. The transcendent experience of pure faith, pure hope, pure love, is not found in the way we dance in the moonlight, but in the way we keep seeking and following our Beloved in the dark.

To persevere in following Jesus into the "breadth and length and height and depth" of love, we have to commit ourselves from the outset, and decide that without looking back, we will keep doing those things to which our faith has led us, those things to which our devotion once impelled us, whether or not we have any feeling of satisfaction or any felt experience of God's presence. Those who commit to this are accepting to be lifted to the "height" of love, where they walk without human supports. They must be willing to "breathe the Spirit pure" in the stratosphere of the spiritual life, where for all their inhaling, nothing seems to be coming in. They must be determined to keep looking for God in liturgies where nothing excites them, in homilies where nothing inspires them, in community activities where nothing nourishes them, in private prayer where nothing is all there is. This is the "nothing," the *nada* of St. John of the Cross, in which we find the All.

This is the paradox of the life of grace. Just as Jesus both hid and revealed his divinity as "Son of God" through the absence of human glory, so we experience most clearly the presence of his divine life within us when it produces no human resonance. In the absence of the human we "drink the Spirit pure." Then we know what Jesus meant when he said, "unless you change and become like children, you will never enter the kingdom of heaven" (Mt. 18:3). When the human voice of the controlling adult within us is silent, then "out of the mouths of babes and infants" God brings forth perfect praise. That is when we experience, not only Jesus, but ourselves as sons and daughters of God.

The key to it all

There is one choice we have to emphasize here, which is *practical*, *challenging*, and *essential*. If we really want to know God, there is a special kind of prayer we have to practice. It is included in what St. Teresa of Avila calls "mental prayer," but we should not let the word scare us off. This prayer can be understood quite easily. It hardly needs to be learned, because it is so natural. At the same time it is not to be taken for granted. I believe that everyone who has a real relationship with God engages in it sometimes, because without it one can hardly be in real contact with God. But I believe those people are rare who engage in it regularly, consistently, and in a committed way. That is why so few people truly "know God" as they should.

The best way I know to describe this prayer is to say what it is not. It is not "saying prayers." It is also not the kind of prayer we make with others in groups: singing hymns, engaging in devotional exercises together (the rosary, the Stations of the Cross, novenas). It is not even — and I say this with sober awareness of how terrible it sounds — the prayer we experience, or that most Catholics appear to experience, at Mass, which is of course the prayer of all prayers. To go to the heart of this description, it is not any prayer in which human words, human actions or the support of others can distract us from personal, face-to-face encounter with God. The prayer we are talking about is time spent dealing directly and personally with God. Its focus is on God, not on anything we are doing.

It is just too easy to identify prayer with "doing something," as if the action itself were somehow an experience of God. We see people who have "said their prayers" and "gone to Mass," and even "received the sacraments regularly" since childhood, but who, upon reaching adolescence or young adulthood, simply drop out of participation in the Church because, as they say, it "just never meant anything" to them.

And it didn't. It was all external. They were not consciously refusing to be involved in the prayers or ceremonies that were part of their life. They just "went along" with the external action, not suspecting there was anything more they should do; just assuming that "this was it," that this was the experience of religion and of what it means to be a Christian. And they did not find God in it.

People can attend church, participate in Bible studies or even retreats, and be untouched by personal encounter with God. They can remain on the intellectual level of listening to the word of God, to a teacher or preacher, or of participating in discussions that may be very stimulating. They can enjoy these activities, and even be emotionally moved by them, and because of this think they are experiencing "religion." But in fact they may be only hearing and thinking *about* God, and *about* God's word, God's love, God's reality. They are experiencing other people, but they may not be experiencing God, speaking to God, hearing God or knowing God. The face-to-face, person-to-person contact with God may not be there. What is there may be nothing but a "meaningful" group activity in which they are taking part. Later they may feel all this was meaningless and describe it, when they look back on it, as a part of their experience that "just never meant anything" to them.

Contrast this with those moments when one is all alone with the reality of God, without book or formula, without any ritual or method to follow. These are the moments when you "go into your room and shut the door and pray to your Father who is in secret" (Mt. 6:6), just you and God alone. These are the "nothing but" moments. They are times of prayer that can be "nothing but" prayer because you have set them up in such a way that nothing else is going on.

For this kind of prayer you "go into your room" — you go apart by yourself. The place is not important so long as you are alone. You sit in the garden, or lie in your bed awake, or just close your eyes to everything that surrounds you. You go into a private place with God.

And you "shut the door." You leave all your props outside. You meet God with nothing in your hands: no book, no crucifix, no rosary, no picture to focus your attention, nothing; not even the Bible. You might use one or more of these props to begin with, to get you started. But you don't limit yourself to them. You are not there just to read, to study, to reflect, to do spiritual problem-solving, to get some deep insights. You are there to deal with God.

In this kind of prayer you look at God and God looks at you and you both are facing what you see. You confront the question, the reality, of who God is for you, who the Father and Spirit are for you, who Jesus is for you. And you talk about what is real. In this kind of prayer you go *mano a mano* with God.

I am not saying that in this prayer you do not think, or even that you do not talk. This is not a kind of wordless, image-less prayer in which you try to "silence" all your human faculties. The prayer I am describing is very natural. All that is excluded are those props and activities that might substitute for personal, face-to-face interaction with God. The point is not to avoid thoughts or words, but just not to be caught up in them for their own sake. As Jesus said, "do not heap up empty phrases as the Gentiles do; for they think that they will be heard because of their many words" (Mt. 6:7). The purpose is to meet God, not to unload on him.

Prayer like this might begin with reading; for example, a passage from Scripture. And the reading might be followed by meditation — confronting what we have read and asking ourselves questions about it in an effort to take a position toward it with our will. We deal with God the way we deal with our fellow human beings: we dialogue with him; we try to understand Christ's words by asking questions about them and trying to answer them. We activate our wills, responding to him, taking a personal stance toward what we have seen, making his teachings and values our own through decisions and choices. But the reading and thinking and deciding must not remain just an intellectual, character-forming exercise within ourselves. It must lead us into eye-ball-to-eyeball contact with God. Frequently while we are thinking, when we are approaching a conclusion, or after we have come to a decision, we take time just to look at God, to talk to him, to sit there in silence with him, sharing the moment, aware of the communication between us.

This is the kind of prayer that makes God real to us, that gives us a conscious, personal, intimate relationship with him. But we need to spend time on it, at least a few minutes every day. If we give it the time, it gives us the experience of God.

Oddly enough, as we persevere in this kind of prayer our deepest experience of God might become identified with what appears to us to be no experience at all. This is to be understood in the light of everything we have said above about the divine revealing itself in the absence of the human.

The clearest experience of encounter with God is the "nothing-but-ness" of the experience. When prayer is completely arid, for example; when we meditate and cannot get a thought; when we can't think of any concrete decisions to make that we haven't made already, and we don't feel any devotion at all, then we inevitably ask ourselves, "What am I doing here?" And the answer is, "I am waiting on God in faith, in hope and in love. That must be what I am doing, because I am certainly not doing anything else!" It is then that we know we believe.

When prayer is humanly rewarding or pleasant; when we are getting great thoughts and insights, or making decisions which we know are putting our behavior on a higher level, then we really don't need deep faith to motivate our prayer. At these times it is obvious to us that what we are doing is producing results, is helping us. But when nothing seems to be happening at all, and yet we are persevering in solitude with God, we know that every minute we spend is an experience of "nothing but" divine faith, hope and love. The absence of human motivation is the experience of empowerment by God.

I have dealt with at least one authentic mystic in my life. She was a nun in a teaching order, but she had special permission to spend three or four hours a day in silent, contemplative prayer. I asked her once what went on during her prayer. She answered, "Nothing, just pain."

I knew she didn't mean physical pain, and assumed it was in some way the pain of longing for God. So I asked her, "Well, if nothing is going on, how do you know anything is going on?"

She answered, "If you are lying in the sun, you must be getting sunburned."

This is the experience of God.

CHAPTER THREE:
GOD PRESENT IN ABSENCE
"Son of God" — Matthew 21:12-16

Summary

When Jesus enters Jerusalem as king, the absence of all the means which would have enabled him to establish his reign as a human being tells us he is entering to establish it as the Son of God. In this, as in other passages of Matthew, it is *the absence of the human that reveals the presence of the divine.*

This helps us understand why we don't find more satisfaction in our religion. It is because Jesus calls us to a level of life that is divine, not just human. It is not easy to make the transition from responding to God in a way that is mostly natural, although empowered by grace, to a way of responding that is so dependent on the power of grace that it doesn't feel natural at all.

To take us beyond what is just human and natural goodness, God purifies us through the "dark nights of the soul." To persevere through these we have to keep praying and responding to God by what seems to be nothing but sheer will power and commitment. But we are in fact experiencing the power of grace, unaided by human feelings, working through pure faith, hope and love. The absence of human motivation is our experience of the reality of these divine gifts active within us.

The experience of "ordinary mysticism," is available to everyone who chooses to respond to God in a way that is *personal, total, integral* and *transcendent.*

The key to personal relationship with God is the commitment to spend some time every day in the kind of prayer that is direct, personal encounter with him — alone and without props, just face-to-face with God, confronting the reality, of who God is for you and who you are for God.

Have you understood?

What is it about Jesus' entry into Jerusalem that indicates he is "Son of God" and not just a prophet? Why does the absence of the human sometimes reveal the presence of the divine?

What are the "dark nights of the soul," and how do they help us grow? From what do they purify us?

Why do the "natural religions" sometimes have more appeal for us, or appear more satisfying, than Christianity?

What is "ordinary mysticism"? What does it take to make our response to God *personal, total, integral* and *transcendent*?

Why is it so important to spend deep time in prayer with God each day? Is it possible to have an intimate personal relationship with God if one does not do this? Why?

What is the challenge of this chapter? To our faith? To our hope? To our love?

Making it your own

What are the key thoughts in this chapter? (Jot them down and give the page number where each is found).

What questions do I have about this chapter? (Bring them up in discussion or ask someone who should know the answers).

What struck me the most in this chapter? After reading this chapter, what do I understand better than I did before? What do I appreciate more?

What do I think is the point of the whole chapter? What response does Matthew want to evoke from those who read or hear this part of his Gospel?

What can I use as a visible reminder (a symbol) to keep me aware of the challenge of this chapter? Where will I put it?

Questions for prayer

How do I feel about the way Jesus entered Jerusalem? What doe it say to me that he refused to use power?

Do I enjoy praying? Participating in Eucharist? Does my commitment keep me faithful to prayer and Eucharist when I find no devotion in them?

Am I an "ordinary mystic"? Do I want to be? Why? For me, what would be a first step to becoming one?

Have I decided to give at least fifteen minutes a day to deep private prayer? Why?

How can I apply to my life what I have come to see by reflecting on this chapter? What concrete action do I choose to perform to express my belief in what I have seen?

FOOTNOTES

[1] This verse as cited in the Gospel is translated differently than it is in the modern translation of Psalm 8:2. The word translated in the Gospel as "praise" literally means "strength." And the *Jerome Biblical Commentary* (35:26 on Psalm 8) explains that the general idea behind this verse is that "God's power is the more evident because of the modest means (*babes*) he uses." This is the principle we will see below: that the absence of human means is sometimes a sign of God's power at work.

[2] See the *Jerome Biblical Commentary*, 43:143 and 146, on Mt. 21:10-17 and 23-27. I disagree with the author's opinion on Mt. 21:12-17 (42:125) that Jesus' prophetic gesture of casting the merchants out of the temple is "the only incident in the Gospel that connects Jesus with violence." The imagination of artists has led us to assume that Jesus used a whip on the moneychangers. It would be more natural to understand that the whip was used as whips normally are used for herding animals, and that Jesus used no violence whatsoever, either on people or on the animals he herded. The prophetic gesture of overturning the tables was certainly intended to show anger, but that does not necessarily make it a violent act. Jesus is not using force. The only power he shows here is the power of truth and righteous indignation. No one resisted his intervention; they all knew it was simply a prophetic gesture, and that they could all come back and set up shop again the next day, which they undoubtedly did. For an explanation of Jesus' transformation of the Ten Commandments from laws of good human behavior into guidelines for living on the level of God, see the Semon on the Mount, Matthew, chapters 5 to 8, as explained in my book *Make Me A Sabbath Of Your Heart*.

[3] See *The Spiritual Exercises* of St. Ignatius of Loyola, #196: the fifth point in the first contemplation of the Third Week.

[4] There are some striking parallels in the passages which, according to the outline we are following, present Jesus under the title "Son of God." The passage on the virgin birth (1:18-25) is matched by the curing of the centurion's servant from afar, without physical contact (8:5-13). The sending of the disciples without provisions (10:9-10) is echoed

in the shocked question of the people of Jesus' home town who could not understand how he could preach so eloquently without carrying any "baggage" of education: "Is this not the carpenter's son?... Where did he get all this?" (13:55-56). Peter's recognition of Jesus in a way "flesh and blood" could not have done (16:17-18) is paralleled by the transformation of marriage into an irrevocable covenant beyond the power of unaided flesh and blood to preserve (19:7-9). And finally, the honor given to Jesus by the little children shouting "Hosanna!" (21:4-16) is matched by the honor shown him by the woman who poured the "alabaster jar of very costly ointment" on his head (26:6-7).

[5] See *Ascent of Mount Carmel*, Bk. 2, ch. 17. Nos. 3 and 4. I am indebted to Michael Joseph Buckley, S.J., for this explanation of the dark nights.

[6] See *The Dark Night*, Bk. 1, ch. 8, nos. 3 and 4. For a definition of "consolation" and "desolation" see St. Ignatius of Loyola, *The Spiritual Exercises*, "Rules for the Discernment of Spirits," nos. 316-317.

[7] See *The Dark Night*, Bk. 2, ch. 16, no. 1. St. Thérèse of Lisieux, the "Little Flower," went through this dark night intensely toward the end of her life. She gives us just a hint of what it was like:

> My Beloved Mother, it might seem to you that I am exaggerating my trial. And as a matter of fact, if you judge by the feelings I express in the little bits of verse I composed this year, I must seem to you to be a soul filled with consolations — one for whom the veil of faith is almost torn apart. The truth is, it is no longer a veil for me; it is a wall that reaches to the heavens and blocks out the sky and the stars. When I sing of the blessedness of Heaven, the eternal possession of God, I feel no joy at all in it, because I am only singing about what I WANT TO BELIEVE. Sometimes, it is true, a tiny ray of sunshine comes down to enlighten my darkness. Then the trial ceases for *a moment*. But afterwards, the memory of that ray of light, instead of giving me joy, makes my darkness even more impenetrable....
>
> ....This trial took away everything that might have given me any natural satisfaction in the desire that I had for Heaven.

On the preceding page she tells how she handled this trial: "[Jesus] knows that, not finding any joy in the Faith, I try at least to keep doing its works. I think I have made more acts of faith during this past year than in my whole life." (Translated from pages 259-261 of chapter 9 of her autobiography, *Histoire d'une Ame*, ed. Conrad de Meester, Carmel-Edit, Moerzeke, Belgium, 1999. This is from manuscript G, written for Mother Gonzaga).

[8] "Declaration on the Relationship of the Church to Non-Christian Religions," no. 2. Unless otherwise indicated, all citations from Vatican II are from *The Documents of Vatican II*, ed. Walter M. Abbott, S.J., America Press, 1966.

[9] See John 1:16; Romans 15:29; 1Corinthians 10:26; Galatians 4:4; Ephesians 1:10; 1:23; and 3:19; Colossians 1:19; 2:9; and 2:10.

[10] *Spiritual Canticle*, Stanza 6; my translation.

[11] This may also explain some of the fundamentalist zeal in converting people: they believe that if they convince someone to "accept Jesus," by that one act the person is saved for all eternity. It is highly motivating to be able to believe at the end of the day what a youthful minister once declared to me, "I have saved four people today!" A Catholic who did the same work would probably say instead, "Well, I got four people interested; let's hope they persevere!"

[12] See *The Ascent of Mount Carmel*, Bk. 2, ch 4, nos. 3 and 4.

[13] See St. Ignatius of Loyola, *Spiritual Exercises*, the tenth rule for the discernment of spirits, no. 323: "Let those who are in consolation think how they will act later on in desolation, gaining fresh strength for it."

[14] See Vatican II's document on *The Church* no. 40. See also no. 11, no. 42, and *Ecumenism*, ch. 1.

[15] I owe the concept of "ordinary mysticism" as personal, total, integral response to Fr. Ernest Larkin, O. Carm., in class at Catholic University, Washington, D.C., 1966-67. I added the dimension of *height*, or "transcendent" response.

Chapter Four
Interacting Humanly with Jesus
Jesus is "Emmanuel" — Matthew 21:5-8, 12-14

Christianity is kept authentic by a constant balancing of
contrasts: Jesus is human, yet divine. Jesus entered Jerusalem in triumph, but to be defeated. His defeat on the cross
was his victory. Christ's divine power is revealed in his
human weakness. Jesus alone is Savior of the world; yet the
rate of redemption depends on the human cooperation of
people who are his body on earth. Our awareness of the
presence of God within us grows deeper through the experience of his absence.

And now we consider yet another contrast: the same God
who reveals himself through the absence of the human has
revealed himself and continues to reveal himself precisely
through what is human. In the human words and actions of
Jesus, both before his resurrection and now in the Church,
his risen body on earth, we experience "Jesus-Emmanuel,"
Jesus as God humanly present and visible among us, God
dealing with us and inviting us to deal with him through
human actions. And paradoxically, through Jesus' death,
resurrection and ascension into heaven, contact with him in
his humanity has become, not less experiential and available to people, but more.[1]

In the scene of Jesus' triumphal entry into Jerusalem, Matthew first establishes for us what the human presence of
Jesus is, what it means for us to call him "Emmanuel: God-
with-us." Jesus enters Jerusalem "humble, and mounted on
a donkey."

In spite of the majesty that Jesus is claiming in this
scene, he appears here as God on ground level: "Emmanuel: God-with-us" — God present to his people, close
to them, God with them as one of themselves: "Tell the
daughter of Zion, Look, your king is coming to you, humble, and mounted on a donkey, and on a colt, the foal of a

donkey." There is nothing in his triumphant entry into Jerusalem as king which inspires fear and awe, or keeps people at a distance; nothing of the Jesus whom Peter, James and John saw transfigured on the mountain top, his face "dazzling as the sun," his clothes "as radiant as light," when they fell down in fear at the sound of the Father's voice (see Mt. 17:1). Jesus enters Jerusalem to inaugurate a kingdom in which this world's symbols of prestige and power will have no place. He enters as a king who is one of his people, close to them, available; not separated from his followers by protocol or distanced by demands for deference. He comes into Jerusalem on a borrowed donkey with homemade pomp improvised by enthusiasts cutting branches from the trees and spreading their coats on the ground. And when he arrives at the temple the blind and the lame feel free to approach him, and he cures them.

"God-with-us" in a new way

Once in the temple, Jesus drives out the money changers and at the same time changes the nature of the temple forever. The full significance of this action is not spelled out in Matthew's Gospel, but in John's account it is clear that Jesus is replacing the presence of God in the temple with his presence in the living body of his Church:

> The Jews then said to him, "What sign can you show us for doing this?" Jesus answered them, "Destroy this temple, and in three days I will raise it up."
>
> The Jews then said, "This temple has been under construction for forty-six years, and will you raise it up in three days?" But he was speaking of the temple of his body.
>
> After he was raised from the dead, his disciples remembered that he had said this; and they believed the scripture and the word that Jesus had spoken (John 2:18-22; and see John 4:19-24; 14:15-23; 15:7; 17:21; and Luke 19:41-44).

John is proclaiming here that in the Church, his risen body on earth, Jesus, with the Father and the Spirit, will dwell forever in a way that God's presence in the temple, and before that, in the Ark of the Covenant, could only remotely foreshadow.

Through Jesus' death, resurrection and ascension into heaven we lost that unique presence of God made flesh which we saw in the body Jesus received from his mother Mary. At the same time, we gained a new presence of Jesus in his Church; a presence in word and sacrament, and a human, physical presence multiplied in all those who would offer their bodies to him in Baptism to be his living body on earth (see Rom. 12:1-5). In the living members of his Church Jesus continues to be "Emmanuel: God-with-us." And although the distortion of Jesus' truth and goodness in those members can be at times the greatest obstacle to perseverance in the faith, it is still true that there is no greater help to perseverance and spiritual growth than continuing interaction with Jesus speaking, ministering and challenging us through those who are his real, if imperfect, body on this planet. In them he continues to be "Emmanuel" for us now, "God-with-us" where we are: in the loving members of our family, in the thoughtful neighbor next door, in the people we work with, in the priest who hears our confession and anoints us when we are sick, in everyone in whom the Spirit of God dwells and through whom the Spirit speaks.

Recognizing the divine in its human appearance

Jesus founded his Church to perpetuate the easy accessibility that people had to him in the Gospels. He sent his disciples out to all the towns and villages, instructing them to travel without provisions and to lodge simply in the homes of the people who received them. The Church was not established to inspire awe by using the status symbols and power protocol of this world, but to give a simple, human form to the awesome presence of God in the world; to let Jesus continue to be *Emmanuel*, "God-with-us" in unassuming lowliness and accessibility in all the members of his body on earth (see Phil. 2:6-7; Mt. 10:9-11; 18:1-4; 23:1-12).

Jesus confirmed and reemphasized this "option for lowliness" when, before announcing his way of saving the world through the cross, he turned over his authority to Peter — a man camped with him on the side of the road in the desert, so poor, so powerless, and so culturally unimpressive that the bestowal of the "keys of the kingdom" on this "rock" of impulsiveness and human weakness could have been interpreted as a joke (see Mt. 16:13-20).[2]

And it probably appeared to many as a joke when Jesus staged his entrance into Jerusalem as king. There is certainly something comic in this ragtag procession of believers escorting a barefoot, dusty-robed prophet on a mule into Jerusalem with shouts of "Hosanna! Save us!" Any Roman soldiers looking on must have been laughing so hard they could hardly hold their spears straight (see Mt. 21:5-9). But we know that this was a scene of contrasts which reveals Jesus to us as "Emmanuel": the infinitely distant God come close, the awesome, majestic God made one of us, human and accessible.

Accepting Emmanuel as he is

If we want to grow into intimate knowledge and love of Jesus Christ on earth, then like the blind and the lame who approached him without fear in the temple, we need to persevere in recognizing him as divine while dealing with him as human. This is to accept Jesus as "Emmanuel: God-with-us."

And if we want to transform the world as stewards of Christ's kingship, we need to remain united to the risen Jesus by persevering in dealing with him through the human interactions of "word and sacrament." There are generous idealists who have "left the Church," but who give themselves, for a time at least, to serving the poor and working for social justice. If they have gone so far as to give up all faith in God, or in Jesus as Savior, they are offering the world a salvation without a soul. They can offer no ultimate comfort to the afflicted, no lasting good news to the poor. They are not "Emmanuel" — just human beings trying to repair humans' inhumanity to humans without offering that union with divinity which alone can make humanity whole.

If they are still partial believers; that is, if they have kept some faith in Jesus but have just broken off their interactive relationship with him in the Church, his body on earth, they are still not "Emmanuel" in a fully authentic way. They are handicapped in ministry because they are trying to do the work of Christ in separation from the full body of Christ. They are trying to function as organs without the rest of the body. This is a radical denial — in action — of the true reality of the Incarnation. God did not take flesh to act as an isolated individual in independence of the human race. And he does not call people to be members of his body today to act as isolated individuals in independence of the rest of the body. Jesus himself, from the beginning of his ministry, worked through, with and within a community of disciples united to him in faith and commitment (see Matthew 4:17-22; Mark 15:). If we refuse community with the members of Christ's body on earth we are refusing community with Christ. We are trying to play the game without being members of the team. That isn't the way Christ plays it.

When people leave the Church they do not necessarily think of themselves as leaving Jesus. And in fact they may continue to interact with Jesus the Son of God in heaven. But they are very definitely parting company in greater or lesser degree with Jesus-Emmanuel: the Jesus who is still "God with us" in the human members of his body on earth. They recognize the historical Jesus, the Jesus who walked and spoke and ministered in Galilee. They may pray to him and draw inspiration from his words. They may gather together with other partial believers for mutual support and ministry, forming "churches" ("assemblies") of their own under the headship of Jesus the Son of God in heaven. But they are parting company with "Emmanuel," with the physical reality of the post-resurrection Jesus who after his ascension into heaven continued and still continues to walk and speak and minister in the community he established to be his body on earth.

There is no doubt about what the word "church" meant to the authors of the New Testament. Whether they were speaking of local churches or of the Church as a whole, the "church" was the community that gathered around the apostles and remained united to them through shared faith, shared Eucharist and shared ministry. Any assembly ("church") that was not united to the other churches through union with the apostles in faith, Eucharist and ministry was simply not what the New Testament authors meant by the church of Jesus Christ. And anyone today who breaks off from this community to do Christian minis-try to others is breaking off from the ministerial body and team that Jesus established. Legitimacy in ministry comes from union with the "twelve foundations" on which are written "the twelve names of the twelve apostles of the Lamb" (Revelations 21:14). This is what the bishops at the Council of Nicea (325 A.D.) meant when they put into the profession of faith which Catholics recite at Mass every Sunday the words "We believe in one holy catholic *and apostolic* Church." The Church we believe in is the Church that can claim to continue the ministry of the original twelve apostles by being in union with those who for the past two thousand years have been and still are in union with them.

It is significant that all four Gospels end on this note. The synoptics — Matthew, Mark and Luke — all conclude with Jesus appearing to "the eleven" (Judas not yet having been replaced) and sending them to be "witnesses" and to "pro-

claim the good news to the whole creation." It is to them
and to those united with them that the mission is entrusted.
John's Gospel has no pre-ascension scene, but ends instead
with Jesus' special mandate to Peter: "Feed my lambs...
Tend my sheep... Feed my sheep." The mission of proclaiming Jesus is entrusted, not just to anyone who reads
his words and believes them, but to the community established under the headship of Peter and the other apostles
"who were chosen by God as witnesses, and who ate and
drank with him after he rose from the dead" (Acts 10:41;
1:21-22).[3]

To part company with that community is to part company
with the risen Jesus ministering in the body he has made his
own on earth.[4]

Can we say that those who give up their dedication to the
Church but dedicate themselves to serving Christ in others
— in the poor and the needy — are failing to recognize Jesus? After all, Jesus himself said to those who cared for the
hungry and thirsty, for strangers, for the naked, sick and
imprisoned, "Truly I tell you, just as you did it to one of the
least of these who are members of my family, you did it to
me!" Do we have to belong to the Church to serve Jesus in
the poor, the afflicted and the oppressed?

Of course not. But to serve Jesus in the poor is not always
the same as to *recognize Jesus* in the poor. It is quite possible — and quite good — to serve the poor just because they
are poor, and to help the afflicted just because they are suffering human beings. And God is certainly pleased with
that, just as he is pleased with the worship of those who do
not know his Name or the revelation of his Person in the
Word made Flesh. The question is whether someone who
has rejected the real presence of Jesus in his whole body on
earth can truly recognize that presence in any of his members. One might wonder about someone, for example, who
recognized the presence of Christ in a pope but not in a
prostitute. But one should wonder equally about someone

who recognizes Christ in the prostitute but not in the pope.

Frequently the underlying mistake of those who leave the Church is one we have already seen: it is the unconscious identification of the "Church" with those in public positions of power and authority rather than with the whole body of Christ. The "Church" should mean for us the whole Church: the saints and the sinners in the pews, the exploited and the poor, the contemplatives in the monasteries and the activists demonstrating in the streets, the mothers with children at home and the college students in mission to the needy during Spring breaks. The "Church" is in the faces of those coming up to Communion during Mass, in hands that are callused by labor, in the patient smile of a gate agent, in feet that are dancing on a date. To "leave the Church" is to leave the father's arm that held you when you cried, the teacher's voice that taught you who Jesus was, the ear of the priest who listened to your sins, the baby you held at the font for Baptism. It is to break with all the Saints down the ages, and with the uncanonized saints of our day: with Archbishop Romero, shot to death on the altar for exposing atrocities against the poor; with Dorothy Day and the Catholic Worker movement; with Fr. Maximilian Kolbe dying in place of a married man in the starvation bunker at Auschwitz; with César Chavez defending migrant workers in California; with Lech Walesa challenging the communist yoke in Poland; with Edith Stein, Jewish intellectual and Carmelite nun, gassed by the Nazis in retaliation for her bishops' courageous defense of the Jews; with Chico Mendes, rubber worker and labor organizer in the Amazon forest, winner of the United Nations Global 500 Award for Environmental Protection, assassinated for preserving the rain forest. The list goes on and on; it reaches backwards for two thousand years. The people it proclaims bring together every country and corner of the earth. And in their lifetimes they all "gathered" with the bishops and assembled with the Church for Eucharist. This is what they all recognized as the fundamental source and expression of their unity with Christ, with each other and with us.

All these people are the Church; it is of them that we should think when we ask what "the Church" is doing today. And when we think of leaving the "Church" we should be aware that we are parting company with them. We are no longer playing on the same team with them.

Jesus lives, works and reigns on earth as the head of a body, his body. He is Emmanuel, "God-with-us" in the flesh, even today. To truly know him as Emmanuel, and to authentically make him present as Emmanuel in our own flesh, we have to accept him in all who are his living body on earth and be one with him by being one with them. As soon as we try to make our identification with Jesus an exclusively one-on-one relationship, we lose our understanding of him and of ourselves as Christians.

Jesus is not a "lone ranger," an isolated Savior. He fulfills his mission completely and authentically only in those who surrender themselves to him in mind and body, in spirit and in flesh to be members of his body on earth. This means accepting him in his human reality, in word and sacrament and Church, as fully as we accept him in his divinity.

Giving full value to the human and divine

As time goes on it can become difficult for us to balance — or better, to keep giving full value — to both parts of the name Emmanuel: "God," and "with us." Jesus is in fact God, the Second Person of the Blessed Trinity, God the Son. He is infinitely more than just a prophet or a human being especially chosen and empowered by God; he is God Himself. At the same time, the name Emmanuel emphasizes the fact that Jesus is God *with us*: God in human form, God dwelling among us in the ordinariness of human life and activity, God inviting us to interact with him humanly in all our actions, to take him with us in all the commonplace activities of daily life.

The challenge in this is to maintain both intimacy and reverence; to deal with Jesus as a human being without forgetting he is divine. The easy accessibility of Jesus in the sacraments, especially in Eucharist and the sacrament of Reconciliation, should not lead us into forgetting that in these sacraments the one we are dealing with is God.

The "divine" without the human

In past ages reverence for the awesome mystery of the Mass was maintained by means that did more harm than good. These means achieved their purpose by falsifying the true nature of the Mass as a communal prayer and an act of the whole congregation. In the western Church Latin was originally adopted as the language of the Eucharistic celebration because it was the only language that was more or less understood by all the various nations in the Roman Empire. But Latin was retained for centuries throughout Europe and in all the countries that were evangelized from Europe, long after it had become unintelligible to everyone but the priests. This was due partly to inertia and partly to the fact that Latin was a foreign and therefore a mysterious language. Its very unintelligibility made the Mass appear more sacred. And since only the priest understood the words, the Mass became a mysterious rite which the priest "said," "offered" or "celebrated" while the people "heard," "attended," or just "went" to Mass, remaining reverently silent.

In order to keep from being totally bored, the people occupied themselves by default with private prayers. Some said the rosary. Others followed the Mass prayers by reading a vernacular translation in their missals, each person privately. Not only did the language make communal participation impossible, it also taught Catholics, falsely, that the Mass was something they were not even supposed to have an active part in, and especially not as a united, vocal, participating congregation. It was a sacred ceremony which each person followed individually, worshipping in private. Pope Leo XIII actually encouraged this distorted understanding of the Eucharistic celebration by prescribing the recitation of the rosary during Masses celebrated in October, the month dedicated to the rosary.[5]

The "silent Mass" had its advantages. For people who did not take time at home to pray in the way Jesus prescribed for private prayer — "go into your room and shut the door and pray to your Father who is in secret" — the Mass became their "quiet time." The church was a place to be alone with God in the midst of a congregation where no one interacted with anyone but God. For those who attended Mass daily this was a precious time. By contrast Sunday Mass was less prayerful because it was more crowded, noisy and distracting.

Since communal participation was impossible, it is understandable that Catholics began to sit as far as possible from each other in church, in order to be alone and undisturbed with God. No one would dream of doing this at a family meal or at any gathering of friends. But the distorted Mass affirmed apartness. Also, because Catholics did not really understand the Mass as a communal celebration, they did not think of themselves as having personal responsibility for the ceremony. They thought their only role was to be quiet, be reverent, and try to pray privately as best they could. That is why Catholics to this day think they are free to sit together or not, vocalize the responses or not, and join in the singing at Mass or not, according to their personal preference. They don't see themselves as members of a worshipping team; they are spectators. This also explains why many will leave Mass before the final hymn is over. The actors in a play would not dream of walking off the stage during the final number; nor would players in a ball game leave before the final whistle. But Catholics at Mass think of themselves, not as members of a cast or of a team, but as spectators who are free to leave whenever they feel that the main event is over for them.

Restoring the human

When the bishops at Vatican II called for a reform of liturgy which would teach again the authentic nature of the Mass, they were restoring the human side of this divine-human celebration. Human beings communicate in a language all can understand. When human beings celebrate something together, they naturally sit together. Not to do so would be a sign of isolating oneself from the group. In human celebrations people sing songs everyone knows, and all try to learn the new ones. Human celebrations are embodied in the language, the symbols, the emotional spirit of the participants' particular culture. They are something people can easily and naturally enter into, not only intellectually, but affectively. All this was the human dimension of the Mass that the reform of the liturgy tried to restore *in order* to help people enter more fully into the divine mystery that the Mass really is.

There were abuses, of course. Some people tried to make the Mass more human by making it less divine. They deliberately downplayed the sacredness of the ceremony. Wild stories were circulating in the heady heydays after Vatican II of Masses celebrated in college dorms with students sitting on the floor in their pajamas drinking coffee. Small groups did not just stand around the altar; they leaned on it to show how comfortable they were with "good ole buddy Jesus." Naturally, there was a reaction to this. Pressure groups began clamoring for the "old Mass" again, and many bishops began to teach error in their dioceses by re-introducing the old distorted liturgy that had falsified the true understanding of the Mass in the first place. And so in our day, just when pastors in the United States are straining all their resources to celebrate Mass in Spanish so that the new wave of Hispanic immigrants can participate at Mass in a language they understand, we see the anomaly of

American Catholics deliberately making the language of
the Mass unintelligible to themselves by insisting it be
celebrated in Latin!

This is the history of the Catholic Church. Because we are
the Church of "Emmanuel: God with us," we are constantly
swinging back and forth between trying to save the divine
in our religion by making it less human and trying to save
the human by making it less divine. We emphasize faith by
denying reason. Then we base everything on reason to the
practical exclusion of faith. We insist on obedience to
authority so much that we downplay responsible judgment
and deaden initiative. Then we institute a process of decision-making that involves everyone, but in such a way that
authority is reduced to nothing but chairmanship of the
board. When we fight against legalism we open the door to
anarchy. When we try to restore order we make an idol of
the letter of the law. And in liturgy, to make the Mass relevant we sacrifice reverence; then we try to regain reverence
by making a value out of irrelevancy.

This pendulum movement can be seen in the earliest councils of the Church. When Christians were trying to come to
clarity about the person of Jesus "Emmanuel," the pendulum swung back and forth between those who insisted on
the "God" part of "God-with-us" by denying Christ's humanity, and those who insisted on the "with us" part by denying his divinity. Was Jesus really just a human being especially favored by God? Or was he really just God who
took on the appearance of a human being without actually
becoming one? This was fought out through several councils of the Church that spanned the fourth and fifth centuries. What is important in this is the Church's consistent
response: Jesus was *fully human and fully divine*, one divine person existing in two natures, one human, one divine.
And the same principle must guide us in our practical living
of Christian spirituality. In everything we do, we must give
full value to the human and to the divine, never saving one

by sacrificing the other, but saving the mystery of our divine-human religion by giving full value to both. "Either-or" is the trap; "both-and" is the saving solution.[6]

Finding Jesus on earth

In the Church Jesus continues to be present to us, first of all, in "word and sacrament." If we persevere in reading his words and receiving his sacraments, we will remain in a life-giving contact with Jesus himself which will confirm our faith, maintain our hope and nourish our love.

The Church believes that both in the inspired words of Scripture and in the sacraments Jesus is really present, speaking and acting.

> ...Christ is always present in his Church, especially in her liturgical celebrations. He is present in the sacrifice of the Mass, not only in the person of his minister... but especially under the Eucharistic species. By his power he is present in the sacraments, so that when a [human person] baptizes it is really Christ himself who baptizes. He is present in his word, since it is he himself who speaks when the holy Scriptures are read in the church. He is present, finally, when the Church prays and sings, for he promised, "Where two or three are gathered together for my sake, there am I in the midst of them"....
>
> From this it follows that every liturgical celebration, because it is an action of Christ the priest and of his Body the Church, is a sacred action surpassing all others. [7]

And again:

> The Church has always venerated the divine Scriptures just as she venerates the body of the Lord, since from the table of both the word of God and of the body of Christ she unceasingly receives and offers to the faithful the bread of life, especially in the sacred liturgy.... For [the Scriptures]... make the voice of the Holy Spirit resound in the words of the prophets and apostles... For in the sacred books the Father who is in heaven meets his children with great love and speaks with them.... [8]

We can interact with Jesus humanly through his words because, first of all, he is truly present and speaking to us when we read his words.

Secondly, we can understand him, because the words of Jesus are human words, which he spoke as a human being to other human beings. What God knows divinely as God he expressed humanly in Jesus Christ. We can understand what Jesus means when he uses words, just as we can understand what other human beings mean when they use words. And when Jesus reveals his mind and heart to us through his words, we can come to know him through the way he expresses himself, just as we come to know other human beings through the way they express themselves. We just have to deal with Jesus the way we deal with other human friends.

Our choice

The only question is, do we choose to? Do we choose to really believe that the living God is speaking to us when we read the words of his book? Do we choose to believe he will speak to us personally if we reflect on his words? Do we choose to put enough faith in him to invest time in trying to get to know him? Do we choose to love — that is desire friendship with — Jesus enough to invest time in human communication with him, just as we invest time getting to know other people through human communication?

And if we hit a snag, run into something we don't understand, or find Jesus expressing in the Gospels some attitude or way of behaving we can't accept, will we just give up? Will we stop reading and stop reflecting? Or will we persevere the way we do with other friends we really want to keep, asking more questions, seeking advice from others who know our friend, trying to understand and accept, trying to become one in mind and heart with this other who is important to us?

If we dealt only with a purely spiritual God, a God far removed from us in the incomprehensible transcendence of his divine being, we might find it harder to persevere in dealing with him. (And then we could not legitimately think of God either as "him" or as "her," but simply as a totally indefinable "It"). It is hard to interact humanly with a God who has no body, no shape, no form of any sort, and no kind of physical presence on earth. It can be done — through various forms of wordless, imageless prayer, for example — but it is more difficult and not usually where we begin. [9]

But once God chooses to interact with us in human ways, to reveal himself in human terms, everything becomes easier. Dealing with God becomes as simple as picking up the Scriptures every morning and reading them. We may not feel great devotion or get any brilliant thoughts, but we will be interacting authentically with God if we do three simple, human things: 1. *confront* some sentence or idea we read in the Scripture; 2. *ask questions* about the meaning it has or can have in our own lives; 3. *make a decision* to do something that will express our response to what we have seen. The key to the whole process is step three: if we get no inspiring thoughts at all when we ask our questions, all we need to do is ask, "What can I *do* that will show my belief in this?" Then we will arrive at the meaning this passage of Scripture has for us here and now.

Because God has made it possible for us to deal with him humanly, perseverance in dealing with God is no more complicated (though admittedly it takes more faith) than perseverance in reading the newspapers or jogging around the block every day. We just have to keep dealing with Jesus in human ways — reading his words, talking to him, interacting with him in Eucharist and in the sacrament of Reconciliation, making decisions based on what we have come to know he desires, counting on his help, carrying out his mission, and persevering in all this without depending on feelings or visible results.

The words of Jesus in Scripture are there; they are real; they are available; there is nothing to stop us from reading them — and from persevering in reading them — except our free choice. If we make the choice to persevere in dealing with Jesus-Emmanuel, God-with-us-through-his-words, we will find that he is faithful to his promises. He will reveal himself to us, and we will grow into intimacy with him (see John, chapter 14).

Keepers of the word

To persevere in this choice is also to persevere in *faithful stewardship*; it is to take *responsibility* for the words Jesus has left us, the treasure he has entrusted to us. The faithful steward invests the master's treasure, appreciates it, puts it to work, draws a profit from it, lets it generate more treasure and bear recurring fruit in every season, according to the needs of every time and place. God's words will do this if we let them. In his words God comes to us like the "radiant dawn": the same sun, the same light, eternal and unchanging, yet dawning anew in every sunrise, unique in the colors and form it takes as it shines through every morning's different atmosphere. Like God himself, God's words are "ever ancient, ever new," always the same yet always surprising, always able to cast new light on changing questions and situations. But if the "stewards of the word," which we are, do not let his words shine through us, through our minds and reflections and judgments, through the unique physical embodiment that every individual's particular words and choices can give them, then God's words, like a sun that cannot penetrate the clouds, will not have a place on earth. And we, the unfaithful stewards of God's word, will be responsible for not letting Jesus be "Emmanuel," God with us in our times. But if we do persevere in reading and reflecting on his words, then Isaiah tells us "your light shall break forth like the dawn, and your healing shall spring up quickly.... Nations shall come to your light, and kings to the brightness of your dawn." (See Mt. 5:16; 24:45-47; 25:14-29; Luke 1:78; Isaiah, chapters 58 to 62).

God being physical

The same is true about our dealing with Jesus through the sacraments. What we call "sacramental graces" are simply graces, favors, or new ways of being in relationship with God which we receive through specific, physical ways of interacting with God and each other in his Church. We are reborn through the pouring of water; reconciled to God by human words of confession and absolution; strengthened, consecrated and healed by anointing with oil; given mystical experiences of spousal love with Jesus Christ through physical sexual relations transformed by the sacrament of matrimony. Through the physical ritual actions of two sacraments, the joining of hands in Matrimony and the laying on of hands in Holy Orders, we take on specific roles of ministry to other people, specifying in particular ways the all-embracing ministry to which we were dedicated by the consecrating oils of Baptism and Confirmation. And in every Eucharist we are spiritually nourished by physically receiving the body and blood of Christ under the appearances of bread and wine.

What is "sacramental" about these graces is the fact that they are given in and through physical, human actions. Some of these graces God can and does give nonsacramentally also; that is, without passing through any human interaction with the Church. There is, for example, "baptism of desire," by which a person can be reborn as a child of God and a member of the body of Christ without ever having heard of Jesus and without any recognized, visible association with the assembly of believers on earth. People can become sharers in the divine life of God (receive the grace of salvation) by "following their star" as the

Magi did, in an unconditional surrender of faith and trust and love to some specific invitation God extends to them in a language or under a symbol to which they can respond. And God is constantly forgiving the sins of people who repent in their hearts and ask him to do so, without any human interaction in sacramental confession.

Not less but more

The coming of Jesus did not limit our way of dealing with God. We can still interact with God in a "purely spiritual" way. We can still "confess our sins directly to God" as people of all religions, Christian and non-Christian, have done since the beginning of time. We don't need to hear the voice of the incarnate Jesus, speaking through the priest, saying to us, "Your sins are forgiven; go and sin no more." We can still ask God in silent prayer for healing when we are sick, or for faith and strength in times of trial, as people of all religions do, without calling on a priest to physically touch us and anoint us with oil. And we can invite God at any time to unite us more deeply to himself. The fact that we are also able to receive his body and blood physically in Holy Communion does not cancel out the way all people of faith can receive Christ in a purely spiritual way by inviting him into their hearts. The sacraments do not limit our ways of encountering God; they simply add a way of encountering him that would not be available to us if God had not taken flesh in Jesus Christ to deal with us in physical, human ways. In the physical, human words and touches of the sacraments Jesus is still "Emmanuel," and we are able to hear his voice and feel his touch and know that he is "God-with-us" until the end of time.

This is a fundamental characteristic of the Christian religion: that God was made flesh and became a human being to deal with us and let us interact with him in human, physical ways. God forgives sins in every religion; it is only in Christianity that he speaks to us with a human voice saying,

"Your sins are forgiven." God comforts and heals the sick in every religion; but it is only in Christianity that the incarnate God, acting through a minister whose hands and voice are his real hands and voice on earth, touches us himself and anoints us with consecrated oil.

We can believe that God communicates the gift of his divine love through every human act of love on earth. But it is only through the sacrament of matrimony that two people are made consciously aware that their bodies are Christ's body, separately and together, and that their physical gift to each other has been declared explicitly divine. Then in their sexual relations with each other they know that Jesus Christ is saying in, with and through each one of them, in the unique, physical and passionate way that is sexual intercourse, "This is *my* body — and my self — given for you." This is sacramental sex. It is a physical expression of love adopted by Jesus Christ to express his divine love.

Finally, God comes to dwell in every human heart that is open to him through surrender to the invitations of his grace. But it is only in the sacrament of the Eucharist that Jesus, as "Emmanuel, God-with-us," takes bread, blesses it, breaks it, and gives himself to us physically, saying, "Take this, all of you, and eat it: this is my body."

It is only in Eucharist that we in response physically lift up the cup of Christ's blood and drink to the Covenant, pledging ourselves individually and together to be faithful to the "new and everlasting" alliance that makes us one with him, one with each other in him, one for each other and the world.

The sacraments are physical, human actions which are real encounters with the living God made flesh in Jesus Christ and physically interacting with us still. To persevere in receiving the sacraments is to persevere in the physical expression of our faith. And this expression keeps our faith alive.

Treating Jesus as a human being

There is a very simple choice offered to us in Christianity. It is based on a very simple act of faith. But it is a choice that is deep, fundamental and life-altering. It is the choice *to interact humanly* with God offering himself to us in Jesus-Emmanuel.

To interact humanly with God means that we interact with Jesus Christ exactly as we would interact with another human being who is our deep friend, and in every possible way. For example:

- We say good morning to him when we wake up, and good night before we go to sleep.

- We ask his opinion about things; things that are important to us and things that are not. We follow his advice, because we trust him.

- We read the letters he writes us; for example, the ones in the Scriptures that he signed as "Paul."

- We read his book. And we take it seriously; we think about his opinions, trying to understand them.

- We argue with him, challenging what he says, identifying our difficulties, raising objections, trying to answer them, listening to his answers.

- We count on his help; we ask for it as a matter of course, from little things like helping us to find a parking place to big things like standing by us in moments of serious trouble or grief.

- We trust him when we don't understand the way he is treating us.

- We spend time with him.

- We visit him where he lives; we bring him into our home; we make him a part of our personal or family life.

- We talk about him a lot.

- We keep mementos of him in our room: his picture, reminders of special times we have spent with him, of special things he did for us.

- We remember days that are special to him; we do something special for him on those days. We go to his parties. (Think of the Eucharistic celebration as a party, not as an "obligation").

- We praise him and appreciate opportunities to say aloud how good he is; for example, in the *Gloria* at Mass.

- We do favors for him; we do favors for his friends. We look for chances to please him.

- We think about him a lot, remembering things he said, things he did. We enjoy admiring him, laughing at his humor. Sometimes we get angry or sad because of the way he is treated; it makes us want to please him more.

- We look forward to times of being with him. We think about what we are going to do then, how we are going to enjoy it and make it enjoyable for him — in the Eucharistic celebration, for example.

- We look back on special moments with him after they are over, analyzing what went on, appreciating what he did for us, savoring what it says about our relationship — for example, after receiving a favor from him, or an insight in prayer, or after receiving the sacrament of Reconciliation.

- We dream about things we can accomplish together with him, working as a team. We let his vision, his goals and ideals inspire us. We have the courage to undertake things because of his support, his friendship.

- We think of all the things we do or would like to do for our friends, and we do them for him.

If we decide to deal with Jesus Christ consistently in all the human, physical ways we deal with other people whom we love, it will transform our lives. It will bring our relationship with him to a new level of experienced, constant, and at times passionate interaction with God.

CHAPTER FOUR:
INTERACTING HUMANLY WITH JESUS
"Emmanuel" — Matthew 21:5-8, 12-14

Summary

Christianity is kept authentic by a constant balancing of contrasts. Jesus is human, yet divine. In the scene of his triumphal entry into Jerusalem, Matthew shows us what it means to call Jesus "Emmanuel: God-with-us." He enters as a king who is one of his people, not separated from his followers by protocol or distanced by demands for deference. Jesus enters Jerusalem to inaugurate a kingdom in which this world's symbols of prestige and power will have no place.

Once in the temple, Jesus drives out the money changers and at the same time changes the nature of the temple forever. Jesus is replacing the presence of God in the temple with his presence in the living body of his Church. In the living members of his Church Jesus continues to be "Emmanuel: God-with-us."

Although the distortion of Jesus' truth and goodness in his members can be the greatest obstacle to perseverance in the faith, there is no greater help to perseverance and spiritual growth than continuing interaction with Jesus speaking, ministering and challenging us through those who are his real, if imperfect, body on earth.

Jesus lives, works and reigns on earth as the head of a body, his body. To truly know him as Emmanuel, and to authentically make him present as Emmanuel in our own flesh, we have to accept him in all who are his living body on earth and be one with him by being one with them.

The underlying mistake of many who leave the Church is their identification of the "Church" with those in public positions of power and authority rather than with the whole body of Christ. The "Church" should mean for us the whole Church: the saints and the sinners in the pews, all those who throughout history have gathered with the bishops and assembled with the Church for Eucharist. When we think of leaving the "Church" we should be aware that we are parting company with them.

Because we are the Church of "Emmanuel," God human and divine, we are constantly swinging back and forth between trying to save the divine in our religion by making it less human and trying to save the human by making it less divine. The principle that must guide us in our practical living of Christian spirituality is that we must give full value to the human and to the divine, never saving one by sacrificing the other, but giving full value to both. "Either-or" is the trap; "both-and" is the saving solution.

If we decide to deal with Jesus Christ consistently in all the human, physical ways we deal with other people whom we love, it will transform our lives. It will bring our relationship with him to a new level of experienced, constant, and at times passionate interaction with God.

Have you understood?

How does the contrast of the divine and human in "Jesus-Emmanuel" appear in Jesus' entry into Jerusalem?

How is Christ's presence in his human body the Church an obstacle to perseverance in faith? How does it help?

How has God's presence in human flesh in Jesus, continued in his Church, made it possible for us to deal with him humanly? In how many ways can we do this?

Do the sacraments limit our ways of interacting with God? What do they add?

In what ways do we try to save the divine in our religion by making it less human and try to save the human by making it less divine? What should be our guiding principle in this?

What is the challenge of this chapter? To our faith? To our hope? To our love?

Making it your own

What are the key thoughts in this chapter? (Jot them down and give the page number where each is found).

What questions do I have about this chapter? (Bring them up in discussion or ask someone who should know the answers).

What struck me the most in this chapter? After reading this chapter, what do I understand better than I did before? What do I appreciate more?

What do I think is the point of the whole chapter? What response does Matthew want to evoke from those who read or hear this part of his Gospel?

What can I use as a visible reminder (a symbol) to keep me aware of the challenge of this chapter? Where will I put it?

Questions for prayer

In how many human, physical ways do I interact with Jesus-Emmanuel?

What do I do for or with my close friends that I do not do with Jesus? How could I interact with him in these ways?

Do I believe that by just treating Jesus as I would a human friend I can enter into intimate relationship with him? To me, is this worth the time and energy I would have to give to it?

How can I apply to my life what I have come to see by reflecting on this chapter? What concrete action do I choose to perform to express my belief in what I have seen?

FOOTNOTES

---

[1] For some mathematical observations on this, see my book *Saving Presence*, His Way Communications (fourth printing 2000), chapter two. p. 17.

[2] See my book *No Power but Love*, His Way Communications, 1999, chapter one.

[3] See Matthew 28:16 and 18-20; Mark 16:14-15; Luke 24:33, 48; John 21:15-17). In Luke he appears to "the eleven and their companions gathered together"; in Acts 1:2, to "the apostles whom he had chosen."

[4] If we focus on other Christian churches in separation from the main body and Rome, this is a very painful subject to deal with, and it is not simple. Vatican II, in the document on the Church (*Lumen Gentium*, no. 8), declares that the

unique Church of Christ which in the Creed we avow as one, holy, catholic and apostolic.... *subsists* in the Catholic Church, which is governed by the successor of Peter and by the bishops in union with that successor, although many elements of sanctification and of truth can be found outside of her visible structure. These elements, however, as gifts properly belonging to the Church of Christ, possess an inner dynamism toward Catholic unity.

Fr. J. M. R. Tillard, O.P., maintains that the significance of these words "has not been properly grasped":

At one and the same time the Catholic community affirms that in her resides the unique Church of God in all that is needed for her fullness — sacramental, institutional and spiritual — and also recognizes that this Church can exist outside her own boundaries, although without that fullness. The grace of God is at work there too. It is therefore important to take with all seriousness what ecclesial groups beyond the Catholic frontiers say when they declare their will to recover universal *koinonia* [communion, fellowship]....

Those who ask these questions, being led by the Spirit of God in their search for unity, have no intention but the good of the one and only Church of God which subsists in the Catholic community but which exists also at the universal level broken in pieces, and which the Spirit wishes to lead back into complete communion. (*The Bishop of Rome*, Michael Glazier, Inc., 1986, p. 15).

Vatican II, while refusing to say that the Church of Christ is simply *identified* with the Catholic Church, as if it could in no way exist outside of the Church's visible structure, does affirm two things. First, the Church of Jesus Christ is not made up of many incomplete churches which, like parts contributing to a greater whole, have each appropriated or retained some portion of the message and means of salvation given by Jesus while none can claim to have retained them all. No, in the Catholic Church "resides the unique Church of God in all that is needed for her fullness," even though it is often only too painfully evident that the gifts with which God has endowed the Church are not made available to all of her members by the clergy and hierarchy, and frequently are not accepted when they are. Secondly, the Council affirms that a sign of the presence of the Spirit in the separated groups is their "inner dynamism" toward restoring unity to the whole body of Christ. Great efforts and great progress have been made in this direction since Vatican II, especially in the dialogues between American Lutheran and Catholic theologians, completed in 1974, and between

Anglican and Catholic theologians, completed in 1975. Both Anglicans and Lutherans "recognized the value of an office of universal primacy such as the bishop of Rome alone has exercised and alone still does exercise. And they agreed that in any future union the bishop of Rome would be the appropriate one to hold such an office." But neither group could accept the papacy with its present autocratic and bureaucratic method of governing the Church (Thomas Bokenkotter, *A Concise History of the Catholic Church*, Doubleday, 1977, chapter 32, pp. 408; but see 404 ff.).

What these Protestants are objecting to is not the papacy so much as the actual abuse of papal power; it is not the pope as such that they reject but a pope who is trying to be "more than a pope." See chapter five below, p. 117 with footnotes 7 and 8.

[5] See Bernard Botte, O.S.B, *From Silence To Participation*, tr. John Sullivan, O.C.D., The Pastoral Press, Wash., D.C., 1988, p. 24. On pages 2-3 Botte describes what things were like "in the old days" in his Belgian home town:

> The people remained quiet and passive, doing whatever each one liked, saying the rosary or losing oneself in [devotional prayers]. As for communion, it was distributed.... every fifteen minutes.... This sounds strange to us, but we ought to keep in mind the ideas then current. Mass was no longer the prayer of the Christian community. The clergy prayed entirely in place of and in the name of the community. As a result, the faithful were only remotely involved and paid attention to their own personal devotion. Communion appeared to be a private devotion without any special link to the Mass.

[6] See the Arian, Nestorian and Monophysite heresies, condemned respectively in the councils of Nicea (325), Ephesus (431) and Chalcedon (451). The Arians compromised the divinity of Christ by making "the Son of God the highest of creatures, greater than we but less than God." The Nestorians said there were "two separate persons in Jesus Christ, the one human and the other divine. Therefore, Mary was the mother of the human Jesus only... [They] emphasized the humanity of Christ." The Monophysites taught that "the human nature of Christ was totally absorbed by the divine nature.... [They] emphasized the divinity of Christ." See Richard P. McBrien, *Catholicism*, Study Edition, Harper San Francisco, Glossary, pp. 1238, 1250, 1251.

[7] See "Constitution on the Sacred Liturgy," no. 7. Because Catholic belief about the Mass is widely misunderstood, both by Protestants and by Catholics, we point out here that the sacrifice of Calvary is not *repeated* during the Mass, as if Jesus were being offered again and again. Jesus offered himself once and for all on the cross, and that sacrifice neither can be repeated nor needs to be. In the Mass one and the same sacrifice is *made present* in our time and space, so that Jesus is truly present offering himself, and we are truly present to the one and unique sacrifice he made of himself on the cross on Calvary. The question this raises is not, "How can the sacrifice of Calvary be repeated?" but "How can the sacrifice which took place 2000 years ago be really present in our time and space today?" The answer lies in the time-transcending mystery of that act of offering on the cross, which took place in time around 33 A.D., but which was and is the central moment of history, the timeless moment around which all time and history revolve.

[8] The "Dogmatic Constitution on Divine Revelation," no. 21.

[9] See Teresa of Avila's autobiography, chapter 22. I think it is safe to say that even when a Christian contemplates God as God, in the inexpressible mystery of God's Being, the reality being contemplated without words or images is nevertheless inseparable from and known through the manifestation of God the Son incarnate in Jesus Christ, and through his revelation of God as Father, Son and Spirit.

Chapter Five
Where Is The Center Of The Church?
Jesus is Universal Lord — Matthew 21:12-17

When Jesus drove the moneymakers out of the temple, he actually did four things:

• He asserted his authority and thereby established his identity, not only as Messiah and Son of God, but also as Universal Lord, the King and Savior of the whole human race.

• He canceled out the restricting identification of his religion with the Jewish people or with any other particular race or culture.

• He replaced the physical temple in Jerusalem with the flesh-and-blood temple of his risen body the Church as the dwelling place of God on earth.

• He rejected the natural human tendency to make some particular building, monument, place or person the animating symbol, center and core of his religion.

Jesus is Universal Lord

We have already seen (chapter 3, above) that Jesus' act of cleaning out the temple was more than the gesture of a prophet; it was the act of a Son restoring the dignity of his Father's house. And when the children acclaimed him as Messiah under the title "Son of David," Jesus identifies their praise with words in Psalm 8 which clearly refer to the praise of God himself.

Jesus' reference to Psalm 8, however, does not just identify him as the divine son of God; the Psalm's main focus is on the universality of God's reign and on human beings' responsibility for establishing it. The Psalm begins with the phrase: "O LORD, our Sovereign, how majestic is your name in all the earth!" And it ends with the same words,

"How majestic is your name in all the earth," repeating the theme of universality. The focus is creation-wide: God is the Lord of all that exists, and he has made human beings the stewards of all creation: "You have given them dominion over the works of your hands; you have put all things under their feet."

St. Paul will apply this last phrase specifically to Jesus. God "has put all things under his feet and has made him the head over all things for the church, which is his body, the fullness of him who fills all in all." Jesus, then, is Lord of the whole universe, and through the stewardship of his Church he will continue working in the world, establishing his reign, until everything in heaven and on earth is brought together into unity under his headship. This is "the mystery of [God's] will", that he has made known to us, his "plan for the fullness of time, to gather up all things in him, things in heaven and things on earth" (Eph. 1:1-10, 1:22).

The instrument for establishing God's reign throughout the earth is the Church: "All authority in heaven and on earth has been given to me. Go therefore and make disciples of all nations..." (Mt. 28:18-19). But repeatedly in his Gospel Matthew has made the point that God is not limited to acting through the human intermediary of cultures and religions. He can and does speak directly to every person.

• In chapter two of Matthew God called the Magi to Jesus as universal *Savior* through a star, using a symbol from their own religious tradition, but speaking through it as the God whose "voice goes out through all the earth, and [his] words to the end of the world" (see Psalm 19:1-6).

• In chapter ten, when Jesus sent his disciples out on mission as his *Church* he warned them not to think that people's first experience of God was coming through them! Rather, they were to look for signs that the Spirit which "fills the world, is all-embracing, and knows the utterances of every heart" has preceded them: "As you enter the house, greet it. If the house is worthy, let your peace come upon it; but if it is not worthy, let your peace return to you" (see Mt. 10:11-13 and Wisdom 1:7).

• And in chapter sixteen, when Peter recognized Jesus as Messiah and "Son of the living God" just before Jesus announced his way of saving the world through the *cross*, Jesus said, "Nothing of flesh and blood has revealed this to you, but my heavenly Father himself." It was not his Jewish culture or background which enabled Peter to recognize Jesus for who he was, but the voice of God who can and does speak directly to every human heart. Then Jesus spoke of building on Peter his "church," which would replace the ethnic religion of Israel, and of giving to him, not to the established Jewish leaders, the "keys of the kingdom of heaven" (see Mt. 16:17-19).

All these examples speak of God's universal presence, and of his ability to communicate with every human heart, calling people to his Son from every nation and culture. Now in chapter twenty-one, in Matthew's description of the purification of the temple, and especially in his use of Psalm 8 to explain why the little children are crying out "Hosanna to the Son of David," we can see a recurrence of Matthew's way of presenting Jesus as the Lord, not just of the Jews, but of all nations and peoples, of every human heart: "How majestic is your name in all the earth!"

This is a clear call to the Church today to persevere as *stewards of his kingship*, working to *establish the reign of Christ over every area and activity of human life on earth* until Christ comes again. And it is a promise of victory.

Canceling ethnic identification

In Jesus' act of purifying the temple by driving out the moneymakers, a new note is added to the theme of universality. The temple is not just being purified; it is being replaced, as later events make clear. Jesus is already giving here a preview of the temple's destruction as a symbol of the cultural religion of Israel, and of its restoration in the living flesh of his body on earth, the universal — that is, "catholic"— Church. The temple as a visible, material symbol of ethnic Judaism is going to be replaced by a new, a spiritual temple, which will be a "house of prayer for all peoples" (see Mt. 21:19; 23:38; 24:2 and Mt. 26:60-61 with its obvious parallelism in John 2:18-21. See also John 4:19-24).

What Jesus was doing here would not be clear to his followers until later; not, in fact, until the assembled Christians in Jerusalem made the momentous decision to allow Gentile converts into the Church without requiring them to adopt Jewish laws and observances. After that, for the first time since Yahweh spoke to Abraham, one could become a member of the Chosen People without becoming a Jew. There was still a definite, visible community to join, an identifiable "assembly" ("church") of people to which one belonged. There were still structures and rules and observances, and a governing authority to preserve the community's identity by passing judgment on beliefs and practices (see, for example, 1Cor. 7:17; 1Timothy 5:17). But now in order to take on the identity of a Christian it would no longer be necessary to adopt the particular, cultural laws and practices which identified one as a Jew. This was decided in what has been called the "first council of Jerusalem" (see Acts 15:1-32). But it was already foreshadowed when Jesus made the gesture which spoke of replacing the temple in Jerusalem, symbol of Judaism, with a new temple which would be a "house of prayer for all peoples." What Jesus did was break the restricting identification of his religion with the Jewish people or with any other particular race or culture.

Replacing the temple made with hands

We might ask here why Matthew, in his account of Jesus' purification of the temple, omits the words "for all peoples." These words, which foretell Jesus' outreach to the whole world, are in the text Matthew cites from Isaiah, and Mark does include them: "my house shall be called a house of prayer *for all peoples*" (see Isaiah 56:7 and Mark 11:17). Matthew certainly agrees with the reality foretold here, because he makes the point repeatedly that Jesus came to be Lord, not only of Jews, but of all people and nations.[1]

The *Jerome Biblical Commentary* suggests that Matthew may have deliberately left out this phrase, not to deny that Jesus is Lord of all peoples and nations, but to avoid giving the impression that authentic worship of the Father "in Spirit and truth" would come through acceptance of the Jewish temple rather than through acceptance of the person of Jesus himself as Messiah. It was not, in fact, the temple in Jerusalem which became a house of prayer for all peoples, but the living temple of Christ's Body on earth, the Church (John 2:18-22).[2]

Henceforth the presence of God will be associated, not with any special place, building, shrine, caste or class of people, but with any and every human person who, by baptism into the Church, the risen body of Christ on earth, is filled with the indwelling presence of the Holy Spirit. Those who share in the life of God through graced union with Jesus Christ will find God in their hearts. They will worship him present there in a way transcendentally different from the way God is present in nature, in the universe, or in any temple or shrine made by human hands (see Mark 14:58). Even in the Eucharist Jesus is not united to the church building. His presence there is for the sake of union with the *church*, the "assembly" who gather in that building, within whose hearts he dwells as truly as in the tabernacle. Because of the indwelling presence of God in believers, Christians recognize every member of the body of Christ as a "temple of the Holy Spirit" who is by that fact more sacred than any building or place on earth.

Seeing what is sacred

There is, of course, a sacredness attached to things and to
people who are made "holy" — that is, "consecrated," "set
apart," "dedicated" — by being assigned to the performance of a particular function. A chalice is more sacred than
an ordinary wine glass because it is specifically consecrated, set apart, for use in the Eucharistic liturgy. Shrines
are set apart, made into "holy ground" to commemorate
some event that took place there. A mother has a special
sacredness because her body has been consecrated to the
task of giving and nurturing life. (Many people recognize
this sacredness in any woman's body because of its obvious
and overall orientation to the function of giving life. Logi-
cally the same sacredness belongs to the male body also,
but because it is less obvious it is less recognized). Christians also attach a special sacredness to those people who
by religious vows have consecrated themselves in a special
and public way to God, and to priests and deacons who by
the sacrament of Holy Orders have been "ordained" — that
is, ordered, directed, consecrated — to a particular sacred
function in the Church. It is very important to bear in mind,
however — and the more so because our way of expressing
ourselves culturally obscures it — that the basic sacredness
or holiness of all Christians comes from the indwelling
presence of the Holy Spirit in each one, and from the fact
that by baptism all have been consecrated, set apart, made
holy by a fundamental dedication of their bodies to be the
body of Christ and to continue his presence and work on
earth (see Rom. 12:1). Once a person has been "set apart"
to be the body of Christ and made "holy" by his or her consecration as Prophet, Priest and King "in Christ," the essential sacredness is there, and no further consecration can
add to it except in relatively minor ways.

To say this is not to downplay in any way the sacredness of
that special consecration which is given through the sacraments of Matrimony and Holy Orders, or through religious

vows; it is just to say that in comparison to the sacredness
which comes through Baptism anything these consecrations
give is in a different and lesser league altogether.

In practice this means that it is a distortion of the faith to attach more sacredness to the particular consecration of any
caste of Christians — the ordained clergy, for example —
than we do to the fundamental consecration which all
Christians have through baptism into the body of Christ.
And we fall into this distortion when our cultural expressions of reverence — the titles we use, the external deference we show — make it appear that certain categories of
Christians are considered sacred while others are not. The
fundamental sacredness which comes from being consecrated by baptism as a member of the body of Christ and a
temple of the Holy Spirit is so overwhelmingly superior to
that which comes from any other consecration that there is
simply no comparison between them. But in practice,
judging by the expressions of reverence we give to secon-
dary consecrations as compared to the fundamental one of
baptism, it would appear that just the opposite is true.

It might be argued that consecration as a deacon, priest,
bishop or nun *adds to* the consecration one has as a member of the body of Christ, and hence calls for greater reverence from the Christian community. In response to this we
have to ask whether "adds to" is the most precise choice of
words. It might be more accurate to say that these further
consecrations *specify* the overall consecration we have as
members of the body of Christ by determining, as Matrimony does, how this individual man or woman will live out
in concrete detail the all-embracing gift of self made in
Baptism. Then we would say it is not a question of more or
less consecration, but simply of how one lives out a gift of
self that is already total. Total gift cannot be surpassed; it
can only be specified.

We might also question whether it is possible to character-
ize any one consecration in the Church as "higher" or

"more holy" than another. Is the ordained priesthood a "higher" vocation than motherhood or just a different one? Is it "more holy" to minister at the altar than to nurse the sick in a hospital or show hospitality to the homeless in a Catholic Worker house? Does a dedicated ordained priest do more to establish the reign of God on earth than an equally dedicated Christian in business? Who forms people better into the likeness of Christ: a good preacher in the pulpit, a good teacher in the classroom, or an exemplary role model in the workplace?

The answer, of course, is, "It depends on each one's union with Christ in mind and will and heart." All are members of the body of Christ, and Christ works in and through them all in the measure that each one is his willing instrument through surrender to the inspirations of his Holy Spirit. To differentiate between vocations by speaking of "higher" and "lower" is to risk obscuring what all Christian vocations have in common: the indwelling presence of Christ which is the source and summit of sacredness in all.

By replacing the temple "made with hands" by another, "not made with hands" (see Mark 14:58), Jesus did not abolish the sacredness which came from the indwelling presence of God in the temple; he relocated it. And he diffused it. Now the presence of God is to be sought, not in one central monument or shrine, not in some holy city or place, but in every living person who is a member of the body of Christ and a temple of the Holy Spirit anywhere and everywhere in the world.[3]

Rejecting any single centralizing symbol

The temple was already a source of division between the Jews and the Samaritans, who both belonged to the Chosen People. The Jews observed the law of Deuteronomy that sacrifices should be offered only in the temple in Jerusalem, while the Samaritans, in spite of the prohibition, offered sacrifice on Mount Gerizim.

When the Samaritan woman in John's Gospel asked Jesus which was the right place to worship, he answered by removing the source of division: "Believe me, woman, the hour is coming when you will worship the Father neither on this mountain nor in Jerusalem... The hour is coming, and is now here, when true worshipers will worship the Father in Spirit and truth; and indeed the Father seeks such people to worship him" (see John 4:19-21).

Jesus is not only striking down the identification of his religion with any particular culture: Jewish, Samaritan or (coming down to our own prejudice) Roman! He is also countermanding the tendency, so natural in us all, to identify the soul and spirit of our religion with its cultural expression in a particular city or place, and to fill that place with signs and symbols which speak to us of its splendor. Henceforth it is not the temple of Jerusalem — nor St. Peter's Basilica in Rome! — which will be filled with the "glory of God," but a temple "not made by hands," the Body of Christ, the Church, the "catholic" people scattered throughout the whole earth (*kata-holos*) in whom his Spirit dwells. [4]

Roman is not catholic

We have to face here our own temptation to see the sign of Christ's universal reign, not in the *koinonia*, the "communion in the Holy Spirit" evident in all the local Churches (dioceses) and parishes who gather together in faith around their bishops throughout the world, but in the pomp and splendor of a new temple (St. Peter's Basilica) located in a new holy City (Rome). This tendency has several bad effects.

First, it encourages the temptation to think of the "catholic" Church as the Roman Church — as if the Latin rite were more important than any of the other thirteen or more rites which recognize the bishop of Rome as having special authority over the universal Church and are in communion with each other through communion with him.

The very phrase "Roman Catholic Church," besides being an affront to the Armenian Catholics, the Byzantine Catholics, the Coptic Catholics, the Syro-Malabar Catholics, etc., is an obvious contradiction in terms. "Roman" refers to the particular diocese of Rome, and "catholic" refers to the Church *kata-holos*, the Church expressing herself in different cultural forms throughout the world. To speak of a "Roman-catholic" or "local-universal" Church is a verbal contradiction.

It is also theologically inaccurate. If we are the "Roman" Catholic Church, what other Catholic Church is there? Is there more than one Church established by Jesus Christ? Is there another Church which is "catholic" — that is, united "vertically" (in time) with the original community of the Apostles, and "horizontally" (in space) with all the other local churches (dioceses) *kata holos*, throughout the world?

Catholicity and communion go together. The "catholic" Church is the worldwide Church in which all the local churches are in communion with one another. But to have *koinonia*, which we translate as "fellowship" or "communion" in the Holy Spirit, means that each local church, "the Church of God 'which is at' one place (1Cor. 1:2), *recognizes itself* as identical with the Church of God which is at another place." This catholicity and communion are only realized in those churches which, while distinct and even different from each other according to rites, practices and the government of their individual bishops, are nevertheless able to recognize in each other one and the same faith, one and the same Eucharist, and one and the same commissioning to ministry dating back to the twelve apostles. There is only one such "catholic" church, and it is recognizable by the union which all of its members, priests and bishops have maintained with each other and with the bishop of Rome since Jesus ascended into heaven two thousand years ago. This Church is no more Roman than it is Alexandrian, Antiochan, or for that matter, Parisian or Memphian (as in Tennessee!) It is just catholic, the Catholic Church.[5]

It would be accurate to speak of "the Catholic (universal) Church in union with Rome." And it would be acceptable for those who are members of the Latin Rite to call themselves the "Roman *Rite* of the Catholic Church." But to speak of the "Roman Catholic Church" is not just grammatically incorrect and theologically inaccurate; it is also pastorally misleading. It fosters the illogical but widespread assumption that the particular, cultural way in which the religion of Jesus Christ is embodied and expressed in the Latin rite and even in the diocese of Rome is "most" Catholic and should be normative for the Church throughout the world.

If we think of the whole Church as being "Roman Catholic," we begin to think that Roman ecclesiastical dress and ceremonies, Roman protocol, Roman forms of devotion, Roman pastoral practices, Roman ecclesiastical policies, and even Roman theological positions should be normative for the whole Church! We are not speaking here of definitive dogmatic teaching or of laws officially promulgated from Rome to be binding on the universal Church. We are not calling into question the pope's responsibility and authority with regard to the Church as a whole, or his right to intervene with authority in particular cases anywhere in the world when necessary. We are not even forgetting the particular responsibility which the bishop of Rome has, as head of the Latin Rite, to exercise leadership within the community ("college") of bishops who belong to that rite. We are simply reflecting on how damaging it is to our understanding of the Church as "catholic" when we speak of "Catholic" as if it meant the same as "Roman." And we are asking whether our tendency to do this does not owe more to the visual impact of Roman pomp and grandeur than it does to authentically Catholic devotion and theology.

Taking the medium for the message

In the light of this, we have to ask seriously whether we are not falsifying the true image of the Church, as much in our own eyes as in the eyes of others, by making Vatican City a showcase of pomp and splendor.

Visitors to the "Holy City" — called so because of saints Peter and Paul, who died there, not because of the lifestyle found there — can be so impressed by the artistic and architectural magnificence of the buildings, and by the majesty of the costuming and ceremonies surrounding the pope, that they might almost unconsciously fall into the error of seeing in these symbols of power the authentic image of Christ's reigning presence on earth. From this attitude it is a very natural, if non-theological, step to slide into another assumption — one followed more in practice than affirmed in teaching: the assumption that the greatest energy, power, and direction of the Church must be coming from the place where there is the most evident display of prestige and power. If the pope lives in a palace while bishops live only in mansions; and if the pope is costumed more richly and elaborately than the bishops and treated with even more deference than they are, then the pope must be the one to whom we should look for the most spiritual power as well.

Many people assume, without any reference to the Church's actual teaching or to history, that the pope must be the person in the Church who has the clearest guidance of the Holy Spirit in all things and whose life must be the holiest. From the way the pope's theological and pastoral opinions are publicized and quoted, we are left with the impression that, even when there is no question of Church law or of definitive teaching, the pope's preferences — or even the attitudes and practices which appeal to those people who work under him in the Vatican — are to be respected over those of any local bishop or national conference of bishops. The source of this assumption is not in Church teaching. In fact, the pope, in union with the whole Church, rather clearly teaches a view quite contrary to this.[6]

To assume that spiritual preeminence must accompany political preeminence is just about as logical as presuming that spiritual riches must accompany material riches. Like a focus on the temple instead of on the worship that is conducted there, this is a confusion of symbol with reality (see Mt. 23:16-17).

To make a cultural symbol, such as the temple in all its glory or the Vatican in all its grandeur, the sign of Christ's reign over all nations, rather than the less impressive and more diffused reality of Jesus present and acting in his Body wherever the Spirit is gathering the local Church together, is to fall into the very attitude Jesus contradicted by his lowly-triumphal entry into Jerusalem: the attitude which values the external symbols of prestige and power more than the reality of spiritual union with God.

Whenever we do this it is a triumph of facade over reality, and of protocol over theology. It focuses the confidence of the Church, not on God's Spirit conferring spiritual authority on all the bishops of the Church *kata-holos*, the "Church catholic," and giving graces of leadership to all the faithful throughout the world, but on one central figure around whom an artificial aura of holiness and oracular wisdom has been created through the use of costuming, ceremony and pretentious protocol. It makes the splendor of the pope on his throne, rather than the humility of Jesus on his donkey, the model of Church authority and the symbol of her security and power.

Seeing through dazzle to doctrine

Papal positions should not be given more weight than is justified by Church teaching. And if we look to the pope for leadership outside of the strict exercise of his authority, let it be for sound theological reasons, and not because we are impressed by the pomp and splendor which over the centuries have attached themselves like barnacles to his office.[7]

The pope does have a special function in the universal Church. Whoever is chosen to be bishop of Rome has the responsibility and the authority to look after the common good of the Church as a whole. He has the last word, if it should come to that, in the settlement of doctrinal disputes. And he is responsible for making laws binding on the whole Church, or even to intervene in particular cases, whenever that might be necessary or truly beneficial.

The pope's office is an essential role in the Church. But, theologically, it does not make the bishop of Rome responsible for providing or directing pastoral initiatives in other bishops' dioceses, much less for monopolizing decision-making authority over matters which would be better decided upon locally. It is the fallacy of over-centralization to believe that it is one's *job* to do everything one has the *authority* to do. For the sake of preserving unity within the Church the pope has almost unlimited authority. But when he uses it to do what it is not his job to do, he is being more than a pope. This is one of the greatest problems in the Church and the principle obstacle to restoring unity with the separated Christians.[8]

When the symbols of prestige and preeminence surrounding the pope are taken to mean what they would mean in a secular pecking order of authority (as in practice they tend to be), the result is a tendency to think of the pope as the Chief Executive Officer in the Church, and the bishops as his branch managers. It is then considered normal for the pope to select a priest from any diocese to be bishop in another, and to move bishops around, transferring them at will, just as large companies transfer and promote their subordinate executives.[9]

The practice of transferring bishops from one diocese to another obscures the Church's teaching that a bishop is the true head of the local Church (diocese) and encourages bishops to look upon themselves as little more than executors of policies formulated in Rome. It also opens the door to ambition and careerism. In the Council of Sardica (342 A.D.) it was already pointed out: "Almost no bishop is found who will move from a large city to a small one.... Whence it appears that they are inflamed by the heat of avarice to serve ambition." And Pope Saint Julius I wrote in reference to the same Council:

> If therefore you truly consider the honor due to all bishops to be the same and equal, and... do not measure the dignity of a bishop by the greatness of his city, it is fitting that he who has been established in a small city should remain there.... and not move to another not entrusted to him, that by despising that which he was given by God he should foolishly hope for the approbation of men.[10]

The practice of transferring bishops from one diocese to another is a good example of how an abusive policy creates a distorted theology. This practice was condemned repeatedly in Church Councils. It was forbidden by the Council of Arles (314), the Council of Nicea (325), the Council of Antioch (c. 328), the Council of Sardica (343) and by the Council of Chalcedon (451). Pope Damasus, citing canon 15 of Nicea, joined the enemies of St. Gregory of Nazianzus in demanding that he resign the see of Constantinople because of his previous consecration for the diocese of Sasima.

This prohibition was not considered just a matter of canonical discipline. It was based on a theological vision that saw the relationship between a bishop and his diocese as a "mystical union existing between the bishop and his see which was expressed as being akin to the marriage bond." This explains why the Council of Alexandria (338) said that a bishop who accepted a transfer from one diocese to another was an adulterer. It also explains why it was taken for granted that a bishop could not be imposed on a diocese without the consent of the people: "Like the assent of the partners in a marriage, the [local] church's 'yes' must be freely given." Current practice in the appointment of bishops is obviously in glaring contradiction to this theology. But instead of crying out against the policy like faithful stewards of the kingship of Christ, we have passively remodeled our theology to fit theory to practice. It is commonplace for bishops at their installation ceremony to thank "the Holy Father" for the confidence he showed in them by appointing them as bishops, as if it were normal for the pope to bestow bishoprics the way kings of old bestowed lands and titles of nobility upon their subjects as a reward for loyal service. No wonder the laity by-pass their bishops and look directly to Rome for motivation and guidance in their lives.[11]

Where is the "center" of the Church

The tendency to focus on the Vatican as the centerpiece and symbol of the Catholic Church has another destructive effect: it encourages the centralizing tendency present in all organizations or societies which acknowledge one unifying authority. There is a natural tendency in more universal authorities to reserve more and more decisions to themselves, to make more and more laws restricting the autonomy of local authorities, and to foster the impression that they are the natural center and principal source of energy and direction for the whole society within which they serve. This tendency goes contrary to Catholic teaching about the role of the papacy in the Church.[12]

Father Raymond Brown emphasizes the importance of acknowledging "the importance of the local Church [diocese]... its place in the Christian scheme of redemption":

> It has often been said that most Catholics view the Church from the top down — a pyramid with sides sloping down from the pope to bishops to priests to laity. The principle of subsidiarity [that is, the Church's teaching that it is improper for higher authority to assume functions and services which can be performed on a lower level] suggests that we view the Church from the bottom up, with centralized authority seen as rendering a useful service but *not as constituting the core of the Church*. An anecdote is appropriate here. When groups of priests are in Rome, frequently a visit is arranged for them to the offices of the administrative units of the Church (the Congregations of the Roman Curia); this visit is partly for pedagogical purposes and partly for public relations to improve the image of the administration. On one such visit the Roman prelate who administered the particular office was explaining to a group of American priests how things were done there "at the center of the Church" with an appeal that the principles be properly explained and applied "on the outside." He was interrupted by a puzzled priest who stated that, when he was administering the sacraments to the people in his parish and preaching the Gospel to them, he thought he was at the real center of the Church and that the Roman administrative offices, however necessary, were really on the periphery of what the Church was all about. An oversimplification, to be sure, but not without its eloquence in phrasing a different concept of the Church. The principle of subsidiarity, when applied to the functioning of the Papacy, could modify the tendency toward centralization so prominent in the last one hundred years and go far to allay Protestant fears about the possible abuse of unified leadership. No Catholic wants the pope to become merely the chairperson of the board; on the other hand, a constant stress on monarchical imagery will do little to unify the churches.[13]

Center without centralization

We can say truly, but in different senses, both that the local church of Rome is the "center" of the Catholic, the universal, Church, and that it is not.

Rome is obviously not the center from which Christianity began; that is Jerusalem. Nor is Rome the "center" in the sense that Rome is the main source of activity and energy in the Church, so that we would expect pastoral initiatives to begin in Rome and spread out to all the other local churches (dioceses) in the world. In this sense, it is the local bishop, and the local bishop alone, who is the "center" of every local church. This does not mean the bishop acts in isolation from the clergy and laity, or even independently of other bishops, but rather that the local bishop, not the bishop of Rome, is by right the true center and source of pastoral activity in his diocese.

We can say that Rome is the "center of unity" in the sense that what is proclaimed in Rome as authentic Catholic doctrine is "an obligatory point of reference" for all who teach and govern in the Church. The bishop of Rome is "the one who preserves unanimity within the body of bishops." He is the link, not only in *space*, between all of the bishops presently serving on earth, but also in *time*, between the contemporary Church and the Church of the Apostles. (All bishops are this link, but the bishop of Rome in a special way). The pope's role is to assure that the Church of today preserves a living continuity with the Church of every time and place.[14]

The Pope's special role in the Church is defined by his responsibility to defend the Church against division. It is not the pope's job as bishop of Rome to direct the ordinary life and ministry of the Church throughout the world. For this we look to the bishop who is the head of the local Church in each particular diocese, whose responsibility it is to supervise parish ministry, on which the vitality and spiritual growth of the Church depends.[15]

The real center *of the Church* is found, not in one place, but in each and every diocese. This perspective is more in accord with Vatican II's teaching about the role of bishops and with the theological description of the Church as a "communion of Churches." In a diocese the people and the priests gather around their bishop as head of the local

Church in a way that the bishops do not gather around the pope when they assemble with him in Rome. The bishops are not "helpers" and "assistants" to the pope the way deacons, priests and pastors are to the bishop. They do not represent the pope in their dioceses but Jesus Christ himself, because they are vicars of the Apostles, to whom Jesus in a special way entrusted his mission. And although, through their communion with the bishop of Rome they make visible the communion of the local church with all the churches (dioceses) throughout the world, it is not the function of the bishops to make the pope present the way the local clergy make the bishop present. The pope, therefore, is not at the head of the universal Church in the way that the bishops are at the head of each local Church; nor is he the center of the universal Church in the way that each bishop is the center of his diocese.[16]

The pope is not the center of the Church

Once Jesus replaced the temple in Jerusalem with the temple of his body spread "throughout the whole" earth (*kata holos*), he took out of the Church any one geographical center located in a particular place. The church of Rome, and the pope as its bishop, can serve as a unifying symbol because of the united witness that Peter and Paul gave there through their martyrdom. But a more common symbol is the crucifix, the image of Jesus on the cross, which is found in every Catholic church and in almost every Catholic home throughout the world. More profoundly and theologically, of course, the one great unifying symbol in the Church is Eucharist. It is in the celebration of the Eucharist that the unity of the Church is expressed, made present and preserved. It is Eucharist, with the Holy Spirit present in every Christian believer and assembly, that is the real unifying power and source of energy throughout the whole Church.[17]

The role and reminder of unity

What is the pope's role in the Church? And of what, precisely, is the city of Rome a symbol?

Sacramentally, the pope is the bishop of Rome. There is no sacrament of papacy. Whoever becomes bishop of Rome by sacramental ordination accepts by that fact a special responsibilty that belongs to the head of that diocese. Rome does not get its importance from the fact the pope is there. The pope's special importance comes from the fact that he is the bishop of Rome. Why is this?

In a nutshell, it is because Peter and Paul died there.

The bishop of Rome is the bishop who has the special function of unifying the churches because Rome is the city in which both Peter and Paul died, united in their testimony to one and the same faith.

In the early Church, Peter and Paul were the natural candidates to split Christianity in half. Peter was the leader of the Twelve apostles. To him Jesus had entrusted the "keys of the kingdom," the task of "strengthening his brothers" in the faith (Luke 22:31-32), and a special care for the flock: "Feed my lambs.... Tend my sheep.... Feed my sheep" (John 21:15-17). Peter was the first, the *protos*, within the special group of historical witnesses who had been with Jesus from the beginning (Acts 1:21-22). He had received his authority from the mouth of Jesus himself, and he had a special responsibility for and authority over the whole Church.[18]

Paul, on the other hand, so far as we know, had never met the historical Jesus. He was called and commissioned by the voice of the risen Jesus speaking to him on the road to Damascus (Acts 9:1-16; and see 1Cor. 15:5-9). But he is an apostle, and he insists on it. He introduces himself as "Paul an apostle — sent neither by human commission nor from human authorities, but through Jesus Christ and God the Father, who raised him from the dead" (Galatians 1:1). He is "an apostle of Christ Jesus by the will of God" (2Cor.1:1).

And not only that; Paul knows himself to be "an apostle, set apart for the gospel of God" (Romans 1:1), but in particular, and in contrast to Peter, as "an apostle to the Gentiles" (Romans 11:13). And this is by the command of Christ himself: "For he who worked through Peter making him an apostle to the circumcised [the Christians of Jewish origin] also worked through me in sending me to the Gentiles" (Galatians 2:8).

Peter and Paul were two leaders in the Church who both knew themselves to be directly commissioned by God. From this fact alone there was potential for division.

 Fr. Tillard speaks of "two primacies": Peter, the apostle to the Jews (Galatians 2:6-9), "represented the authority of the original church, the first witness to that basic *kerygma* [announcing of the Good News] which unites all the apostolic preachers." Paul, however, the apostle to the Gentiles, had what Fr. Tillard calls a different kind of "primacy": one that was "charismatic rather than institutional. Paul was the one who bore witness to the absolute, radical authority of the Word over everything and everyone." Peter and Paul could have divided the early Church. But they remained united and died in communion with each other in the same city. For that reason the church in that city has been entrusted with the special task of keeping all the churches in the world faithful to the unity to which their death bore witness. And for the same reason the bishop of Rome needs to reflect the charism of Paul as well as that of Peter: "Paul seems indeed to have been raised up by the Spirit of the risen Lord to bear witness above all to the primacy of an inward communion of faith and love, the perpetually new work of the Spirit... Because his church is founded on the witness of Paul, the bishop of this city [Rome] receives a quality which should mark his ministry: permanent openness to the Spirit, the care of non-believers, the priority of

the Spirit over the letter, the total transcendence of the
Word over all structures."

Tillard continues:

> The two primacies did, however, meet at Rome, intermingling in
> the blood of martyrdom. There, the 'glorious witnesses' welded
> into one communion the leadership of the *protos* [Peter, the first
> among the apostles] and the authority of the prophet [Paul]. The
> Christian community at Rome, the church of their witness, had in-
> deed existed before the Spirit impelled them there. It now became
> the place of total, perfect confession of the apostolic faith, with no
> split in its faithfulness both to its roots in the historical group
> which Jesus had gathered during his earthly ministry [through Pe-
> ter] and to the new experience of the Spirit of the resurrection
> [through Paul]. Hence the privilege of this local church, and so of
> her see and *cathedra*. Hence also her special calling: the *commun-
> ion* of the witness of Peter and that of Paul which had been en-
> trusted to her — engraved in her, so that she became the 'living
> memory' among all the churches. Her bishop would have the re-
> sponsibility of becoming the guardian of and spokesman for all
> that is implied by such a privilege and calling.[19]

The city of Rome is not a symbol of unity because the pope
is there. Rather, the pope is there because Rome is a symbol of unity. And it is this because Peter and Paul both died
there in witness to a unified Church.[20]

The Church is not unified by gathering around the pope,
but by gathering with their bishops and other believers in
Eucharist and around the deposit of faith which has been
handed down within the Church for two thousand years.
The pope's role is to make sure that all his fellow bishops
do that. For this he has the authority to call them together to
confront issues in the light of Scripture and the Christian
tradition. (This is what an ecumenical council is). And if an
individual bishop or member of the Church departs from
the common teaching, the pope is responsible for preserving the unity of the Church by taking the necessary
measures to correct the error. He is empowered to do this.
But this does not make the pope the center of the Church or

even the guiding light of theological investigation in the Church. As Catholics, we do not find our unity by centering on the pope or on the particular theological positions that various functionaries in the Vatican are taking at the moment, but by letting the bishop of Rome use his gifts and authority to center us on the faith taught by Peter and Paul in that city and on the action of the Holy Spirit throughout the centuries and throughout the world. The goal is not union with the bishop of Rome as such, but union with all the bishops in the world, *kata holos*, who are kept in unity with each other through their union with the diocese of Rome and by using Rome's bishop as a unifying point of reference.[21]

The challenge of catholicity

The theme of this final portion of Matthew's Gospel is the call to persevere in faithful stewardship, laboring to establish the reign of Christ on earth until he comes again.

This means that all of us, as responsible stewards, must try to right whatever is wrong in God's world; and that includes whatever is wrong in the Church. The call to renew and transform society is also a call to renew and transform the Church.

This call is addressed equally to clergy and laity, because all were equally anointed at Baptism to the triple role of Christ Priest, Prophet and King. If we recognize Baptism as giving to every Christian the unrivaled and overwhelming sacredness of the body of Christ, then we must accept Baptism itself as giving to every Christian a dignity and status to which no other ordination or consecration can add, except in relatively minor ways. But this means that Baptism itself, not the pronouncing of religious vows or the acceptance of Holy Orders, makes every Christian responsible, and equally responsible, for renewing, reforming and upbuilding both the Church and secular society. In this respect the only difference between the hierarchy, the clergy and the laity is in the way that each is called and empowered to exercise that responsibility.

We may think we are being obedient and respectful Catholics by accepting with unquestioning docility every direction that comes from Rome. But it is more likely that we are just taking the easy way out and leaving to remote authorities all responsibility for the direction the Church is taking in our own place. This is a rejection of the catholicity of the Church, which requires that our unity be the fruit of interactive diversity. It is to restrict and localize the Spirit who breathes *kata holos*, "throughout the whole." In the *catholic* Catholic Church to be a silent follower is to be an unfaithful steward of the kingship of Christ.

It is also a formula for failure. For the Church to stay on course, and even more so to deliver the Gospel where it needs to be delivered, those in authority need constant input from all the members. And this is true on every level: parish, diocese and universal Church. The Church is a faith community meant to be guided by communal discussion, prayer and discernment. It is not to one person or category of persons, but to each and every individual that "the manifestation of the Spirit is given for the common good" (1Cor. 12:7). The Spirit speaking in each one needs to be expressed and heard.

Jesus rode into Jerusalem on a donkey and promised to replace the temple "made with hands" by another temple made of living stones (see Mk. 14:58; 1Peter 2:5). In Luke's account, when the Pharisees wanted him to stop his disciples from acclaiming him he answered, "I tell you, if these were silent, the stones would shout out" (Lk. 19:40). It is time for us to be those stones.

CHAPTER FIVE:
WHERE IS THE CENTER OF THE CHURCH?
"Universal Lord'"' — Matthew 21:12-17

Summary

When Jesus drove the moneymakers out of the temple, he actually did four things:

1. He asserted his authority and thereby established his identity, not only as Messiah and Son of God, but also as Universal Lord, the King and Savior of the whole human race. Jesus' reference to Psalm 8 does not just identify him as the divine son of God; the Psalm's main focus is on the universality of God's reign and on human beings' responsibility for establishing it. The Psalm begins and ends with the phrase: "O LORD, our Sovereign, how majestic is your name in all the earth!"

2. He canceled out the restricting identification of his religion with the Jewish people or with any other particular race or culture. The temple is not just being purified; it is being replaced by a new, a spiritual temple, the universal — that is, "catholic"— Church. The Church recognized this when they decided not to impose Jewish religious observances on Gentile converts (Acts 15:1-32).

3. He replaced the physical temple in Jerusalem with the flesh-and-blood temple of his risen body the Church as the dwelling place of God on earth. Henceforth the presence of God will be associated, not with any special place, building, or caste of people, but with any and every human person who, by baptism into the Church, the risen body of Christ on earth, is filled with the indwelling presence of the Holy Spirit. The basic sacredness or holiness of all Christians comes from this, and any further consecration simply specifies how this total gift of self will be lived out in action. There is no "higher" or "lower" caste in the Church.

4. He rejected the natural human tendency to make some particular building, place or person the animating symbol and center of his religion. This calls us today to reexamine the way we think of Rome, and to evaluate the effect its splendor has on us.

The call to renew society is also a call to renew and transform the Church. It is addressed equally to clergy and laity. To leave to remote authorities all responsibility for the direction the Church is taking in our own place is a rejection of the catholicity of the Church, which requires that our unity be the fruit of interactive diversity. In the *catholic* Catholic Church to be a silent follower is to be an unfaithful steward of the kingship of Christ.

Have you understood?

What does "catholic" mean?

How is the Church being catholic and failing to be catholic in our day?

Why do we need to refocus the Church on the action of the Spirit throughout the world rather than on the centralized control which at present characterizes Vatican government? How could this be done?

Do you agree that the laity are just as responsible for renewing and giving direction to the Church as the clergy are? Why?

What is the challenge of this chapter? To our faith? To our hope? To our love?

Making it your own

What are the key thoughts in this chapter? (Jot them down and give the page number where each is found).

What questions do I have about this chapter? (Bring them up in discussion or ask someone who should know the answers).

What struck me the most in this chapter? After reading this chapter, what do I understand better than I did before? What do I appreciate more?

What do I think is the point of the whole chapter? What response does Matthew want to evoke from those who read or hear this part of his Gospel?

What can I use as a visible reminder (a symbol) to keep me aware of the challenge of this chapter? Where will I put it?

Questions for prayer

What contribution am I making to the direction of the Church in my parish, my city, my diocese?

Do I think of priests, nuns or bishops as being more "sacred" than lay persons? Do I treat them with more respect? Why?

Does it encourage me in my faith to know that, yes, in some ways it is

*possible to be "more catholic than the pope"? Does it make it easier
for me to persevere in faith and fidelity?*

*How can I apply to my life what I have come to see by reflecting on this
chapter? What concrete action do I choose to perform to express my
belief in what I have seen*

FOOTNOTES

[1] See Mt. 2:1-12 (the Magi) and 8:5-13 (the Roman centurion); Mt.
10:12-18 (witness to the Gentiles) and 13:57 (not a prophet in His native place); Mt. 16:17-20 (Israel supplanted by the Church) and 19:8-9
(universal law of creation vs. Mosaic Law).

[2] See the *Jerome Biblical Commentary* on Mt. 21:10-17

[3] This takes nothing from the reverence Catholics have for churches in
which the Eucharist is celebrated or preserved. But it is important to
bear in mind that the unique sacredness of any Catholic church comes
from the Eucharistic celebration itself, not from that building's geographical location, cultural identification, history, architecture, devotional statues, relics, or non-Eucharistic ceremonial uses. Without denying any of these values or discounting the sentimental attachment
many people have to "their" churches, we have to insist that the pri-
mary function of a Catholic church is to make possible and to encourage *full, active, conscious participation in the Eucharistic celebration.*
To sacrifice this value to any other is a form of liturgical idolatry.

[4] St. Peter's, of course, is only a basilica, not the cathedral of Rome.
Father Henri de Lubac, S.J., who was later made a Cardinal, quotes Fr.
Louis Boyer, to this effect: "If, after the dissolution of the primitive
Church in Jerusalem... the Roman Church inherited its role as 'Mother
and head of all the Churches on earth,' the Roman Church herself never
gave this title to the offices in the Vatican, but rather to the Lateran
Cathedral, where, down through the centuries, the popes [as local bishops in their own diocese] preached the Gospel to the assembly of believers, baptized, and presided over the common prayer and the Eucharistic banquet." See Henri de Lubac, *Les églises particulières dans
l'Eglise universelle*, Paris, Aubier Montaigne, 1971, ch. 6, note 2, p. 14.

[5] See J. M. R. Tillard, *The Bishop of Rome*, Michael Glazier, Inc.,
1986, pp. 150-154: Tillard points out that the role of bishop

exists at the intersection of two communions which together constitute the necessary guarantee of the community's identity as
Church. The 'apostolic succession' secures the vertical communion, so guaranteeing that the church committed to the bishop shares
the identity of the Church of the Apostles. It is the identity across
time. It binds today with the day of the beginnings and allows the
local church to recognize herself in the features of the apostolic
Church. But there must also be a horizontal communion which will
guarantee the identity of this local church with all the other local
churches here and now dispersed throughout the world: the identity
across space. It allows the local church, working out her faith and
obedience to the gospel in her own situation, to recognize herself
in the other local churches which are working out the same faith
and the same obedience in their own particular situations. The
horizontal communion is just as essential to the Church of God as
the vertical communion....

....In other words, communion with the... bishop of the see of Peter
and Paul is to the horizontal dimension of catholicity... what inclu-
sion in the 'apostolic succession' is to the historical vertical dimension of catholicity.

[6] See Vatican II's teaching about the role of bishops in the *Constitution
on the Church*, chapter 3, especially paragraph 23; and in the decree on
Bishops' Pastoral Office in the Church. See also Vatican II's repeated
endorsement of the "principle of subsidiarity" enunciated by Pope Pius
XI in *Quadragesimo Anno* and applied by the Council to the international community's stimulation of economic growth in developing
countries (*The Church in the Modern World*, article 86, with the footnote in Abbot's America Press edition) and to the state's role in education (*On Christian Education*, articles 3 and 6). The Church is saying
here that both in governmental policy and in teaching, it is an unjust
and harmful "disturbance of right order to turn over to a greater society
of higher rank functions and services which can be performed by lesser
bodies on a lower plane" (Pius XI). This means that it is not more according to Catholic teaching but less — in fact, a "harmful disturbance
of right order" — for local bishops and their dioceses to look to Rome
to generate the theological and pastoral insights which should grow out
of the prayer, reflection and experience of the local church. See also

McBrien, *Catholicism*, Study Edition, Part IV, ch. 23, "The Church and Papal Primacy," p. 835.

[7] Father J. M. R. Tillard warns against accepting every statement of the pope as if it were Catholic doctrine:

> We can only deplore the fact that under pressure from latent juridicism... every intervention of the bishop of Rome is accorded a juridical 'authority' it may not necessarily possess....

> Except in the case of the definitions guaranteed by infallibility... there is no question of according equal importance to these 'universal words' of the bishop of Rome, nor even to all the encyclicals. Nor should we award *a priori* to all such communications a higher standing than that enjoyed by pastoral letters from the local bishop or from the episcopal conference (*op. cit.,* pp. 167-170).

[8] See Tillard's report on Protestant willingness to restore unity. But "this will involve the presence both of a universal primacy to ensure cohesion... and... a healthy conciliarity to guarantee the diversity which catholicity requires" (*op. cit.,* p. 12). On the question of the pope's role, Richard McBrien refers to what is known as *The Venice Statement*, "An Agreed Statement on Authority in the Church," written by the Anglican-Roman Catholic International Commission and published by the United States Catholic Conference of bishops, Washington, D.C., 1977. The authority this document is concerned with, says McBrien, is "the authority of Christ, which is activated by the Holy Spirit to create community with God and with all persons. The model is definitely not political, sociological, or structural, but rather one of *koinonia*, i.e. fellowship of loving service in the truth of Christ. Whatever authority the Church possesses is always and only for the sake of promoting *community*." The Commission agreed that "Primacy fulfills its purpose by helping the churches to listen to one another, to grow in love and unity, to strive together towards the fullness of Christian life and witness; it respects and promotes Christian freedom and spontaneity; it does not seek uniformity where diversity is legitimate, or centralize administration to the detriment of local churches" (*Catholicism*, Study Edition, Pt. IV, ch. 23. p. 827; and see *Origins* 7/30, Jan. 12, 1978, pp. 474-476).

[9] Fr. Bernard Häring reminds us that "For the first thousand years, not one pope — no bishop of Rome — ever thought he had the right to appoint bishops everywhere. These appointments, or rather elections, took place according to the principle of subsidiarity — unless the em-

peror or other secular rulers intervened" (*My Hope for the Church*, Ligouri/Triumph, 1999, p. 32).

[10] One of the problems which follow from confusing symbols with reality is that the order of priorities can be reversed, so that the reality can be made to exist just for the sake of the symbol. One glaring example of this is the ordination of "titular bishops" who have a diocese in title only, but who do not actually serve as bishop of any real diocese. For example, when the pope feels he needs to give a Vatican diplomat some prestige in the eyes of a national government or church, he may ordain the man bishop of some ancient diocese that no longer exists so that he can use the title "Bishop" (or even more fictitiously, "Archbishop"), dress like a bishop, and command the prestige of a bishop in his diplomatic work. To do this is simply to prostitute the sacrament of Holy Orders to political pragmatism. Archbishop John Quinn argues in the same way about ordaining people bishops to serve in the Vatican curia:

> Increasingly there are those who see the ordination of a priest as bishop in order to be secretary of a curial congregation as an abuse of the sacrament of Holy Orders and of the office of bishop. This practice has the appearance of making a priest a bishop in order to give him rank or prestige. It is also an ecumenical problem because it appears to quarrel with the teaching of the Church about the episcopate (*The Reform of the Papacy*, by John R. Quinn, Crossroad (Herder and Herder), New York, 1999, p. 173).

[11] The bishops do not receive the power of jurisdiction over their dioceses by papal appointment. Fr. Tillard reminds us:

> For [Vatican II] the episcopate itself is a sacrament. In view of its function, indeed, the power of hierarchy in the Church can only derive from the sacrament, not from some distinct *ordo jurisdictionis* [chain of command] with its source in the pope.... Everything they [the bishops] need for the discharge of their office comes to them in their sacramental ordination (*op. cit.* p. 39).

For all that is said here about the transfer of bishops and for the identification of words quoted from other sources, see Michael J. Buckley, S.J., *Papal Primacy and the Episcopate*, Crossroad, 1998, pp. 91-94. Buckley's book came out of a presentation he was invited by Cardinal Joseph Ratzinger, Prefect of the Congregation for the Doctrine of the Faith, to give at a theological symposium in Rome in 1996. It was first published by the Libreria Editrice Vaticana, Vatican City, 1997, under the title "*Perpetuum Utriusque Unitatis Principium ac Visible Fundamentum*: The Primacy and the Episcopate: Towards a Doctrinal Synthesis," in *Atti del simposio teologico, Roma, diciembre 1996.*

[12] For a treatment of this topic that is reverent, loyal, theologically precise and historically documented, see the book cited above: *The Reform of the Papacy*, by John R. Quinn, retired Archbishop of San Francisco, Crossroad, New York, 1999. See also Bernard Häring, C. Ss. R., *My Hope for the Church*, Ligouri/Triumph, 1999, esp. pp. 30-35.

[13] Raymond E. Brown, *Biblical Reflections on Crises Facing the Church*, Paulist Press, 1975, pp. 81-82; emphasis added. The local churches (dioceses) are not elements in a single whole gathered around the diocese of Rome as their center. Each diocese contains within itself all that is necessary for the whole Church to exist. If all the dioceses in the world, including that of Rome, were obliterated except one, the Church of Jesus Christ would still exist in that remaining diocese in its entirety, endowed with everything necessary to continue its mission. The function of the church in Rome is to keep this whole "communion of churches" united in faith and love. Fr. Tillard explains:

> It is not the bishop of Rome who has received from the Spirit the charge to build the local church and keep it in faith and communion. It is the bishop of that church. But he accomplishes his mission fully to the extent that he is in communion with the *centrum unitatis* '[center of unity] who presides in charity.' Further, the bishop of Rome is not strictly speaking he who creates unity. That responsibility falls to the local bishop as the instrument of the Spirit. The 'primate' has the task of 'watching' over the unity so that the faith on which it is built remains one with the apostolic faith....

> ...We here touch on the formal reason for the primacy of the see of Peter and Paul. It concerns that bishop's function as 'watchman,' as memory. The *centrum unitatis* does not take over the whole work of building unity. As Vatican II showed... each bishop is a source [or principle] and foundation of unity (L.G. 23). The existence of a centre requires elements to be unified around it. In this case the elements are the churches, in every one of which is to be found the Church of God (*op. cit.*, see pages 150-154).

[14] Citations are from Henri de Lubac, *op. cit.*, chapter VI, pp. 99-103.

¹⁵ See Vatican II: *Constitution on the Church*, no. 28; and *Decree on Bishops*, nos. 28 and 30. Fr. Tillard points out that while Vatican I made clear that the bishop of Rome has, in virtue of his office, the *authority* (*potestas*] to intervene directly and immediately in any bishop's diocese, it is not his *job* [function, *munus*] to do so unless particular circumstances make this necessary in order to preserve the unity and well-being of the Church. During Vatican I there was a

statement often made during the discussions that the pope's function and the power needed for it exist *ad aedificationem Ecclesiae non ad destructionem* [for the building up of the Church, not for its destruction]. This implies that everything which works against the building-up of the Church as Christ willed it and along the ways attested by living Tradition must be contrary to the truth of the papal function, so that the power thus deployed is being improperly used (*op. cit.*, page 28).

This gives special significance to a second principle cited by Tillard, which was affirmed during the Council by Mgr. Zinelli, in the name of the Deputation of the Faith:

'A plenary and supreme authority was conferred on Peter and his successors in the Church, plenary in the sense that it could be limited not by any greater human power but only by natural and divine law.' The principle of limitation for the plenary authority of the Roman pontiff was thus admitted...(*ibid.*).

This would lead to the conclusion that when the pope steps outside of the proper exercise of his office (*munus*) and uses his power (*potestas*) in a way that is destructive for the Church, it is an act contrary to divine law and not a valid exercise of authority. It is also an obstacle to the restoration of Christian unity. Pope Paul VI, in a speech to the Secretariat for Christian Unity on April 28, 1967, said, "The Pope, as we well know, is undoubtedly the gravest obstacle in the path of ecumenism." Fr. Tillard is building on Pope Paul VI and anticipating John Paul II (*Ut Unum Sint*) when he points out that the problem not the papacy as such but the wrong use of papal authority. A reform in the pope's *way of exercising* the primacy might remove the obstacle and eventually restore the unity of a Church divided into East and West, Catholic and Protestant. As Tillard expresses the problem, "The present Catholic vision of the papacy magnifies the office. It makes the pope 'more than a pope'" (*op. cit.*, p.17-19). Tillard sums up his whole book:

The bishop of Rome is *servus servorum Dei* [the servant of the servants of God] and he has the duty (the charge, the commission, the *munus*) to carry out faithfully whatever is needed to keep the churches in *koinonia* [communion, fellowship]. If he does not do so, whether from negligence or from lack of knowledge, it will be *ad destructionem Ecclesiae*. But it is equally 'for the destruction and not the building up of the Church' if in his concern he oversteps the limits of his own primatial power and encroaches on the power of the bishops of other local churches. There, we have suggested, lies the whole problem (*op. cit.*, p. 180. Tillard includes a reference to Denziger-Schoenmetzer, *Enchiridion Symbolorum*, Freiburg, no. 3061).

[16] See Vatican II's *Constitution on the Church*, paragraphs 20, 21 and 28. Tillard says that Vatican II's "shift in emphasis" regarding the pope's relationship to the bishops "ties in with a more profound development without which the real issue at stake would not appear":

It concerns the movement from an ecclesiology starting with the idea of the universal Church divided into portions called dioceses, to an ecclesiology which understands the Church as the communion of all the local churches. In the area of our special concern [the authentic role of the bishop of Rome], this is the great new insight of Vatican II compared with Vatican I.

Tillard then quotes Vatican II's "Constitution on the Church," no. 26, and "Decree on the Bishops' Pastoral Office in the Church," no. 11. He concludes:

This means that the Church of God, seen in its universality, is the *communion* of local or particular churches. The universal Church is not to be identified as a vast whole, divided into portions each one of which is imperfect on its own. It is born from the *koinonia*, in each of which, through its celebration of a true Eucharist, *vere inest et operatur Una Sancta Catholica et Apostolica Christi Ecclesia* [the One, Holy, Catholic and Apostolic Church of Christ truly exists and functions] (*op. cit.*, pp. 37-38).

For further explanation of the phrase "communion of Churches," see Michael J. Buckley, S.J., *op. cit.*, chapter four.

[17] See Vatican II, *Constitution on the Church*, no. 26 and Tillard, *op. cit.* pp. 151, 153, 185 and 189: "The Church is made by Eucharist and

baptism, not by the papacy. The purpose of the papacy is to give the Eucharist its full dimensions."

[18] See Tillard, *op. cit.*, pp. 105-6; 115.

[19] See Tillard, *op. cit.*, pp. 93, 116-117. See also pp. 74-83).

[20] St. Irenaeus (bishop of Lyons, c. 203 A.D.) is a witness to the special place of the church of Rome in the minds of the earliest Christians:

It is with this church, on account of her more powerful origin (*propter potentiorem principalitatem*) that it is necessary that every church should agree, that is the faithful from all sides; (this church) where that which is the tradition from the apostles has been preserved always by those who are from all parts. (Irenaeus, *Adv. Haer.* III, 3, 1-2, cited by Tillard, p. 75-76).

There were other factors, of course:

The hierarchy of the Churches was thus determined in relation not to the story of Jesus, but to the apostolic mission and witness... Its great centres are therefore not the holy places of the Lord's life, ministry and Passion, but those points on the map of the world where in the power of the Spirit the gospel of God took root in order to spread out among the peoples of the world. The local church at Rome is first among the churches because the martyrdom of Peter and Paul there made it the supreme place of apostolic witness, not because it was established before the others. It is certainly true that the fact that Rome was the city, the capital, was not without influence on the directions in which the gospel spread.... Nevertheless, the geographical importance is, as it were, relativized by that of the apostolic witness which 'those whom the Lord had sent' brought to the place (p. 74-75).

[21] To understand the position of the pope with reference to the bishops and their local Churches, it helps to make a distinction between the diocese of Rome and the Vatican. When we look to the pope with faith and reverence as exercising authority over the universal Church, we are looking to him as bishop of Rome, not as head of the Vatican bureaucracy. As Henri de Lubac pointed out, there is a difference. See footnote 4 above.

Chapter Six
The "Earthquake"
Jesus arouses conflict — Matthew 21:10-17

Matthew tells us that the impact of Christ's entry into Jerusalem was "seismic" — like an earthquake. "As he entered Jerusalem, the whole city was *stirred to its depths*, demanding, 'Who is this?'"

We saw in Chapter One above that Matthew uses the same verb (*seio*) two other times: once to describe the effect of Jesus' death, when "the earth shook, and the rocks were split," and then to report his resurrection, when "there was a great earthquake [*seismos*]... [and] the guards shook [*eseisthesan*] and became like dead men (Mt. 27:51 and 28:1-4). In both cases he is writing of events which called the whole world into crisis.

The first "crisis" passage in Matthew is the story of the Magi, whose entry into this same city of Jerusalem with the announcement of Jesus' birth produced an emotional earthquake. At that news, Matthew tells us, "King Herod became greatly disturbed, and with him all Jerusalem" (see Mt. 2:3).

And now, when Jesus enters Jerusalem again, this time as a king about to die, Matthew tells us again that the whole city was "stirred to its depths," or, more literally, just "shaken." The entry of Jesus into anyone's life, anyone's consciousness, is an event which shakes things up, which stirs people to the soul, which will not leave anyone the same.

Jesus leads us into crisis

The proper word for the impact encounter with Jesus has on us is "crisis." Jesus is a recurring "crisis" in our lives in the sense that encounter with him calls for a response, and according to the response we make, our lives are enhanced or diminished. And we ourselves are called into question.[1]

The rejoicing of the crowds and children when Jesus rode into Jerusalem is in sharp contrast to the indignation of the priests and scribes (see Mt. 21:15). Clearly the coming of the Messiah affected people in different ways. And it still does. Each one of us, encountering Jesus, must respond. And our responses will reveal our hearts. This is to experience a crisis.

Every invitation from Jesus calls us into crisis. Our response to him is our "judgment." By the way we respond to his invitation we pass judgment on ourselves. Our response to his truth, his goodness, his ideals, reveals the light or the darkness of our minds, the sincerity or insincerity of our hearts up to that moment (see John 3:16-21; 9:39; 12:46-49).

Not only does encounter with Jesus reveal what we are; it also changes us. By the choice we make in response to him, we either turn away from the light or darkness which has characterized our lives to this point, or we root ourselves more deeply in what we have already embraced. For good or bad, every encounter with Jesus requires a conversion from or a confirmation in what we were before. In either case, we do not remain the same.

That is why encounter with Jesus "shakes" us. When we encounter him, we encounter ourselves. In our spontaneous reaction to his truth, his ideals, his call, we experience the orientation of our own hearts. If our deeds are truly good and our minds sincerely devoted to truth, and if our wills are in fact wholly directed to God and to all that God desires, our hearts will recognize Jesus for who he is and will welcome him with joy. But if our religion is not sincere, we will recoil from his presence, shield our minds against his truth, be offended by his call and threatened by the ideals he teaches.

Discernment of spirits

Every encounter with Jesus shakes us, but not to the same degree. In fact, most of the time he speaks to us so softly, he touches our hearts so gently, that we are hardly aware of encountering him at all. We read or hear something which arouses a tiny reaction in us, negative or positive. We feel slightly inspired or threatened by someone else's behavior or style of life. We are mildly excited or disturbed by some idea which comes into our heads. But we pay so little attention to these feelings, these almost imperceptible reactions, that we hardly remember them afterwards. If we are not seriously bent on receiving and responding to the movements and inspirations of the Holy Spirit in our hearts, we will hardly notice he is there or be aware of any communication from him at all. This is because God respects our freedom too much to make his desires known to us unless we really want to respond to him more generously. He will not push his gifts on us unless we really want to receive them. He does not normally shake us up in a way we cannot ignore unless the fundamental direction of our lives is at stake.

That is why, if we want to keep making progress in the spiritual life, we have to make deliberate efforts to attune ourselves to the movements his Spirit causes in our hearts. The best way to do this is to begin paying attention to what we *feel* — to consciously register moments when we experience peace or disturbance, clarity or confusion, encouragement or fear — and then to go back over these experiences, asking what word, thought, action or perception excited these feelings. If we pay attention to changes of mood and ask ourselves — for example, at the end of each day — what caused our mood to change, we can begin to recognize the "crisis" moments of encounter with Christ throughout our lives.

A whole body of literature exists to help us interpret the reaction of our hearts to particular inspirations. Especially useful are the "Rules for the Discernment of Spirits" found in the *Spiritual Exercises* of St. Ignatius, which he gathered from his own experience and from long Christian tradition. These are solid guidelines, but it takes grace and skill to apply them, because there is nothing simplistic about the human heart, and we could not do justice to these rules if we tried to explain them here. What Matthew's Gospel alerts us to is just that we can expect encounter with Jesus to stir us up, one way or another. Therefore, whenever we notice that some inspiration or idea moves or "shakes" us interiorly — whether it "turns us on" or "turns us off" — we should return to that idea and discerningly pray about it. Disturbance can be a sign of the presence of God. It summons us to notice the movements of our hearts, to listen to them and to grow.

Hopefully, this book will cause some disturbances!

All of us, in every age and place, repeatedly throughout our lives experience the "earthquake" of encounter with this Jesus who calls us into "crisis." The "earthquake" may be a tiny tremor, so faint we hardly notice it. Or it may be something which shakes the very foundations we have built our lives upon. But large or small, every encounter with Jesus is a crisis of *faith*, of *hope*, of *love*. To teach us what to expect and how to respond to Jesus, we have the Scriptural record of the others who have encountered him.

Crisis of faith: (Matthew 21:10-11)

When God called the Magi to his Son, the sign which brought them into the crisis of faith was the *star*. When Jesus sent his disciples out on mission, they themselves — as *Church* — were the sign that brought people into crisis. When Jesus explained to his disciples how he was going to save the world, the *cross* became the "sign of contradiction" which called their faith into crisis.[2]

Now, when Jesus enters Jerusalem as Messiah and king,

but without the power and prestige people expect, this calls the whole city into "crisis": each person will have to decide whether or not to *believe*, to *trust*, to *accept* a Messiah riding in on a donkey.

> And when he entered Jerusalem the whole city was shaken and asked, "Who is this?" And the crowds replied, "This is Jesus the prophet, from Nazareth in Galilee."

The sign which precipitates the crisis of faith in the people of Jerusalem now is Jesus' entry into the city *as a king without human power or resources*, to all appearances nothing but "the prophet from Galilee." The signs they expect to accredit the Messiah are not there. Instead, there is another sign: lowliness, peacefulness, a refusal to use power and violence. And, although the crowds do not suspect this yet, the disciples have been told that Jesus is in fact entering Jerusalem to die. The sign of his victory will be his acceptance of defeat with uncomprehending faith, his going down into death with "hope against hope," and his offering of himself on the cross with absolute, unwavering love. But to accept this sign requires of his followers an act of faith similar to that of Abraham, our "father in faith," who accepted to sacrifice Isaac, the only conceivable fulfillment of God's promise to him, while still believing that the promise would be fulfilled (see Rom. 4:18; Gal. 3:6-14; Genesis, chapters 15, 17 and 22).

This is the faith the Magi invested in the newborn baby of poor parents in Bethlehem (Mt. 2:11); the faith that the first people to join the Church invested in those who came to them without money or purse or a change of clothes, announcing the Good News (Mt. 10:9-15). It is the faith the disciples were challenged to invest in a Savior who would save them from evil by "enduring it with love" in the powerlessness of nonviolence and non-retaliation, and who called them to do the same (see Mt. 16:21-25). This is the faith that we are invited to invest in the King who takes possession of his Kingdom by riding into Jerusalem on a donkey to die.

"When he entered Jerusalem the whole city was shaken and asked, 'Who is this?' The question is still addressing our faith. And it is still an earthquake.

Crisis of hope: (Matthew 21:12-14)

When the procession accompanying Jesus arrived at the temple, the first thing Jesus did was drive out all those who were using the temple for the purpose of making money. This scene is sometimes used as evidence that Jesus did not really renounce the use of force or believe in nonviolence, because he overturned the tables of the money changers and (in John 3:15) drove out the animals with an improvised whip of rope.

In reality, the action of Jesus here was threatening to the established leaders of Israel, not because it was a show of force, but because, on the contrary, it rejected the power that the people of this world rely on.

First of all, the only power at Jesus' disposal here was the power of witness to the truth. He didn't organize his followers into an attack force and tell them to clean out the temple! He made a prophetic gesture, alone and unarmed. The famous whip of rope was not a weapon, but the ordinary tool anyone uses for driving cattle; and Jesus used it on animals, not people. By overturning the stalls and tables he was simply making a dramatic gesture, not attacking anyone. It may be that he got away with the gesture because no one wanted to risk resisting him or having him arrested in the explosive presence of the crowd. But it is certain that Jesus could and would have done the same thing, whether or not he had the support of the bystanders. There is a power in truth itself, and in anyone who is committed enough to proclaim it without regard for consequences. This was the only power Jesus used.

If Jesus had come back every day to clean out the temple,

that would have been different. Then he would not just
have been making a prophetic gesture; he would have been
setting out to effectively disrupt buying and selling in the
temple, and that would have provoked a reaction against
him in force. But he wasn't really trying systematically to
force a change on the temple; he was just bearing witness
to the truth of what they were doing. That was where his
threat to the establishment lay.

Jesus was rebuking the temple establishment for their compromise with wealth and power. Money is power. Those
with money have power, and those who seek the security
this world can provide soon learn to cooperate with the
moneyed class. Churches are no exception to this rule.
Every bishop, pastor and college president; every diocese
and parish, faces repeatedly the temptation to subvert the
work of the Church to purposes other than those of the
Gospel. A Church institution can make its real goal *survival*, for example, and accept means to this which are in-
compatible with the end for which the institution was
founded. Christians are frequently tempted to place their
real hope, not in the power of prayer, of faith and of love,
but in the techniques and resources this world offers to assure "success."

We might reflect here on fundraising techniques. Leaving
aside those which are fraudulent, such as those which sug-
gest that God will reward generous givers with material
success, the key question is whether our focus is really on
raising money or on converting hearts. The two can go together, but there is a real difference between trying to teach
people to take ownership in the Church and to express their
commitment by giving, or just using fundraising methods
that will "work."

Jesus, by attacking the business patrons of the temple, was
striking at the priests' sense of security. And by risking his
own life to do so (it is dangerous to make enemies of the
rich and powerful), he was exposing the cowardice which

kept the priests from defending the temple against those who were turning it into a "den of thieves." In short, the Jesus who drove the merchants out of the temple was expressing exactly what he expressed by entering Jerusalem "meek and mounted on a donkey" — he was rejecting all reliance on or alliance with worldly power and prestige as means for establishing his kingdom.

This calls us into "crisis!"

When Jesus refused alliance with the symbols of money and power, Matthew tells us that "the blind and the lame came up to him in the temple, and he healed them." Jesus' alliance is with the poor and powerless, the outcasts and afflicted — and with any rich who identify with them. This is the sign of his Messiahship, the reality of his reign.

Jesus' dramatic gesture of driving the moneymakers out of the temple summons us to *hope*. This hope, as Mary and Joseph learned in their flight into Egypt (see Mt. 2:13-15), is a hope based, not on the evident signs of God's protection, but on God's promise alone. This is the hope Christ demanded of his *Church* when he sent them out on mission without provisions, warning them that they might be delivered over to imprisonment, torture and death (see Mt. 10:9-10. 16-31). This is the hope required of all those who take up the *cross* to follow Jesus, trusting that by losing their lives they will save them (see Mt. 16:24-25). And it is only this hope which allows us to keep believing in a "loser Lord" who triumphs by entering into Jerusalem to die, and who refuses to establish a reign based on the power and prestige of this world. The hope to which Jesus calls us is a reliance on God alone and on his promises, which becomes most evident, most clear, and most challenging in the absence of any human resources or signs of success on which we can rely.

When Jesus enters our lives, he provokes in us an "earthquake" which lays bare the foundations and the goal of our hope: is our reliance really on God or on the resources of this world? Are our desires fixed on the invisible rewards God promises or on what this world offers visibly here and now?

This is a crisis which invites us to change.

Crisis of love

When the Magi entered Jerusalem, what disturbed Herod and his court so much was their faith. It was clear to Herod that these wise men already believed in the king they sought. They did not say, "We have come to check him out." They said, "We have come to adore him" (see Mt. 2:2-3). It was because rich, important, sophisticated men like these could believe in the unknown newborn they sought that Herod felt threatened. A child who could win faith from people like these could take away his throne. That is why he sent soldiers to kill all the baby boys in Bethlehem. His heart was divided between God and the things of this world. He was called into a crisis of love. It led him to murder.

This wasn't the first or the last time a government official would accept the "collateral damage" of massacring innocents in order to counter a threat to "national security." If the end is important enough to us, we will find ways to justify the means.

And now again, when Jesus enters Jerusalem as king, what disturbs the chief priests and scribes is not any power he displays, but the faith of those who accompany him. When the authorities hear even the children shouting out in the temple, "Hosanna to the Son of David!" they are incensed. If Jesus is accepted as Messiah, their own position and the values they cling to will be called into question. What they see threatens what they *love*, because their love is divided between God and the things of this world. They voice their objection furiously to Jesus, "Do you hear what they are saying?"

Jesus answers, "Yes; have you never read, 'Out of the mouths of infants and nursing babies you have prepared praise for yourself'?" (see Mt. 21:15-16 and Psalm 8:2).

The First Commandment: undivided love

Here again we have to look at the rich suggestiveness of Psalm 8, which Jesus quotes here. According to the *Jerusalem Bible* translation and notes on this Psalm, whoever keeps singing of the universality of God's reign — "Yahweh our Lord, how majestic is your name throughout the world!" — becomes "a fortress, firm against God's foes," because "the divine name confounds all idolatry by revealing the one true God." We overcome the temptation to "serve many masters" on earth (Mt. 6:24) by proclaiming adherence to the one true God who is Lord of all creation.

By citing this Psalm with its opposition to idolatry, Matthew ties us into the theme of the First Commandment: "I, the LORD, am your God, who brought you out of the land of Egypt, that place of slavery. You shall not have other gods besides me" (see Exodus 20:1-5; Mt. 22:34-40 and Deuteronomy 6:4-5). It is a call to reject any attachment to anything — position, prestige, power, any value or accomplishment on this earth — which can seduce us into compromising our undivided loyalty to God.

Jesus' response to the priests, then, calls us into "crisis" on the level of *love*: will we or will we not love the Lord, our God, with our whole heart, whole mind, whole strength — undividedly?

The simplicity of children

In all four accounts of Jesus' triumphal entry into Jerusalem, Matthew's is the only Gospel to explicitly mention children. Matthew may have done this in order to cite Psalm 8 and apply it to Jesus. But he may also be making a connection with another story which he alone reports: that of the children who were massacred in Jesus' place some thirty years before in Bethlehem. The Church celebrates these "holy Innocents" as martyrs, witnesses to the faith by their blood, even though they were too young to believe consciously in Jesus or offer their lives for him in witness. Nevertheless, their deaths too were a fulfillment of the words of Psalm 8: out of the open mouths of their wounds God both showed his empowering strength and "called forth praise."

The martyred Innocents are an example of undivided love. So are the children crying "Hosanna to the Son of David" in the temple. All during the long walk to Jerusalem from Caesarea Philippi, where Jesus first told his disciples that he was going to save the world by dying on the cross, Jesus kept repeating that we have to "become like little children" if we want to have a part in his Kingdom. We have to be totally open, as little children are, to the discovery of new reality. In adults, who are already locked into a whole set of cultural assumptions and values, this requires a willingness to "die" to all programmed priorities and preconceived ideas. In Jesus' Kingdom the "first will be last and the last will be first." Values will be turned upside down. We must be willing to lose or renounce money and possessions, our national and cultural identity, all power and prestige, even family life, should it come to that, if we want to be his disciples. In short, unless we "change and become like little children" in our openness of mind and willingness of heart to accept everything Jesus teaches, and "make ourselves lowly," seeking only that importance which is found in serving others, we "will not be able to enter the Kingdom of God" (Mt. 18:3-4; 19:14, 30; 20:16, 25-27; 23:11).[3]

The Kingdom calls for that purity of heart, that single-minded intentionality, that undivided love, which is the first and ultimate Commandment and the core of all response to Jesus Christ. This is the love which opens our eyes to recognize Christ; it is the love expressed by those who accept to die for him (see Mt. 5:8; Mt. 6:33; Mt. 11:25; Mt. 16:24-25; Mt. 22:34-40; John 15:13; Philippians 1:21).

The children who are shouting, "Hosanna to the Son of David!" are a reproach to the priests and scribes who are too attached to their possessions, their positions and prestige to acknowledge him as Messiah, too afraid to enter into the Kingdom. As such, these little children call the priests — and us — into a "crisis" of love: are we ourselves willing to respond to Jesus Christ with that abandon, to love him with that undivided love, to live for him with that single-mindedness of intention and desire which these little children, consciously or not, like the massacred Innocents who preceded them, are showing here? "Out of the mouth of infants and babies you have called forth praise": it is to such as these that "the Kingdom of heaven belongs!"

This "crisis" is the greatest earthquake of all!

Stewardship and crisis

If we are going to persevere in following Jesus, we must accept to be called repeatedly into crisis. Jesus is not a leader, or a lover, who lets anyone stagnate. And if we are going to persevere in *stewardship*, taking responsibility for realizing the reign of God on earth, we need to take crises for granted. Jesus said, "Every scribe who has been trained for the kingdom of heaven is like the master of a household who brings out of his treasure what is new and what is old" (Mt. 13:52). In a living, dynamic Church that is in constant interaction with the changing reality of this world, faithful stewardship requires us to be at one and the same time arch-conservatives and wild liberals. In our adherence to all that truly belongs to the "deposit of faith," to the body of truth revealed by God and clarified by the authentic teaching of the Church over the centuries, we do not give an inch; we "conserve" it literally with a "conserve-atism" that is absolute. But in our openness to the Holy Spirit, to new questions, new clarifications and developments, new light to illuminate old truth and new ways to live it out in action, our freedom is also without bounds. We are total "liberals" in the root meaning of the word, which is *liber*, meaning "free." This is the only way to remain faithful to the Holy Spirit, who constantly guards the Church conservatively from error and guides her liberally into new understanding of the truth.

A dynamic tension

Our absolute conservatism about matters of divine revelation, and our unrestricted liberalism regarding all things humanly debatable quite naturally leads to tension. It is not always clear to us just what belongs to divine revelation or to the authoritative interpretation of God's revelation by the Church, and what is still open to speculation. Most of the dogmatic or "infallible" pronouncements of the Church have been made in response to intense disagreements and violent debates over the authentic meaning of Scripture, especially when a point in Scripture is extended by reason to its logical consequences. For example, it is clear in the Gospel that Mary was the mother of Jesus and that Jesus was God. But can we conclude from this that therefore it is correct to call Mary the "Mother of God"? The Bible doesn't use this title. Although one and one are in the Gospel, are we correctly adding them up to make two? The Church did not officially come to agreement on this until the fifth century, when the Council of Ephesus (431 A.D.) declared it a dogma of faith that Mary is truly *Theotokos, Dei Genetrix*, or in English "Mother of God."

What this example makes clear is two things: first, that there is no way for Christians to remain united in their interpretation of Scripture (and to persevere in one faith) unless there is some person or body in the Church who can decide between conflicting opinions with an authority conferred and guaranteed by God. The fragmentation of Christianity into innumerable Protestant sects after this authority was rejected in the sixteenth century is confirmation of this.

The second conclusion is that a "dogmatic" Church makes it possible for more intellectual freedom to flourish rather than less. A Church which has the power to decide the outcome of a debate can afford to encourage debate. The more authority the Church has to detect and denounce error, the more freedom she has to explore truth in every direction. By contrast, we observe that those churches which claim no authority as a body to tell anyone what to believe — the fundamentalist "Bible only" churches — often tend to be the most rigid, narrow and anti-intellectual congregations in Christendom. Since there is no way to decide between conflicting interpretations, the only way they have to safeguard their faith is to stick to the letter of the Scripture and ask no questions about it. In practice this means they confer practical infallibility on the classic fundamentalist Protestant interpretations of Scripture which were developed during and after the Protestant Reformation to justify separation from Catholic doctrine and practice. The fundamentalists would never declare these interpretations "infallible," of course, but by adopting a stance of "chosen ignorance" which excludes all other interpretations from thought and discussion they achieve the same end.

A Church with the authority to be dogmatic welcomes crisis; it is a way to grow in understanding and appreciation of the faith. But while the crisis is going on, while questions are still unanswered and doctrine undecided, there is very definitely tension.

Some people, yielding to confusion and discouragement, leave the Church under the pressure of this tension. Is there anything we can say to this? How can we remain faithful in a Church that is constantly drawing us into crisis?

False escapes from crisis

There is an authentic way to deal with the tension between a conservative commitment to be faithful to tradition and a liberal commitment to follow the Holy Spirit wherever that might lead. The solution is to insist on "both-and" rather than to fall into the trap of "either-or." Granted that there are times when one simply has to say "Yes" to one thing and "No" to another, still, as a matter of habitual stance, the "both-and" choice is the first direction to explore. The "either-or" choice is too apt to be a cop-out.

For example, it is very tempting to take the conservative stance only and focus solely on safeguarding the faith. In practice this makes one more ready to "defend the faith" against error than to extend understanding of the faith into more challenging truth. It is a defensive stance, and it inclines one to accept without question whatever condemnations of new ideas or movements are being issued by the "*magisterium*"; "the special kind of teaching authority that is conferred by the sacrament of episcopal ordination and that authorizes the pope and the Catholic bishops to teach in the name of Christ on matters of faith and morals.".[4] Many Catholics bypass the voice of the local bishops entirely and listen only to what is being propagated by the Vatican. They assume (falsely) that any opinion given in the name of the pope is the "one that counts." Another option is not to listen to any new teaching, and just stick with what one learned in grade school, which was certainly approved doctrine at the time. As long as one is willing to live today with the stance the Church took toward last century's problems, a purely conservative position appears to be the safest way to persevere in the faith.

In reality, however, if we decide to accept as true everything that is the official position of a particular bishop, even the pope, or of Vatican officials speaking with the approval of the pope, we are already, by that very fact, going against the clear teaching of the Church and denying the faith in action. Every Catholic should know that the pope is only infallible when he speaks *ex cathedra* ("from the chair"), making it perfectly clear that he is using his full authority as pope to define a dogma of faith. And we know that the popes have only done this twice in the history of the world — to define as dogmas the Immaculate Conception in 1858 and the Assumption in 1950 —and then only after consulting all the bishops of the world to see if this was the universal belief of the Church.

God's absolute guarantee that the Church will not fall into error on a particular point is a "limited warranty" — limited, not in time, but by the conditions required before it can be invoked. The doctrines covered by this absolute guarantee are relatively few, and except for the two exceptions mentioned above, they are all dogmatic declarations, precise statements of belief, issued by the bishops in councils of the Church in unity with the bishop of Rome. Aside from these formally "defined dogmas," the only way to claim that a particular teaching comes under God's divine guarantee of infallible teaching is to show that it is either the clear, indisputable meaning of Scripture, or that it has been taught throughout the whole Church as a "catholic" or universal teaching from earliest times. And this is not always easy to establish.[5]

For example, there is a difference between what has always been *assumed* in the Church, and even lived out in practice, and what has been taught as the revelation of God. The first Christians apparently assumed that it was moral for Christians to own slaves. St. Paul, at least, sent the runaway slave, Onesimus, back to his master Philemon, and wrote Philemon a letter about how to treat him. And as late as the nineteenth century Catholics in the United States, including priests and religious orders, were slave owners with the full approval of the Church. At this time anyone who accepted the "ordinary *magisterium*" or teaching authority of the pope as definitive would have had to affirm that it is not intrinsically evil to own slaves, since Pope Gregory XVI taught in 1839 that "while slavery was a social evil, it was not a *malum per se* — that is, not necessarily an evil for the slave under a kind master, and not a positive detriment to his hope of salvation. At the same time the pope, like previous Catholic authorities, condemned the slave trade."[6]

The point is that the Church never definitively faced the issue of slavery in the light of divine revelation. What she did and taught was mostly by inertia, just following the common opinions of the times. We can say the same thing about what the Church assumed, accepted, taught and practiced for centuries with regard to questions like the morality of war, the death penalty, charging interest on loans, and the ordination of women. Throughout the Church's history the cultural climate of the times kept these questions from becoming the focus of explicit, definitive doctrinal decisions. Some (like the ordination of women) were just ignored in common teaching. Others (like the immorality of accepting any interest on loans) were explicitly and emphatically maintained in teachings that were later reversed in the light of a clearer understanding of the facts. What is clear is that, in the absence of explicit, definitive doctrinal decisions, answers that were (and are) commonly assumed and taught, even for centuries, cannot be automatically proclaimed as the infallible teaching of the Church.[7]

Clearly, in order to persevere in orthodox Catholic belief, we have to distinguish very clearly between what is the teaching *of* the Church and what is only teaching *in* the Church. But to do this we have to accept the effort of doing some homework, and the responsibility of making up our own minds. This is to be called into crisis. There is stress in the responsibility of decision-making. But if we can make only one choice — the choice to simply rubber-stamp whatever the *magisterium* (too often reduced in practice to Vatican officials) is saying at the moment, while ignoring local bishops and serious theologians, we can avoid the tension involved in trying to reconcile conflicting views. Any anguishing over what might be true or false we simply leave to those whose official job it is to safeguard the faith, and we don't feel obligated to think anymore about it. This is unfaithful stewardship; in other words, a cop-out.

We can avoid stress by just refusing to think. This can appear to be a safe way to persevere in the Church. The bishops and the Vatican may not always be on the cutting edge of the Church's exploration into truth, but they are also very unlikely to deny outright anything that has already been clarified by the Church and handed down as tradition. If one is comfortable with the explanations one got in grade school, why put a strain on one's faith by getting involved in the speculations of those who are not? And when the bishops do get up to the cutting edge of prophetic insight in their interaction with the world of today, as they did magnificently during the Second Vatican Council and still do in pastoral letters addressing current problems, one doesn't have to read them. We can crusade for the old and obvious values — crying out against extramarital sex and abortion, for example —while ignoring the burning modern questions the pope and the bishops are calling us to look at today: for example, our culture of violence, war, nuclear testing, capital punishment, the reform of the prison system, racism and the challenge of cultural diversity, ecological irresponsibility, un-self-questioning affluence and international exploitation of the poor.[7]

This, of course, is the problem: those who focus only on safeguarding the faith they grew up with are losing touch with a faith that is growing up without them. The very people who claim to be loyal to the *"magisterium,"* the official teaching voice of the Church, are often the ones most blatantly disobedient to the voices of popes, bishops and Councils begging them to bring the Gospel into contact with the modern world. Can any of us really say we are "persevering" in the faith and in the Church by standing pat while the faith and the Church are both leaving us behind? Can anyone claim to be persevering as a steward responsible for establishing the reign of God in family and social life, business and politics, while refusing to keep in touch with the Church's most enlightened and most modern teaching in these areas?

We can choose to live in the past, but it is not a way to persevere authentically in the Church. It is infidelity to our baptismal consecration as stewards of the kingship of Christ. It is to be in the Church but not of it.

The purely liberal option is another simplistic way to persevere. If one discounts the *magisterium* entirely and is not concerned about remaining faithful to the past, there is no reason to break with the Church in the present. One just adopts a "loose-leaf" theology that allows one to discard any teaching one disagrees with and add any teaching one desires. It is easy to remain in a Church whose boundaries expand as you move. When polls appear claiming that X percent of Catholics say they "do not believe in an after life" or "do not believe that Jesus Christ is God," one wonders what the word "Catholic" means to them. Are these people Catholics with a liberal faith, or just liberals with no faith at all? Whatever they are, they aren't under any tension to reconcile their opinions with the teaching of the hierarchy, and no statements by popes or bishops will make it more difficult for them to persevere in the faith, for they have made that faith too indefinable to deny! This is an either-or option that avoids tension by rejecting the teaching authority of the Church altogether.

Preserving the both-and

Clearly, in order to persevere as fully authentic Catholics, we have to make the "both-and" choice of being totally faithful to the authentic tradition of the past while keeping ourselves totally open to the authentic discoveries of the present. We have to combine fidelity with freedom, certitude with questioning, dogma with discovery. We have to be anchored in the past while we navigate toward the future. This is the ongoing crisis of being the faithful steward Jesus speaks of "who brings out of his treasure what is new and what is old."

We respect the ordinary teaching of the *magisterium*, and ordinarily follow it, because the ordinary way in which God preserves the Church from error is through the vigilance of the bishops. But the teaching of the bishops is not necessarily the ordinary way in which God leads the Church into new and deeper understanding of the truth God has revealed. This belongs to the prophetic, or ground-breaking ministry of those Catholics whose contact with the realities of life in this world, or whose more intensive prayer and study in some particular area enable them to see the application of the Gospel to life from a new perspective. If we avoid the "either-or" attitude as a matter of principle, and lean always toward "both-and," we will be open to the Holy Spirit guiding the Church through both of these ministries in complementary ways. Jesus did not only promise that the Holy Spirit would preserve the Church from error; he also promised that "when the Spirit of truth comes, he will guide you into all the truth" (John 16:13). The Church sees herself as a pilgrim people, ever on the move into deeper intimacy with God, into clearer understanding of God's mind and heart. A moving Church needs both a stabilizing ministry, people empowered by God to keep her from deviating from the path, and a prophetic ministry, people inspired by God to keep her from settling down where she is and stagnating. These two ministries are complementary, and the people called to them must work together, each group respecting the role of the other, each conscious of its own ministry's limits. Ideally, of course, since the Spirit animating both of these ministries is one and the same, every member of the Church should be both prophetic and preservative, open both to preserving structures and to changing or going beyond them.

The ground-level problem

On the individual level the tension is felt most strongly
when one is trying to remain loyal to official teaching
promulgated by authorities in the Church while one's own
experience, common sense or understanding of theology
contradicts it. This is the classic tension between the official and the charismatic elements in the Church. It was the
tension between Peter and Paul — and the fact that they
overcame it, kept the Church together, and both died in
Rome in united witness to the Gospel, is the reason why
that city's bishop is entrusted with the special task of keeping all the bishops in the world united. In the mingled blood
of Peter and Paul the unity of the Church seeped into the
soil of Rome and remains there.[8]

When we disagree with Church authorities (as Paul dis-
agreed with Peter; see Gal. 2:1-14) we will be tempted to
take the *either-or* option. Then we will either just dismiss
the official teaching as irrelevant, or we will simply accept
it on face value and close our eyes to everything else. But if
we take the *both-and* stance, we will try to be obedient to
the truth as it appears to us and at the same time be respectful of the various teaching authorities in the Church.
We will refuse to relieve the tension by a simplistic, black-
or-white solution. This might lead us to do some reading or
studying, or to ask some questions. (Notice that already we
are growing rather than stagnating; the "crisis" is bearing
fruit!). Most likely, in our efforts to reconcile conflicting
positions, or to come to a position ourselves that is respectful of them both, we will learn a lot about the Church, her
real teaching, her true values, and her authentic spiritual
soul. And this, more than anything else, will help us to persevere.

A sample crisis

There may be many ideas in this chapter that have "called you into crisis." Perhaps you stopped to focus on them; perhaps you didn't. But I would like to present one suggestion that can put your whole spiritual life on a different level. Once that suggestion is made. of course, you are in "crisis" — you have to say yes or no (just to ignore the question is to say no) — and the answer you give will be a yes or no to God which will be a step into deeper relationship with him or a step back from that.

To keep this from sounding more presumptuous or threatening than it is, we should be aware that not every suggestion from a human being is a suggestion from God! But when a suggestion concerns our relationship with God, we are already dealing with God when we decide whether it is in fact from him or not. To reject as irrelevant to ourselves something we believe is not from God is to grow in intimacy with him. It is to reaffirm and confirm our conviction that God is dealing with us, and that we are able to identify and follow his voice. This gives confidence, even if we cannot be absolutely certain whether we have made the right decision or not. The point is, we have had the courage to make a personal faith decision, and we trust that if it was the wrong one, God will knock again.

This is the suggestion: take a few minutes each day to notice, identify and respond to experiences that may have been God calling you into "crisis." In other words, ask every day whether God has said something to you. There is a simple, practical way to do this. Here's how to get into it:

The first thing you have to do is keep this exercise in perspective. You are not going to face world-shaking questions every day. Every invitation from God is not an earthquake! And you should not expect clear and certain results every time you try to recognize God's voice. There will be a lot of trial and error in your efforts. But if you persevere in this exercise, you will gradually grow in awareness of what is going on between yourself and God. And this is what it means to live a "spiritual life."

Strictly speaking, everyone has a "spiritual life," because everyone has a spirit. But when we speak of "living the spiritual life" we mean interacting with God in a way that is personal, conscious and active. For this it is not enough just to be very active in our religion: to consciously keep the Commandments, go to Mass, say prayers, try to learn more about the message of Jesus through Bible study and discussion groups. It is possible to do all this without dealing very deeply and personally with God. That is why we say that our "spiritual life" really begins from the moment we realize there is *something going on* between ourselves and God, and we *decide to get involved* in it.

This is of fundamental importance. It is often ignored in pastoral ministry, both in parishes and in Catholic schools. We teach people the doctrines of our faith. We teach them the laws of God. We initiate them into Catholic life through the sacraments. We encourage them to go to Mass and Confession, to receive Holy Communion. All of these are ways of responding to God, but we don't always teach them *as* ways of responding to God. People can do all these things with very little awareness of interacting consciously and personally with Jesus Christ, hardly experiencing a live relationship with him, one that is unique to themselves.

The spiritual life begins when we b*ecome aware that there is something going on between ourselves and God, and we decide to get involved in it.* The exercise I am suggesting is a way to do that.

It is a prayer form. It has been known by many names, the best of which is "the Awareness Exercise," or perhaps "Examination of Consciousness." It takes from five to fifteen minutes a day. People with no time at all can do it in the shower!

• **Preamble**: This prayer begins, as all prayer should, with a conscious *recognition* that we are in the presence of God. God is present everywhere, including in our hearts, but he is not present *to us* until we make ourselves aware of his presence here and now, where we are. And when we do, we should *acknowledge* his presence by some physical gesture: putting our hand on our heart, bowing our head, closing our eyes for a moment. This is a human, and therefore a very Christian, thing to do.

Then we naturally ask him for help. What we are about to do is not some psychological "self-help" exercise, although it could degenerate into that if we do it without interacting with God. This exercise is *prayer*, which means a time of communication with God. But our communication with him is not just in words. No deep communication is. When we communicate with God we need to be listening, thinking, feeling, responding with decisions and choices. That is why we ask him to be involved, to speak to us, to help us hear and understand his voice.

How does God do this? The fundamental assumption of this prayer form is that on a daily basis God speaks to us by causing changes in our *feelings*. He makes us feel peace or disturbs us. He brings about a change of mood in us. And these changes may be barely noticeable. In a normal, busy day we have so many different feelings and mood swings that we cannot pay attention to them all. So we take a "time-out" periodically to look back and see if any of them might be telling us something. No — that would be just psychological self-awareness. We look back to see whether through some of them *God* might be telling us something.

• *First step*: we use our *memories*, trying to recall and identify any change of mood that has taken place during the day; any feeling we had that we did not take time to examine. And we look at what may have caused that feeling. What put us in a good or bad mood? What put some good feeling of peace or some little, nagging feeling of disturbance into our day? When did it happen? What was the "before and after" moment of change in our mood?

• **Second step**: we use our minds, our *intellects*, to ask whether God might have had something to do with the change in our feelings. If we just got fired or promoted, we don't need God to explain our dejection or elation. But sometimes we may notice that the change of mood started right after we made some decision. Then we may realize that we were not really comfortable with that decision, although at the time we didn't stop to focus on that. Or we may realize that the reason we feel so good is that we really are happy with the decision; that everything about it seems right.

It is important that we then we make an intellectual judgment about the decision, or about whatever it was that caused our change of mood. We look at the whole picture of our feelings, at the attitudes, values and priorities involved, at the rightness or wrongness of our reaction. And we relate this to anything we think God has been saying to us recently or throughout our lives. We put our reaction or decision into the context of our total experience of God. Then we decide whether God was giving us negative or positive beeps through what we felt. We don't just make up our minds to go with what we decided or to call it into question; what we do above all is decide whether we believe God has spoken to us.

This is where we allow for error. We don't really decide definitively whether God has spoken to us or not; we decide whether or not to *believe* God has spoken to us and to act on that — at least until we get more clarity about it.

• **Third step**: we use our *wills* to choose the response we will make to what we have seen. We choose explicitly to believe this was or was not an intervention of God in our lives. We choose what we will do, what action we will take, what course we will follow, as a result of our discernment. We make a choice.

• *Fourth step*: we present this decision to God. We ask him to confirm it by giving us a deeper conviction about its truth, a felt peace in the decision we have made. And we close with an appropriate prayer, like the *Our Father*. [9]

Depending on the importance of the decision, this whole process might take less time than it has taken to read about it. And what we examine might not be a decision we made at all; it might be a reaction we had, a feeling, which on examination reveals some attitude in us, some value or priority God may be asking us to call into question. The whole point of this exercise is to get in touch with what God might be saying to us; to look at what is going on between ourselves and God and to interact with him.

So: let's take the first step: How do you feel about the suggestion that you make this exercise an element in your daily life? Does the suggestion anger you? Make you feel sad? Excite you? Give you hope? Open a door for you? Make you feel hemmed in? Disturb you, or give you peace?

Second step: What is your judgment about your reaction? Where is it coming from? What is it based on? How would you feel if you acted against your feelings here and did the opposite of what you feel inclined to? Does that prospect seem to carry with it hope, freedom, joy, peace, the promise of more? Or does it depress and discourage you, make you feel bound up and suffocated, as if you were heading into the narrow end of a funnel? How do these feelings fit with your past experience of being led by God or away from God? Have the courage to decide whether to believe God is encouraging you to accept this suggestion or whether he is saying to ignore it.

Third step: Decide what you will do.

Fourth step: Present that to God. Ask him to let you feel what he feels about it.

There: you have just experienced a "crisis."

CHAPTER SIX:
THE EARTHQUAKE
"Jesus arouses conflict" — Matthew 21:10-17

Summary

When Jesus enters Jerusalem, the whole city is "shaken." The entry of Jesus into anyone's life or consciousness is an event which will not leave anyone the same. Jesus is a recurring "crisis" in our lives. By the way we respond to his invitations we pass judgment on ourselves.

Most of the time God touches our hearts so gently that we are hardly aware of encountering him at all. That is why, if we want to keep making progress in the spiritual life, we have to make deliberate efforts to attune ourselves to the movements his Spirit causes in our hearts. The best way to do this is to begin paying attention to what we *feel* and then to go back over these experiences, asking what excited these feelings. For this we can use the "Examination of Consciousness" daily.

Jesus' entry into Jerusalem calls us into a crisis of *faith* by challenging us to believe in a King who takes possession of his Kingdom by riding in on a donkey to die. Can we accept a Savior who saves us from evil by "enduring it with love" in powerlessness and nonviolence, and calls us to do the same?

Jesus calls us into a crisis of *hope* by his dramatic gesture of driving out the business patrons of the temple. Here he is rejecting all alliance with worldly power and resources as the means for establishing his kingdom. He summons us to place our real hope in the power of God.

When the Jewish authorities hear the children shouting, "Hosanna to the Son of David!" it threatens them, because their love is divided between God and the things of this world. Jesus' response to them calls us into crisis on the level of *love*: will we love the Lord, our God, with our whole heart, undividedly?

If we are going persevere in *stewardship*, taking responsibility for realizing the reign of God on earth, we must accept to be called repeatedly into crisis. In a living, dynamic Church that is in constant interaction with the changing reality of this world, faithful stewardship requires us to keep bringing out of our treasure "what is new and what is old." In our adherence to all that truly belongs to the "deposit of faith" we are arch-conservatives. But in our openness to new questions, to new light that illuminates old truth and shows us new ways to live it out in action, we are total "liberals"; that is "free." This is the only way to remain faithful to the Holy Spirit, who constantly guards the Church conservatively from error and guides her liberally into new understanding of the truth.

We can shun stress by just refusing to think or to keep in touch with the Church's most enlightened modern teaching about family and social life, business and politics. But if we avoid crisis this way, we are failing as *stewards* responsible for establishing the reign of God in these areas.

Have you understood?

What does it say to you that Jesus took possession of his Kingdom by riding into Jerusalem on a donkey to die? Does this call your faith into question? Should it?

What does Jesus' dramatic gesture of driving out the business patrons of the temple teach you about hope? Does this cause you to challenge anything that is taken for granted in your parish or diocese? Anything in your own way of living and working?

Has the uncomplicated response of children to God ever made you ask whether you were rationalizing or compromising in your own response? What is undivided love for God? What would it look like in your daily life?

Why does faithful stewardship mean we will be constantly called into crisis? In what wrong ways do people try to avoid the stress of this? What is the right way to deal with tension arising from uncertainty about what we should believe or do?

What is the challenge of this chapter? To our faith? To our hope? To our love?

Making it your own

What are the key thoughts in this chapter? (Jot them down and give the page number where each is found).

What questions do I have about this chapter? (Bring them up in discussion or ask someone who should know the answers).

What struck me the most in this chapter? After reading this chapter, what do I understand better than I did before? What do I appreciate more?

What do I think is the point of the whole chapter? What response does Matthew want to evoke from those who read or hear this part of his Gospel?

What can I use as a visible reminder (a symbol) to keep me aware of the challenge of this chapter? Where will I put it?

Questions for prayer

In what ways do I embrace powerlessness in my own life? In what ways do I use power or ally myself with power?

Have I decided to practice the "Awareness Exercise" daily? Why? How do I feel about that?

On what issues would I be considered a "conservative"? On what issues would I be considered a "liberal"? If I don't fall into both categories, what does this say about me?

How can I apply to my life what I have come to see by reflecting on this chapter? What concrete action do I choose to perform to express my belief in what I have seen?

FOOTNOTES

[1] See John 12:31-50 for the theme of Jesus as *"krisis"* or judgment. See also John 5: 39-47 and 10:"24-30.

[2] In the call to accept *Jesus* this "crisis of faith" appears in the call of the Magi (Mt. 2:1-12). In the call to accept the *Church,* it appears in the effect the messengers of the Good News have on people (Mt. 10:11-15 and 20-25). In the call to embrace the *cross* it appears in Christ's announcement of the cross (Mt. 16:22-23).

[3] The word Matthew uses when he cites Psalm 8: "Out of the mouth of *infants* ..." is *nepios,* which can also mean "simple" or "unlearned." This is the sense it has in Mt. 11:25: "...you have revealed them to the *childlike.*" This childlike openness which allows people to receive truth from God is connected with the *simplicity* which Jesus urges in Mt. 10:16: "Behold, I am sending you like sheep in the midst of wolves; so be shrewd as serpents and simple as doves" (*akeraioi*; literally, "unmixed, pure"). It is this unmixed purity of heart which enables people

to see truth and reject idolatry. And God promised Solomon that if he sustained it, God would "establish his sovereignty over Israel forever," as he had promised to David. But if Solomon or his descendants turned to false gods, then God would "cut off Israel from the land... and repudiate the temple..." (1 Kings 9:4-7).

4 SeeFrancis Sullivan, S.J., "The Magisterium in the New Millenium," *America* August 27-September 3, 2001, p. 12.

5 The word "infallible" is sometimes used as if it just meant "certain" or "true." This is inexact. "Infallible" refers to an act of teaching. It is never used of a person unless it is followed by the word "when"; as, for example, in "The pope is infallible when he speaks *ex cathedra*." It is bad English and misleading to say, "This doctrine is infallible." Doctrines can be infallibly taught (therefore certain), but they are not infallible. Doctrines are true or false; they belong to the "deposit of faith" (truths revealed by God) or they do not. And it may be declared and taught infallibly that they are in one of these categories. But we use the word "infallible" only to refer to the way something is taught, never to the doctrine itself. If we are strict about this, it will focus us on precisely what we must prove when we speak about what Catholics are required to believe. (See my article, "Infallibility Complex, A Pastoral Response" *U. S. Catholic*, 61/4, April, 1996, pp. 11-13).

6 Theodore Maynard, *The Story of American Catholicism*, Macmillan, 1941, p. 342. Maynard is referring to the pope's Apostolic Letter *In Supremo Apostolatus* of 1839.

7 For example, the current position of the Vatican against artificial contraception and the ordination of women have both been proposed as infallible teaching on the grounds that these have been the stance of the Church from the beginning. The truth is that contraception hardly became an issue as long as infant mortality was so high that parents' main concern was to have children rather than limit them. When decreased infant mortality and increased urbanization made large families a problem, Greeley reports that "Several times the French hierarchy secretly asked Rome for advice on the problem. Each time they were told not to trouble the consciences of the laity." Greeley continues: "St. John Vianney, the Curé of Ars, in his conferences for confessors, repeated the advice, often in fierce language. Pope Leo XIII, in his encyclical on marriage [*Arcanum*,1880], written precisely at a time contraception was widespread in France — and he knew it to be so because

---

of the questions of the French bishops — said nothing on the subject." In 1930 Pope Pius XI wrote *Casti Connubii* and included a condemnation of contraception. But priests hearing confessions generally did not make an issue of it. Then in 1968, when Pope Paul VI wrote the famous "birth control encyclical," *Humanae Vitae*, the ensuing reaction made it clear that this teaching was not accepted throughout the Church as infallible. The responses that national bishops' conferences around the world made to it were marked by reserves and modifications. (See McBrien, *Catholicism*, Study Edition, ch. 27, p. 1024 ff.) And on the ground level of pastoral practice rejection of the teaching grew instead of declining. Of priests surveyed, those who would not refuse absolution to laypeople practicing birth control grew from 67 to 87 percent. Greeley concludes, "It therefore appears that for reasons of demographic transition, contraception became a major problem in the church only in the early years of this [the 20th] century and ceased to be a problem for the laity and the lower clergy by the late middle years (1970)." (See *National Catholic Reporter*, Oct. 15, 1993, pp. 18-21).

In the light of this, we can hardly say that the Church has been addressing the modern question of birth control for two thousand years. It simply had not become the issue it has become today. The same is true of the ordination of women: the cultural climate of earlier centuries kept it from being a real option. The Vatican position on both these issues may be true or false, but neither position is being taught with the infallible authority of the Church.

[8] To keep in touch with the statements of the American bishops, or to obtain a catalog of titles published by the United States Catholic Conference, call toll-free 800-235-8722 or visit the U.S. bishops' Internet site at *www.nccbuscc.org*. One can subscribe to all the USCC publications on a yearly basis.

[9] See Tillard, *op. cit.* pp. 74-83. Fr. Tillard explains that the church (diocese) of Rome was founded on both Peter and Paul, called the "two Coryphaei" or "leaders of the chorus," whose heads are both on the papal seal. For this reason the bishop of Rome needs to reflect the charism of Paul as well as that of Peter. See chapter five above, pp. 123-125.

[10] For the origin of this method of prayer, see *The Spiritual Exercises of St. Ignatius*, nos. 24-43. I drew from George Aschenbrenner,S.J., "Consciousness Examen," in *Review for Religious*, Jan., 1972.

Chapter Seven
The Power in the Word
Jesus triumphs — Matthew 21:18-22

After the conflict aroused by his triumphal entry into Jerusalem and his prophetic gesture in driving the moneymakers out of the temple, Jesus leaves the city and withdraws to Bethany to spend the night.

The next morning, on his way back into the city, Jesus feels hungry. He sees a fig tree by the side of the road and goes up to it looking for figs, but finds nothing on the tree but leaves. He says to it, "May you never bear fruit again!" And the fig tree withers up instantly.

When the disciples see this they are thunderstruck. They say to him, "How did that happen!?" Jesus answers, "Believe me, if you have faith and don't doubt, you will not only do what has been done to the fig tree, but even if you say to this mountain, 'Be lifted up and cast into the sea,' it will be done."

Then he adds, "And whatever you ask in prayer, you will receive, if you have faith."[1]

What is the meaning of this story?

A sign of triumph

Jesus has just had a confrontation in the temple with the leaders of Israel. He is going back into Jerusalem, where he will confront them again, and soon after that be handed over to death. His enemies are going to triumph over him, to all appearances, and they are the very ones who are keeping God's Chosen People from bearing the fruit they should bear. They are going to have Jesus killed in order to defend the sterile structures and pretentious practices they have imposed on Israel — the facade of religiosity which, like leaves on a barren tree, gives the appearance of life and fruitfulness where there is none. And when Jesus goes down in death, those who have the appearances of religion without bearing its fruit will also have the appearance of victory over Jesus — but it will not be a real victory; only the appearance of one. This is the meaning of Jesus' prophetic gesture with the fig tree.

In the withering of the fig tree Jesus is giving a sign of the withering of Israel, at least under the form its leaders wished to preserve. He is performing a miracle as a sign of his power, and of his eventual triumph over his enemies. But the point is, this is just a sign. What the disciples actually see is the destruction of a fig tree — not of the power structure of Israel. What they will see in just a couple of days, however, is the real destruction of Jesus' body on the cross, brought about by that same power structure. All Jesus is giving his disciples here is a sign to which they can cling in faith when to all appearances he is defeated by his enemies. Like his triumphant-ridiculous entry into Jerusalem, his triumph here is a triumph only to those who are willing to put more faith in God's words and signs and promises than in what they see with their own eyes happening all around them here and now.

That is why Jesus adds, "Whatever you ask for in prayer, you will receive, if you have faith." The disciples are going to have to believe, not only that Jesus has triumphed, but that they themselves, as Jesus' Church, have the power to prevail over the combined opposition of Israel and Rome. But they will prevail through prayer and faith; not through the power of the world, but through the power of the word. And they must not insist on seeing it.

The power of prayer

They will not see instant results. The fig tree withered up instantly at Jesus' word, but human institutions and cultures, with their attitudes, values and policies, will change only very gradually in response to the preaching of the Gospel.

Prayer has power, but it is not like the power of this world. Prayer is an act of free human beings addressed to a free God who respects human freedom. The prayer that changes people is a power which will not sweep aside anyone's freedom, whether it be of those praying or of those prayed for. Therefore those who pray for the conversion of others (or for their own!) must have enough faith in God to wait for results — just as God has enough faith in human beings to wait for their free response.

Truly, prayer can "move mountains." But it may appear to be at the pace at which the glaciers moved: almost imperceptibly from year to year, extending from one generation to another.

Down through the ages, the Church will have to keep believing that she has the power to move mountains — to prevail over the mountainous distortions and entrenched dominion of cultures both religious and non-religious. At different times and places the Church will be opposed by wealth, by military power, by prevailing trends in education, entertainment and social life, by laws and customs, by the seemingly irresistible tides of cultural and sociological trends. And to oppose these forces she will have nothing to rely upon but *faith*, *fidelity* (faith lived out in action), and *prayer*. If she tries to win by acquiring wealth and power herself, she will lose. If she tries to manipulate minds by marketing and advertising techniques, she will lose. If she allies herself with the business establishment, the military and the politicians, she will lose.

And if she looks for reassurance to those signs of power and success which the world — and we — spontaneously believe in, she will lose heart. For the Church today, as for the disciples who saw Jesus dragged off to execution, and who later were dragged off to execution themselves, there is no ultimate reassurance to be had from anything but

God's promise. Anything that appears to be success according to the standards of this world should sound a warning bell.

Oh, from time to time God will work some miracles. And frequently (constantly, for those with eyes to see) there will be the same consoling signs of Jesus' power that he offered to John the Baptizer when he was tempted to doubt: "The blind are receiving sight, the lame are walking, lepers are being cleansed, the deaf are hearing, the dead are being brought back to life, and the poor are having the Gospel preached to them" (see Mt. 11:4-16). There will always be fruitful ministry taking place in the Church for those to see who look for spiritual conversions and growth. But even while individuals are beginning to see by faith, to hear truths to which they were deaf before, and to walk along paths where they used to just stumble and fall, the population as a whole (and even at times the Church in her most visible policies and practices) may appear to be sliding downhill. Though sinners continue to be cleansed of their sins, and young and old to be born again to divine life, what tends to be most visible (or noticed) is the number of people who, in appearance at least, are refusing or falling away from grace. The Church is always preaching the Gospel to the poor — but this is seldom the activity of the Church which is most publicized! Those whose faith in the power and presence of Christ in his Church is based on evidence of success as the world measures success are headed for disappointment. And when we do see some minor triumph, we should recognize it as just a sign, a preview and promise of the triumph that is to come.

Faith is the triumph; prayer is its sign

To give his disciples a sign of his power, Jesus spoke one word and the fig tree withered up instantly. In Mark's Gospel nothing happened when Jesus spoke, but the next morning the disciples found that the tree had withered (see

Mark 11:12-25). In both Gospels the point is the same: the power is *in the word of Christ itself.* The particular moment when that power becomes visible through its effect is not important. The power of Jesus was exercised when he spoke his word, not when the fig tree withered. The separation of the word from its effect in Mark tells us that a difference in time is not a difference in reality: the fig tree was doomed from the minute Christ spoke. The simultaneity of word and effect in Matthew simply gives us a strikingly visible sign of the triumph of Christ already present in his word.

In the same way, the power of Jesus is present and is exercised whenever the Church speaks her words in prayer. The power of Jesus is present *in the faith of the Church itself;* and the visible sign of that power is not in the results that we see, but *in the fact itself that the Church is persevering in believing and in prayer.*

When the Church prays, the power of Jesus is already present and visible in her words. But the power made visible in prayer is not the power to accomplish here and now this or that particular thing for which the Church may be praying; it is the power of faith itself. The Church may pray for peace, and war may break out; but the power which will bring about, and is already bringing about, the peace of the world is already present when the Church prays. That is the power of faith. Where there is faith there is power, regardless of how or when the effects of that power become visible. The important thing is that the Church should persevere in faith, and manifest her faith by persevering in prayer. When the Church is praying she is moving mountains, regardless of when we see the scenery change.

Where faith is made visible, the power of Christ is made visible, because what he really came to do was convert the human heart to faith, to hope and to love. This is that "life to the full" which he came to give (see John 10:10). Jesus triumphs when we begin to share in God's own divine life;

when we begin to see with the eyes of God and love with the heart of God, because the work he came to do was to join us to himself through grace. Everything else that appears to be a triumph, everything the Church accomplishes or seems to accomplish on earth, is a real triumph only in the measure that it reveals her own union with Christ in faith, hope and love, and brings this same union to completion in others.

When the Pharisees asked Jesus, "What must we do to be doing the works of God?" Jesus answered, "The work of God is this: that you should *believe* in the one he sent." We can interpret this to mean both that believing is the work God wants us to do, and that believing is the work God does in us. The "work of God" which Jesus himself came to do is that we should believe. And so, in the faith itself of the Church, in her hope, in her love, the triumph of Jesus' work is already present and visible (see John 6:28-29. See also Luke 12:49; John 1:31; John 9:39; John 10:10; John 16:27; John 17:8).

Obviously, this faith must be carried out into practice. Faith in Jesus as Lord, for example — our faith that he really has triumphed over sin and broken its power on earth — is expressed in *fidelity*; that is, in faith lived out in action, faith expressed in persevering efforts to extend God's reign over every area and activity of human life on earth. Because we believe Jesus has triumphed, we do not give in to discouragement or fear; we keep trying to transform the institutions and structures of our society, to reform, reshape and renew human life on earth.

A parallel: Herod

We believe that even in the moment of apparent defeat Jesus is triumphing. This is the lesson of the cross, and it sets the pattern for the Church's life today. When we are losing we are winning. And we know that the enemies of Christ, even in their moments of greatest victory, have already lost.

There is a preview of this principle in the very first account Matthew gives of Jesus triumphing over the opposition of his enemies. Joseph and Mary have fled as refugees to Egypt, saving Jesus from Herod's raid on Bethlehem. Now the angel appears again to Joseph in a dream and tells him to return to Israel because "those who wanted to kill the child *are dead*" (Mt. 2:19-23).

There is more here than just fact. In the words "are dead" Matthew is touching on the general principle that, regardless of appearances, those who set themselves against Jesus are already "dead." They may appear to be in perfect health, triumphant and powerful, but in their opposition to Christ they are already excluded from the final reality of existence. They are discounted; they count for nothing. Even in his enemies' most powerful acts of opposition against him, Jesus is already triumphant.

The reality is that Jesus *is life* — in him, as members of his Body, we share in his life, his divine life. Even if we are being put to death we are alive with the life of God which lasts forever. On the other hand, those who are outside of him, apart from him, are dead, even when they seem to be most alive. Herod, with all his power, was already "dead" when he attacked God's Anointed One, and the entrenched establishment of Israel was already uprooted and withered when it rejected Jesus as Messiah — just as Jesus was already victorious in the act of dying, defeated, on the cross.[2]

Another parallel: the Church

In the same way, when the preaching of the *Church* arouses opposition and persecution, Jesus assures his disciples that, regardless of appearances, they are winning, not losing. When they are arrested, flogged in the synagogues, driven out of one town after another, lied about, betrayed by their own parents or children and handed over to death, they must not be intimidated. There is nothing to fear from those who can only deprive the body of life. The only one there is any reason to fear is God. God is the Father of Jesus, and Jesus promises, speaking already as triumphant Lord, "If you declare yourself for me before others on earth, I will declare myself for you before my Father in heaven" (Mt. 10:16-42).

The triumph of Jesus is taken for granted in the closing words of this first missionary instruction to the Church: "Anyone who receives you receives me.... and *shall not go unrewarded*." The victory is not in question; the rewards are already Christ's to dispense. Jesus is not "counting his chickens before they are hatched," because the hatching is not in question, any more than the emergence of Jesus from the tomb was in question on the day he was laid in it. No wonder Christian culture has chosen an egg to be the symbol of Easter! The tomb is just something we emerge from, a matrix of life. In the life of the Church, as in the life of Jesus, the tomb is really a womb, and moment of death and resurrection are the same. The death of Jesus and his rising were both "his hour" — of defeat and of victory.[3]

Parallel in the doctrine of the cross:

Jesus takes his triumph for granted in the same way when, in one and the same breath, he speaks to his disciples about his approaching passion and death and goes on to say, "For the Son of Man will come with his angels in the glory of his Father, and then he will repay all according to their conduct. Amen, I say to you, there are some standing here who will not taste death until they see the Son of Man coming in his kingdom."

Then he took Peter, James and John up the mountain and was transfigured before their eyes. He wanted these three, who would see him crushed in weakness and fear during his agony in the garden, to see him first appearing visibly in "the glory of his Father" — the glory that was already his, that was his "before the world began" (see John 17:5), and would be his throughout the humiliations and defeat of his passion, regardless of appearances (Mt. 16:27 to 17:9).

"Moving mountains"

Now, when Jesus withers the fig tree and tells his disciples, "If you have faith, you can move mountains," the context again is one of triumph. Jesus is asking them to believe, not just that his way of saving the world works, but that it has already worked; that his triumph is a fact, and that when they pray, they are already moving mountains.

In the withering of the fig tree Jesus is giving a sign of his triumph over the leaders of Israel. He is telling his disciples not to worry when they see him defeated by the chief priests and leaders of the people; these enemies are already defeated; the power structure of Israel is dried up and blown away. The fig tree is a sign of it.

But as we have already pointed out, this sign is the only destruction of his enemies they are going to see — at least for the next forty years, until the Roman army levels Jerusalem. And typically — that is, as a general rule — the only triumph of Christ's Kingdom which the Church will see in any given age is the triumph made visible in her faith, and in the faith of those who listen to her preaching. Evil will still appear to reign in politics and business, in society's institutions and social customs. But the power of evil is already broken, just as the power of the chief priests and Pharisees was already withered up when Jesus pronounced his word of condemnation. Whether it takes forty years or forty centuries, the triumph of Jesus is already a fact.

Forty years after Jesus withered the fig tree as a sign, his disciples saw the actual "withering up" of the political structure in Israel when the Roman army destroyed Jerusalem. The Gospel writers saw in this terrible event a "dress rehearsal" of the upheavals that will precede Christ's return in triumph at the end of the world, and wrote about the two events as if the descriptions of the destruction of Jerusalem and of the end of the world were interchangeable. Over the splendor of Jerusalem's temple, over the "glory that was Greece and the grandeur that was Rome," and over the massive monuments to wealth and power in our own modern cities, the words of Jesus are already spoken, and their fulfillment is assured: "You see all these things? Amen, I say to you, they will all be thrown down. There will not be left of any of them a stone upon a stone!" (see Mt. 24:1-42).

Jesus withers the fig tree as a sign. But when the disciples are impressed by the miracle, he tells them that what they really should find impressive is faith. Faith can move mountains. Whatever they ask for in prayer, persevering in faith, "continuing in believing," they will receive. Jesus is putting the focus on believing and on praying. And he is saying that if they are believing and are praying, then they should take it for granted that they are moving mountains, whether they see visible signs of it or not. He is asking them to have faith in faith itself as the sign of their triumph and his until he comes in glory.

The faith which will "move mountains" is faith that the Kingdom which Jesus really did come to establish is in fact being established here and now, in spite of all appearances to the contrary. It is faith that the triumph of Jesus is present and is taking place wherever and whenever the Church is persevering in faith and expressing that faith in prayer.

The triumph of Jesus consists in the fact that the force which is actually and inevitably bringing about in reality right now the transformation of society and the conversion of the human race is visibly present and active here and now — not in the fact that it is visible to us. But it is visible to those who have eyes to see. That force is the faith, the hope, and the love which are revealing and expressing themselves in the persevering prayer and labor of those who are dedicated to establishing his reign on earth. Where there are hearts united to Christ's in faith, hope and love — and expressing this union in action; where there are lives surrendered to him in the sharing of his divine life — and living out his life in mission — there the triumph of Jesus is real and we should rejoice in it. There the word of his power is being spoken and the victory is assured; all that remains is for the results to become visible in time (see Eph. 1:15-23; 1Thess. 2:13-20).

Conclusion

This section of Matthew's Gospel leaves us with the question: "Can you accept to *persevere in faith and fidelity*, believing in the triumph of Jesus (and in the triumph of the Church taking place right now), when all you see around you appears to be defeat? Can you keep believing in his triumph on the basis of no more evidence than the words of Jesus, his promises and the signs he has given?"

The bottom line is, we do not believe that Jesus has triumphed because we see that our efforts to save the world are succeeding; we believe that our efforts are succeeding because we see ourselves *believing* and *expressing* that belief in prayer and in persevering efforts to bring his triumph to completion. We do not look for healing miracles to confirm this faith. Even if the world continues to hurl itself destructively into fire and water, as long as we live, we will keep at it — at prayer and sacrament, bearing public witness to the truth, believing with faith that the mountains can be moved; believing that Christ's promise stands. This is what it means to be a faithful steward of the kingship of Christ. [4]

CHAPTER SEVEN:
THE POWER IN THE WORD

"Jesus Triumphs" —— *Matthew 21:17-22*

Summary

By withering the fig tree Jesus gave a sign of the withering of Israel
and of his eventual triumph over his enemies. But what his disciples see
is just a sign, not the reality. The sign is what they will have to cling
in faith when to all appearances Jesus is defeated by his enemies. Like
his triumphant-ridiculous entry into Jerusalem, his triumph here is a
triumph only to those who are willing to put more faith in God's words
and signs and promises than in what they see happening all around
them here and now.

Jesus said, "Whatever you ask for in prayer, you will receive, if you
have faith." But we will not see instant results. The power of Jesus was
exercised when he spoke his word, not when the fig tree withered. In
the same way, the power of Jesus is present whenever the Church
speaks her words in prayer. The power is present *in the faith of the
Church itself.* The visible sign of that power is not in the results that we
see, but *in the fact itself that the Church is persevering in believing and
in prayer.*

Jesus triumphs whenever we are sharing in God's own divine life; seeing with the eyes of God and loving with the heart of God, because the
work he really came to do was to convert the human heart to faith, to
hope and to love; to join us to himself through grace. This is the "work
of God" Jesus came to do and the "life to the full" he came to give.

Obviously, this faith must be carried out into practice. Faith that Jesus
has triumphed over sin and broken its power on earth is expressed in
fidelity; in faith lived out in action through persevering efforts to extend
God's reign over every area and activity of human life on earth.

The triumph of Jesus does not consist essentially in the visible conversion or transformation of society here and now, but in the fact that the
force which is actually and inevitably bringing about the transformation
of society and the conversion of the human race is visibly present and
active here and now. That force is the faith, the hope, and the love
which are revealing and expressing themselves in the persevering
prayer and labor of those who are dedicated to establishing his reign on
earth.

This section of Matthew's Gospel leaves us with the question: "Will you accept to *persevere in faith and fidelity*, believing in the triumph of Jesus and of the Church taking place right now, when all you see around you appears to be defeat? This is what it means to be a faithful steward of the reign of Christ.

Have you understood?

What was the withering of the fig tree a sign of? When did the result it promised actually take place? What is it a sign of to us in our day?

What is the significance of the fact that in Matthew the fig tree withers instantly while in Mark it withers overnight?

What is the sign and proof to us that the power of God is at work in the Church right now?

How would you answer someone (or yourself) who is discouraged by the fact that evil seems to be triumphing all around us and the Church seems to be having little effect on society?

What is the challenge of this chapter? To our faith? To our hope? To our love?

Making it your own

What are the key thoughts in this chapter? (Jot them down and give the page number where each is found).

What questions do I have about this chapter? (Bring them up in discussion or ask someone who should know the answers).

What struck me the most in this chapter? After reading this chapter, what do I understand better than I did before? What do I appreciate more?

What do I think is the point of the whole chapter? What response does Matthew want to evoke from those who read or hear this part of his Gospel?

What can I use as a visible reminder (a symbol) to keep me aware of the challenge of this chapter? Where will I put it?

Questions for prayer

Am I willing to keep working for the transformation of society regard-

less of how hopeless it seems? Why?

Do I consciously and deliberately draw courage from my belief that Christ is triumphing by the very fact that I am praying and working for his reign? How could I encourage myself more?

What signs of the triumph of Christ do I see around me? In myself? In others? In the Church as a whole?

How can I apply to my life what I have come to see by reflecting on this chapter? What concrete action do I choose to perform to express my belief in what I have seen?

FOOTNOTES

[1] Literally, this line reads, "Whatever you ask for in prayer, continuing in believing (*pisteuontes*, the present participle), you will receive."

[2] See my book *Why Jesus?*, chapter eleven; and in chapter twelve, the commentary on Mt. 8:18-32 (on not having a place to lay one's head, on the storm at sea and the deliverance of the Gedarene demoniacs and the drowning of the pigs), explaining that security and insecurity are based on union with Christ, not on being in a secure environment. See also John 1:4; John 3:36; John 5:24; John 6:47-54; John 14:6; John 17:3; Romans 8:6; 2 Corinthians 2:16; 1 John 3:14.

[3] See the *Jerome Biblical Commentary*, 63:60, on John 2:4: "The 'hour' of Jesus is that of His glorification, the crucifixion, death, and resurrection by which salvation is achieved." See John 2:4; 7:30; 12:23-27; 13:1; 17:1.

[4] See Fr. Dan Berrigan, S.J., "On being a prophetic peacemaker in the imperial state," quoted in my book *No Power But Love*, end of chs. 11 and 12.

Chapter Eight
A Call to Declare Ourselves
Jesus calls to conversion — Matthew 21:23-27

When Jesus rode into Jerusalem amid the acclamations of the crowd and purged the temple of the moneymakers, he was obviously acting with an authority no simple citizen of Israel — even a prophet — could claim. The point was not lost on the chief priests and elders of the people. They approached him as he was teaching and said, "By what authority are you doing these things? Who gave you this authority?"

Jesus knows their minds are closed. But he gives them a chance to convert to faith in him, even though he knows they won't take it. At the same time he puts them on the spot in front of the crowd. He says to them: "Let me ask you one question. If you answer it for me, then I will tell you by what authority I do these things. John's baptism: where was it from? Was it from God or of human origin?"

The priests and elders discuss this among themselves and see their dilemma: "If we say 'From God,' he will say to us, 'Then why didn't you believe in him?' But if we say, 'Of human origin,' we have to worry about the crowd, for they all think of John as a prophet."

So they refuse to answer. They say to Jesus, "We do not know."

And Jesus replies in turn, "Then neither will I tell you by what authority I do these things."

Call to conversion: call to choose (Matthew 21:23-27)

Matthew shows us repeatedly in his Gospel that conversion to Jesus requires a human act, an act of choice.[1] If we make a choice, then whether it is good or bad, God has something to work with. Any response we make is an entrance into dialogue with God. A bad choice reveals the orientation of our hearts and God can use it to shock us into repentance. But if we refuse to respond at all we are closing ourselves to further communication. To "stonewall" God is to "harden our hearts." And in Scripture that is presented as a very bad thing to do. It is one of the acts which in the Gospels moves Jesus to anger. For example, when the Pharisees refuse to answer his question about whether it is lawful to do good on the Sabbath by healing, Jesus, weighed down by their hardness of heart, looks around at them "with anger" and says to the man with the withered hand, "Stretch out your hand." He stretches it out and is cured (see Mark 3:5).

What Jesus says to us is, "Stretch out your hearts! Even if they are withered up, respond to me! Answer. Make a choice!" If we will act, if we will put our human natures into motion, he can help and direct us. But if we refuse to answer we are refusing to be human. That leaves God nothing to work with.

First refusal to be human: "I cannot know"

God created our human natures to be capable of entering into dialogue with him. We were designed to be able to know and love God. To do that, however, we must accept our human power to judge and to choose what is true and good. That means accepting our ability to know truth. We cannot love what we do not know. If we deny our power to decide what is true, or refuse to use it, we deny our humanity at its root. And that is to cut off at the root our capacity to respond to God.

An atheist is one who says, "There is no God." An agnostic is one who says, "We cannot know if there is a God or not." The true agnostic, as distinguished from someone who is simply ignorant or a seeker, is one who says, "There is no way to know if there is a God; it is just impossible to be sure." The agnostic is guilty of the greater sin.

The atheist accepts to be human; accepts the responsibility of making a rational human decision about truth and a free choice based on that decision. The agnostic, by refusing the risk and responsibility of decision, denies in practice both God and humanity. The atheist denies God. The agnostic denies the very means for knowing God. Like Pilate, the agnostic dismisses dialogue with God by asking a question which is not intended as a question at all but as an act of denial to forestall all answers: "What is truth?" (see John 18:37-38).

To make clear to the priests and elders what they are doing when, in answer to his question, they say, "We do not know," Jesus replies, "Then neither will I tell you by what authority I do these things." The penalty for agnosticism —not its punishment but its natural consequence — is the silence of God.

Second refusal to be human: "I will not choose"

It is possible to deny our humanity, not only by refusing to take a stance toward the truth of God, but also by refusing to take a stance toward the will of God. When prompted by the Spirit to "convert" in some way, to make a prophetic choice, a life-altering moral decision, we can just turn away without declaring any decision at all. We take refuge in indecision. This is not a refusal to choose if we continue to think about the matter, weighing the pro's and con's, asking advice, and trying to discern the voice of God by examining the movements in our heart, because then we are positively working toward a decision and we intend to make one. But when we simply "table" the question indefinitely by putting it out of our minds, that is in fact a choice not to choose. We do not want to take responsibility for saying "No" to God, so we just don't choose at all.

Not to choose at all is worse than saying "No," because it is a refusal to be human. What makes human beings like God is the power we have, like God's, to know and to choose. We have intellect and free will. To refuse to use either one of these is a refusal to be human. And since humans are designed in the image of God, to refuse to be human is in a very radical way a rejection of God himself. We cannot refuse to be like God without in some way rejecting what God is.

To say this in another way, when we refuse as a matter of principle to use our intellects we are revealing that we do not love truth as such; and not to love truth is not to love God who is all Truth. In the same way, when we refuse to take responsibility for free choices, we are refusing to use our wills in order to choose what is good. And this reveals that we do not love goodness as such. This is a rejection of God who is all Good.

Legalism: a chronic refusal to choose

The refusal to make choices can become chronic. This is not as uncommon as we may think. The most dangerous tendency in religion, judging by the space the Gospels give to combating it, is *legalism*, which was the sin of the Pharisees.

Legalism, at its root, is nothing but a refusal to take responsibility for personal decisions and choices. Legalists follow the letter of the law because they will not take responsibility for recognizing the goal of the law and trying in every way they can to achieve it. Legalistic pastors will pay employees the "going wage" established by the culture, or the exact wage required by civil law or diocesan policy, without asking whether it is enough for a particular employee's family to live on. Legalistic Catholics will faithfully "attend" Mass, but they will not enter enthusiastically into the celebration with that "full, conscious, active participation" which makes the celebration fruitful for themselves and others. (After all, the law just says they have to "be there"; it doesn't say they have to sit up front with other people and sing!) And many Catholics will be scrupulously dutiful about having a baby baptized, but they will not take personal responsibility for coaching the child into conscious knowledge and heartfelt love of God as it grows. They will do what the law says, but not what the law intends; they will not do what is necessary to achieve the goal of the law. This is legalism, the sin of the Pharisees.

In most cases, the letter of the law is something we can live with; but the goal of the law is something we have to live for, and that is a challenge we frequently fear to accept.[2]

Third refusal to be human: "I cannot commit"

Every choice is a moment of freedom embraced, an act of freedom lived. And every commitment is a moment of freedom that endures.[3]

People fear commitments; they fear to bind themselves; they see it as a loss of freedom. In reality, freedom without commitment is like a bird without wings: it cannot go anywhere. And any free choice which does not express the committed orientation of our hearts is a choice in which freedom is stripped of its full value.

The true purpose and value of freedom is self-creation. By our free choices we shape our souls; we give the unique meaning to our names; we create ourselves as the persons we will be for all eternity. The importance of our choices lies in the fact that we become what we do; at least, what we freely choose to do.

If I choose to tell a lie, I am choosing, at least for that moment, to be a liar. If I "change my mind" (the basic meaning of *metanoia*, or "repentance") and choose to tell the truth, then I cease to be a liar; I am instantly an honest person; at least I am if my choice is a full commitment. I may not succeed instantly in telling the truth always (any more than the choice to tell a lie means I will lie constantly), but if I truly choose this as my ideal, and sincerely commit myself to it, that committed choice already determines who I am as a person. In the measure that I am interiorly committed, I already am what I choose to be.

We cannot judge the interior reality of a person by external actions, because performance is not always proportionate to commitment and does not always express a person's deepest free choice. What we do does not always express who we really are. As we will see later, many factors intervene between person and performance, between commitment and action. All we are trying to establish here is that the true reality of a person's soul, of what one is as a unique, self-creating individual, is determined by the reality of that person's free and lasting commitments, whether to good or to evil. As persons, we are characterized by the goals and ideals we have chosen to embrace.

And so, to commit ourselves is not to lose freedom; it is to discover and experience what freedom is all about. Every free choice is an act of self-creation; every commitment is an act of self-creation that endures. The fear of making a commitment is in reality a fear of freedom itself: we are afraid to take the responsibility of creating ourselves. But unless we take this responsibility we cannot be human, and we cannot be like God.

The two words used in Scripture to best describe God are *hesed* and *emet*, which are variously translated as "grace and truth," "kindness and fidelity," "steadfast love and faithfulness," or simply as "enduring love." When they are translated as "grace and truth," the word "grace" means "redeeming love," and "truth" means "faithfulness to his promises." The meaning is that God is that One who freely chooses to love and save us, and God never goes back on his word. Love and commitment are the two most identifying characteristics of God. To be like God we must give ourselves above all things to committed love.[4]

The God we know, the God who has revealed himself to us, is a God of covenant. Because he is a God of love, he enters into a covenant with us. Because he is a God of fidelity, he is faithful to his covenant. And if we accept to respond to such a God, to deal with him and enter into relationship with him, we must give him committed love. The proof of our commitment is perseverance. And perseverance means perseverance in *trying*, because trying is loving, regardless of how well we succeed.

The power to commit

God our Father gave us life as a free gift, unilaterally. But to share God's life in its fullness we have to do something; we have to act. The reason is that God's life is loving, and loving is a free act. To have "life to the full," then, we must act; we must make the free choice to love.

And we must choose to love as God does, totally and undividedly: "with all our heart, and with all our soul, and with all our mind." This is the formula for living which we receive from our Father. If we recognize God as the source of our life, we will recognize God's teaching as an action through which he is giving us life still. We will accept his words as life; we will listen to them and bend all of our strength to obey them. To "honor our Father" is to say to him what Peter said to Jesus, "You have the words of eternal life" (John 6:68; see also John 5:24; 6:63; 8:51). It is to accept his words as the "word of life" for us (1John 1:1).

What God commands us, however, is not just to love; it is to persevere in love. The love that gives us the fullness of life, which is God's life, is the love that is like God's love; that is, a love that is "kindness and fidelity," steadfast love, enduring love, persevering love.

And this is where we balk. We think it is beyond our capability as human beings to commit ourselves to a definite way of acting for an indefinite future. Change is intrinsic to living; it is part of human life. Situations change, people change. We don't know how we will feel twenty years from now about something we are doing now or about someone with whom we have a good relationship now. "Forever" seems a rash word to pronounce.[5]

If nothing were involved but our human condition and powers, there might be a reason to drop "forever" from our vocabulary. Life itself — at least as we know it on this earth — does not go on forever. But when Jesus Christ made us sharers in his own divine life by grace, "forever" became the natural dimension of human existence. We share in God's eternal life. And we share in God's own power to pronounce "forever" words, words of eternal commitment. On the day of our baptism we, or our parents and godparents in our name, spoke words that committed us forever. These were divine words, spoken not by us alone, but by us in union with Jesus Christ, who joined himself to us and spoke with us, in unison with us, from within our hearts.

The power to speak "words," words of commitment, words that create us, words that will endure, is the power that makes us most like God. And through our union with God by grace, our human words become one with God's divine words and share in their divine power. We draw our confidence from this.

God's words, our words

From the first chapter of Genesis, when God said, "Let there be light" and there was light, Scripture is filled with the theme of God's producing whatever effect he wills by the power of his word. The creation story echoes with the chorus, "And God said, 'Let there be…' And it was so." God's word is the expression of God's self, and the power of his being is in it:

> The LORD said to Moses, "Is the Lord's power limited? Now you

shall see whether my word will come true for you or not" (Numbers 11:23).

"So shall my word be that goes out from my mouth; it shall not return to me empty, but it shall accomplish that which I purpose, and succeed in the thing for which I sent it" (Isaiah 55:11).

This is the power the Gospels ascribe to Jesus' words: Jesus "cried with a loud voice, 'Lazarus, come out!' [and] the dead man came out." During a storm he said to the sea, "Peace! Be still!" And at his word "the wind ceased, and there was a dead calm" (John 11:43-44; Mark 4:39). He said to the fig tree, "May you never bear fruit again!" And the fig tree withered up instantly (Mt. 21:19).

This power is ours when we speak words of self-orienting choice and commitment. What we choose to be, we are. We speak a word of choice and we become what we have chosen to be. In this our words are like the words of God: we say "Let it be" and it is.

There are differences, of course. First, our choices as such do not affect any reality outside of ourselves; we change ourselves through choices; we change everything else through actions.

Secondly, we cannot choose with our whole being at once. Our human natures have parts, and so we can be in conflict with ourselves. For example, with our mind we may approve of dieting; with our will we may choose it; but our body has its own guidance system, and our appetite will cry out for food when the body signals it to do this. This means that there can be influences at work within us to reverse any choice we make. St. Paul is a witness to this fact of our human condition:

I do not do the good I want, but the evil I do not want is what I do.... I see in my members another law at war with the law of my mind, making me captive to the law of sin that dwells in my members (Rom. 7:19-24).

Finally, we who live and act in time cannot make choices that are permanent by nature. We can will them to be so;

we can commit ourselves; but as long as we live on this earth — that is, in time — we remain free to change any choice we have made. It is possible for us to break our commitments. No word of self-orientation that we speak in this life is by nature our last word until we speak our final "Yes" to God in the act of surrendering our whole being to him at the moment of death, which is our passage from time into eternity.[6]

This is the human condition. But nevertheless, because we are in union with God by grace, sharing in his divine life, we can speak irrevocable words of commitment. And as long as we remain in union with God we will be empowered by God to persevere in them. That is what gives us the confidence to speak them.

This does not mean, however, that God simply removes us from the human condition and makes our performance instantly identical with our persons. Our commitments do not always take flesh in action exactly as we intended them to do. Only in God are being and action one and the same reality. In human beings what we do is not always the perfect expression of who we are. And so, if we are going to feel comfortable with commitments — especially with "forever" commitments — we have to accept human life as a growing reality, and come to terms with the fact that growth is only possible from a starting point of imperfection; that is, of incompleteness. Through perseverance we grow into the fullness of our commitments. And in human beings perseverance takes the form of commitments repeatedly renewed.

Commitment does not give instant perfection

In this life no choice is irreversible; that is what makes "conversion" possible — for better and for worse. If I choose to tell a lie, I make myself a liar until I "repent" and embrace again the ideal of truthfulness. In many cases, however, choice and repentance are simultaneous. This is not a contradiction in terms. St. Paul testified about himself, "I do not understand my own actions. For I do not do what I want, but I do the very thing I hate" (Rom. 7:15). To hate what one is doing while one chooses to do it is to experience sin and repentance at the same time — both of them incomplete — which is the reality of a divided heart. In these cases the particular choice to do or not do something may not express a real change of ideal; just a momentary departure from what we really want to be. Many sins are "sins of weakness," which means that the person committing some particular sin may not really be choosing to abandon commitment to the ideal, but just yielding to the pressure of the moment and failing to live up to it. We can commit sin without committing *to* sin. Many people, because they do not understand this, condemn themselves unjustly, confusing their persons with their performance. When St. Paul said, "I do not understand my own actions," he was recognizing the difference between who he chose to be and what he was choosing to do. In Catholic tradition this reality is recognized in the teaching that, in order to commit "mortal" sin, a person must have "full consent of the will." We may not always be able to say whether we have given "full consent" or not, but at least we know it is a relevant question, and it should keep us from changing the image we have of ourselves or of others too quickly.

Youth in white water

This is a very important point when we are talking about perseverance. How do we explain the phenomenon of devout and apparently committed young Christians who suddenly "leave the Church" or "lose the faith" when they go off to college or face one of the other challenges of adult life, like entering into a sexual relationship through love or getting caught up in a career that pressures them to compromise their ideals? In many cases we might suspect that

they never had "sufficient understanding" of what Christianity is or gave "full consent of the will" to being a Christian; that it was never a wholehearted personal commitment
for them, just an element in their culture that they accepted
superficially without thinking very much about it. For people on this level of awareness, the choice to give up the
faith may be equally superficial, just another act of letting
themselves be swept along wherever the culture of their
present peer-group carries them. When they grow up some
more or enter a stage of life (such as marriage) which
makes them aware of other values, they may "come back"
to the practice of their religion, and perhaps rediscover —
or for the first time discover — the faith they grew up with.

A new experience of sin

But this doesn't explain all the cases. Frequently those
young adults who turn away from the Church and the faith
are not people we would think of as superficial. Frequently
they are the "best and brightest," leaders in their peer group
and models of good behavior.

This too can be cultural conditioning, of course. What appeared, even to them, to be religious fervor may have been
an unconscious desire to please their parents or to excel in
whatever role their culture assigned them. But without ex-
cluding any of these possibilities, we ought to recognize
another possibility, one which is only speculation, but
which finds some support in observable facts. It may be
that for many young people their good self-image was their
undoing. They grew up unchallenged by serious temptation; not because the temptations weren't out there, but because they themselves were so caught up in healthy things,
things they were able to succeed in — school and family
life, friends who supported them — that the temptations
never became proximate issues of personal choice to them.
They really had no experience of significant moral failure;
they were always good and they took for granted they were

good. This wasn't pride; it was a true evaluation based on performance.

But the day comes when this changes. They go to college and— to take an example typical for this age group — they fall in love. For the first time sex becomes a real temptation for them, because it is not just "fooling around" now, but the expression of a mature relationship that is very important to them; one that has begun to absorb their lives. They fall into what they have always believed was "sin." And they don't know how to deal with this.

In a sense much wider (and deeper) than the literal meaning of the phrase, they have "lost their virginity." They have entered into a whole new world, in which they can no longer identify themselves as the persons they always thought they were. Also, they cannot recognize what they are doing as "sin" in the simplistic way they were taught to understand sin: as something simply ugly and bad. The sin they are committing is sin on another level. It is the sin, not of doing something that is simply bad, but of doing something that is not simply good: something that is good, but in an incompletely authentic way. To them, however, the inauthenticity is not clear. They are experiencing sex, not as a weak act of selfish gratification, but as an expression of love. They are experiencing sex in (almost) all of its goodness and power. For the first time sex has power over them because it has power for them: power to express what they want to express, power to unite them to a person they never want to be without. And it calls into question their whole world: their judgment of right and wrong, their trust in everything they were taught, their relationship with their family and Church, the image they have of themselves.

It is too much for them. They cannot, will not make the choice to give up the relationship that means so much to them or the sexual expression that is so much a part of it. And they think that the only alternative they have is to give up everything else.

Remember, we are talking about people with no real experience of sin; people who have always been "winners," who have never had any reason to think of themselves as anything but good people and good Christians. They don't know how to live as sinners. What they are experiencing now is something they don't know how to deal with. If they stick with the moral principles they grew up with, they think they have to say that what they are doing is "bad" and that they themselves are "bad." That is too absolute to accept. It is also not true to reality.

They have been taught that sins can be forgiven in the sacrament of Reconciliation. But for this they have to be "truly sorry" and have a "firm purpose of amendment" — a determined intention to stop committing the sin. But they cannot say they are "truly sorry" for what they are doing, because too much of what they experience in it is good; so good that they are not ready or willing to let go of it — or completely convinced they should. They cannot honestly say they have a "firm purpose of amendment." They think it would be hypocritical to go to confession, and they believe that sacramental absolution would be invalid if it were given.

And because they have been taught that what they are doing is "mortal" sin, it follows in their minds that they cannot receive the Eucharist. This calls into question their relationship with the Church. If they cannot live according to Catholic belief and teaching, and cannot express their communion with the Church by receiving Communion, what relationship is left?

The answer is, "the normal one"; the one Jesus seemed to be most comfortable with: the relationship of sincere but struggling sinners to Jesus as Savior and to the Church as his healing, sustaining, saving presence on earth. Jesus said to those who were shocked at the kind of people he would eat with (the parallel to Communion at the "Lord's Supper" is obvious), "Those who are well have no need of a physician, but those who are sick. Go and learn what this means,

'I desire mercy, not sacrifice.' For I have come to call not the righteous but sinners" (Mt. 9:12-13).

The situation we are describing here is almost a textbook example of something we should not automatically declare "mortal" sin. Leaving aside the question of whether the actions involved are evil enough to constitute "grave matter," we have strong grounds for suspecting that there is neither "sufficient knowledge" nor "full consent of the will."

The young people involved are confused. They are, for the first time, experiencing sin, not as something that is just bad, but as a real human value that is "falling short" of authenticity.[7] And they may not have — probably do not have — sufficient depth of understanding or practical experience to know why, or even that, it is falling short. They just know the Church teaches it is wrong. They believe in the Church; they don't want to cast off its teaching; but they can't reconcile in their own minds what the Church is saying with what they are experiencing. It can be argued that in this case they simply don't have "sufficient knowledge" to be guilty of mortal sin. They are too confused.

Nor can we be sure they have "full consent" of the will. It is true they are doing what they are doing as free, consenting adults. They are not being forced. There is, however, an element of passion — not just the flame of a momentary desire, but the consuming fire of a life-transforming relationship and its expression in a way that activates some of the deepest wellsprings of their emotional life. And they are young. They may never have dealt with passion on this level before. It is overwhelming. There is something in them which says, "This is wrong," or at least, "The Church says this is wrong; my parents say this is wrong." And they are not ready to just write off the Church, their parents, and all of their religious teachers as deluded. They are torn between two desires: to remain united to their Church and family in religious communion, and to keep doing what they are doing. They are divided in will, not giving "full consent" to either desire. In practice they keep doing what they are doing, but it could be argued that they are not doing it with sufficient fullness of freedom and consent for this to be "mortal" sin. They are not wholeheartedly committed to whatever sin they are committing.

Because of the way they have been taught, however; and perhaps because they have never really experienced sin on this level before, they see nothing but an "either-or" option: "Either I stop what I am doing and live like a good Catholic; or I leave the Church and stop professing to believe in Christianity." Many choose the second option. And when they do, because the working of our human psychology tends to complicate things, the issue gets very muddled with all sorts of irrelevant factors: anger at the Church and at parents; indignation over faults in the Church that never bothered them before; even intellectual arguments seeking to disprove the existence of God — all rooted in self-justification.

A triple stance

What can we do to save persons caught up in this kind of situation from the trauma of leaving the Church and everything in the Church they once held dear?

For one thing, we need to form ourselves and others to a more theological understanding of what "mortal" sin really means, joined to some basic understanding of human psychology. The Catholic theology of sin is a teaching about the acts of human beings, but frequently it is taught as if it were a teaching for angels. Angels always have "sufficient knowledge" and "full consent of the will." Humans seldom do.

Also, we need to stop thinking about the reception of Eucharist in Holy Communion as if it were a reward and profession of perfect innocence. The Eucharist is for sinners; they are the ones who need it most. The words of institution (consecration) are, "Take this *all of you* ... eat... drink... This is my body... my blood... for the forgiveness of sins." The Eucharist is the "waybread" which sustains us when we are finding it hardest to persevere in faith and in fidelity to God. When we are caught up in sin and struggling to understand ourselves and what is happening to us, that is the time we need the felt, nurturing, understanding, sustaining presence of Christ the most. And Eucharist is where we find it.

In practice, we need to adopt a triple strategy in response to the sins we "just can't stop":

• *First: don't rationalize*; if it is wrong, don't say it is right. If there is something good and something bad in what you are doing, admit it. Truth is the only safe foundation for anything. Rationalization can lead us into a morass of false questions and answers.

• *Secondly: admit your weakness.* Humility is truth, and the truth of human beings is that we grow into perfection slowly, through many trials and errors, failures and re-commitments. To pretend, even to ourselves, that we cannot fail and fail badly is to lose contact with our own reality. And that breaks our contact with everything else. So we admit our weakness and we live with it. If God can, why shouldn't we?

• *Thirdly: keep going to Confession and Communion.* This is not hypocrisy. All God asks of us at any moment is that we say to him sincerely, "I will go as long as I can without sinning." We might not be sure what "sinning" really means in our case. We might not know what "as long as I can" means either. We might believe it means forever, or we might be sure we won't last five minutes. And we might be wrong in both cases! But when we make a promise like this, we should be very conscious that there is a hidden card in the deck: God's. For all we know, God might zap us with a grace so strong we will never sin again. Or we might drop dead of a heart attack in the next instant, in which case we will have kept our commitment until death! The important thing is not to know what we are going to do in the future; it is to desire sincerely to respond to God right now, even if we are confused about what that response can and should be. All Jesus asks is good will. It was Jesus who said, "Do not worry about tomorrow, for tomorrow will bring worries of its own. Today's trouble is enough for today" (Mt. 6:34). We do what we can do in the present and entrust the future to God.

A promise is not a prediction. And a commitment to keep trying is not a guarantee of instant reformation. If we have the realism not to rationalize, the humility to admit our weakness, and the deep desire to love and serve God with undivided hearts, what more does God ask of us except that we should do the best we actually can do at the moment and trust in him for the rest?[8]

Conclusion

We can and must convert to God speaking to us in Jesus; and this conversion, to be worthy of the God of "kindness and fidelity," must take the form of an irrevocable commitment. It may be that, before we can make this act of conversion, we have to convert to believing that human beings can know some things with certitude; that free choices are the highest exercise of our humanity; and that the grace of sharing in the life of God makes irrevocable commitments possible for human beings. And we have to accept all this as good for ourselves: accept decision-making, accept self-creation through free choices, accept the challenge and glory of commitment.

Since, however, we are human beings still growing to perfection, this means we have to accept to make decisions even in the half-sight of imperfect clarity, and to make commitments even when our weakness warns of imperfect performance.

What this all boils down to in practice is the simple choice to *persevere* — to persevere in believing, no matter what remains unclear to us; to persevere in belonging to the Church, no matter what we are still struggling to accept; to persevere in efforts to establish the reign of God in our own hearts and in every area and activity of human life until Christ comes again, no matter what results we see or fail to see.

To accept Christ's call to conversion, each one of us must ask, "Is this a commitment I am ready and willing to make?" Now is the time to ask it.

CHAPTER EIGHT:
A CALL TO DECLARE OURSELVES

"Call to Conversion"" — *Matthew 21:23-27*

Summary

When Jesus purged the temple of the moneymakers, the chief priests and elders asked him, "By what authority are you doing these things?" Jesus answered by posing them a question. When they refuse to answer, Jesus replies, "Then neither will I tell you by what authority I do these things."

Conversion to Jesus requires a human act of choice. If we make a choice, we are interacting with God, and God can enter into dialogue with us. But if we refuse to respond at all we are refusing to be human. That leaves God nothing to work with. We cut ourselves off from further communication.

The first refusal to be human is to deny our *intellects*, our ability to know truth. The penalty for agnosticism is the silence of God.

We can also refuse to be human by refusing to use our *wills* to respond to what is good, or to some indication of the will of God. We can take refuge in indecision. This is worse than saying "No" because it is a refusal to own the choice we have made not to choose.

The most dangerous tendency in religion is that chronic refusal to make choices which is *legalism*. Legalists follow the letter of the law because they will not take responsibility for recognizing the goal of the law and deciding how they can best achieve this goal in particular circumstances. This was the sin of the Pharisees.

A third way to refuse to be human is to refuse to *commit* ourselves. Every free choice is an act of self-creation. Every commitment is an act of self-creation that endures. The fear of making commitments is in reality a fear of freedom itself: we are afraid to take the responsibility of creating ourselves. But unless we take this responsibility we cannot be human, and we cannot be like God..

The power to speak "words" of commitment, words that create us, is the power that makes us most like God. The two words used in Scripture to best describe God are "steadfast love and faithfulness." Love and commitment are the two most identifying characteristics of God. To be like God we must give ourselves above all things to committed love, persevering love.

We think it is beyond our capability as human beings to commit ourselves to a definite way of acting for an indefinite future. "Forever" seems a rash word to pronounce. But through our union with God by grace, our human words become one with God's divine words and share in their divine power. When Jesus Christ made us sharers in his own divine life by grace, "forever" became the natural dimension of human existence.

Because we are human, many factors intervene between person and performance, between commitment and action. Only in God are being and action one and the same reality. And so, to be comfortable with commitments we have to accept human life as a growing reality. We grow into the fullness of our commitments through perseverance.

Have you understood?

Why is it worse to refuse to make a choice than to make a bad choice? (Granted that indecision is a choice in itself).

In ordinary, day-to-day living, what is the difference between not knowing what to do and assuming it is impossible to know what to do?

When does indecision become a refusal to take a stance and choose? How can one refuse to make a decision without facing the fact one is doing this?

Why are we afraid to commit ourselves? What is the answer to this fear?

Why are commitments so important? What is their value?

What is the challenge of this chapter? To our faith? To our hope? To our love?

Making it your own

What are the key thoughts in this chapter? (Jot them down and give the page number where each is found).

What questions do I have about this chapter? (Bring them up in discussion or ask someone who should know the answers).

What struck me the most in this chapter? After reading this chapter, what do I understand better than I did before? What do I appreciate more?

What do I think is the point of the whole chapter? What response does Matthew want to evoke from those who read or hear this part of his Gospel?

What can I use as a visible reminder (a symbol) to keep me aware of the challenge of this chapter? Where will I put it?

Questions for prayer

What is my last experience of making a conscious act of choice (conversion) in response to some word of God? (Scripture, reading, preaching, conversation, inspiration).

Can I think of any choices I have "tabled" or just chosen not to think about? If so, why am I doing that?

What are the most important commitments I have made consciously, personally? How do I feel about them?

What do I think God might be asking of me now?

How can I apply to my life what I have come to see by reflecting on this chapter? What concrete action do I choose to perform to express my belief in what I have seen?

FOOTNOTES

[1] See the preaching of John calling people to accept Jesus as *Savior*: "Change, repent, give evidence you mean to reform!" (Mt. 3:1-12). Later John himself is asked to choose between the Messiah he expected and the Messiah Jesus was actually revealing Himself to be — just as we must choose today between the abstract, ideal *Church* of our dreams and the concrete, human Church that is (see Mt. 11:1-24). And when Jesus finally reveals the doctrine of the *cross* to his resisting disciples, he invokes the image of Elijah, who called upon Israel to quit "hopping from foot to foot" and to choose between Yahweh and Baal. He asks them to choose between the Elijah of power who called down fire from heaven and the Elijah of powerlessness (John the Baptizer) who was abandoned by God to death in a dungeon. This is basically the same choice he is now asking the priests and elders to make: "Accept John the Baptizer as the Forerunner and accept me as Messiah; or reject me and reject John also" (see Mt. 21:24-25 in the light of Mt. 17:9-13 and 1 Kings 18:21-24).

[2] For more on legalism, see chapter nine below, page 226 ff.

[3] For more on the value of free choice and commitment, see my books *An Armchair Retreat* (Our Sunday Visitor, Inc., 1987), chapter three, "I Am Creating Myself By My Choices"; and *The Good News About Sex* (St. Anthony Messenger Press, 1979), chapter ten, "Sex as the Expression of Love."

[4] *The New Oxford Annotated Bible, (New Revised Standard Version,* 1991) uses "steadfast love and faithfulness." See the great revelation to Moses in Exodus 33:17 to 34:7, which is echoed in John's Gospel 1:17, where the 1970 NAB translates these two words simply as "enduring love."

[5] See John C. Haughey, S.J., *Should Anyone Say Forever? On making, keeping and breaking commitments.* Doubleday, 1975.

[6] Fr. Karl Rahner, S.J., teaches that death is the greatest free moment of life. We can die saying "No!," "O.K.," or "Yes! Father, into your hands I commend my spirit." The first is despair, the second is stoic resignation, and the third is total surrender in faith, hope and love. The only Christian way to die is to say "Yes" in an act which bestows our whole being on God. It is the only time in our lives when we can choose him literally, effectively and irrevocably with "all our heart, all our mind and all our soul." That is why it is the greatest free moment of our lives.

Understood this way, death is not something that just happens to us, that we passively and helplessly endure, but a moment of choice in which we become most fully active and alive.

[7] The New Testament word for "sin" in Greek is *hamartia*, which comes from a root meaning "to miss the mark," to fall short, to go awry.

[8] These three responses to sins we "can't stop" were taught to my ordination class in 1961 by Père Girardon, S.J., who was Spiritual Director at the Séminaire des Missions, Fourvière, Lyon, France. It was the best preparation for hearing confessions that we received, and the forty years I have spent following his advice as a priest have confirmed to me over and over again the truth of what he taught.

In corroboration of what is said here about "mortal sin," see Richard P. McBrien, *Catholicism* (Study Edition), Harper-San Francisco, 1981, Part IV, ch. 21, p. 742, and Part V, ch. 26, pp. 953-960;. See also Ronald Rolheiser, O.M.I., *The Holy Longing: The Search for a Christian Spirituality*. Doubleday, 1999, chapter five, p. 93, with footnote 12, p. 251. I also recommend my book *The Good News About Sex,* (St. Anthony Messenger Press, 1979), available through His Way Communications, Monastery of St. Clare, 1310 Dellwood, Memphis TN 38127. (www.hisway.com or 901 357-6662).

Chapter Nine
Response and Experience
The experience of God — Matthew 21:28 to 22:14

What is blocking the experience of God in the Church? Why do so many people stop going to Mass? They may not actually reject the Church or embrace another religion, but they stop being active Catholics. They don't leave the Church; they just leave it alone. And the reason many give is that their religion just never "meant anything" to them; it never gave them the experience of God. All their religious activities were just something they "did" or were "at," but in them they did not experience a real, person-to-person contact and interaction with Jesus Christ or with God.

There can be many explanations for this, and it is true that none of them relieves the individual of responsibility. No one "gives" us the experience of God; we experience God in the act of responding to him with deep, personal faith. God is only "real" to those who personally take him for real. If we have not done this; if we are not conscious of personally interacting with God in all of our religious acts, then that is a place to begin. The fact is that every act of receiving the sacraments can and should be an experience of interacting with God. We just need to receive them with awareness and with conscious faith, hope and love. If we never experience God as real for us in the Eucharistic celebration, we should take a deep look at what we are doing during Mass.

However, our experience of the Church as an "assembly" or community does affect us. What we see around us, the attitudes and responses we absorb from others without even being aware of it, can help us do what we need to do to experience God, or it can mislead us. In particular there are three attitudes prevalent in the Church which can distort our perception of what the Church is, of what Christianity is, of what religion itself is all about. Each one is an obstacle to the experience of God, because each is a way to avoid true, personal interaction with God. And to experience God we need to interact with him through choices. In fact, this is what the "experience of God" really is: the experience of consciously interacting with God.

Conversion and experience

In Matthew's Gospel the experience of God is linked to conversion. In every act of converting to God more deeply we realize more clearly in faith both who God is for us and who we are in relationship to God. The prime example of this is the experience Jesus had after expressing his "conversion" into solidarity with the sinful human race by asking John for baptism. At that moment he heard the voice of the Father calling him "my Son, the Beloved, with whom I am well pleased" (see Mt. 3:13-17). This was an experience of identity through relationship.[1]

But if we refuse the call to conversion, we lose this experience. That is why the failure to respond to God is so serious. And if we keep refusing to listen, we become deaf to his voice.

If the chief priests and elders had answered Jesus' question about the credibility of John the Baptizer, he could perhaps have shown them through their answer who they were: what they were choosing to be in relationship to himself and to God. And he could perhaps have won them into a life-giving relationship with himself. But when they just refused to answer, his response was, "Then neither will I answer your question; I won't tell you by what authority I do the things I do." When God speaks we must answer — or we experience the silence of God.

Nevertheless, Jesus gives the priests and elders another chance. In spite of their refusal to answer his question, Jesus doesn't stop trying. He approaches their closed minds with three stories, three parables designed to bring home to them how the failure to convert results in exclusion from the experience of the Kingdom. If they choose to listen they will recognize themselves in the stories.

These three stories serve to bring out the meaning of three words which every Christian — and especially every Catholic — needs to know in order to understand what we must avoid in today's Church if we want to keep our religion alive. They are three attitudes which distort our perception of Christianity; and they are major obstacles to true, personal conversion.

The man who brought this triple distortion into focus for us was Bishop Emile De Smedt of Bruges, who during the first session of Vatican II brought about a new agenda for the Council by pointing out that the agenda originally drawn up by Curia officials in the Vatican was characterized by *triumphalism, clericalism* and *legalism.* These are three common ways of making ourselves spiritually deaf and blind by refusing to enter into dialogue with God. "In their concrete manifestations," Fr. Avery Dulles has observed, "they tend to fuse into one." In a nutshell, they constitute the stance of those who believe they are good Christians because 1. they are in the right church; 2. they profess to do everything authorities in the church (clerics) tell them to do; 3. they keep all the laws and commandments of God. This is a combination package of triumphalism, clericalism and legalism.[2]

The parable of the two sons: triumphalism
(Matthew 21:28-32)

Matthew's first parable addresses triumphalism: it strikes at those who are basking on laurels they have not won. And the laurels may not even be there.

"What do you think about this?" Jesus said: " A man had two sons. He said to one of them, 'Son, go out and work in the vineyard today.' The son answered, 'I won't,' but afterwards he thought better of it and went."

"The man found his second son and gave him the same order. This son said in reply, 'Yes sir. I'm on my way,' but he didn't go. Which of the two did his father's will?"

The chief priests and elders answered, "The first one."

Then Jesus said to them, "Let me tell you something. The tax collectors and prostitutes are entering the kingdom of God ahead of you. When John came, offering you an authentic way of holiness, you did not believe him. But the tax collectors and prostitutes did. And even after you saw that, you did not change your minds and believe him."

How do we explain this story?

The second son did not think of himself as disobedient. He saw himself as a good son, and therefore he took for granted that he was obedient, because this is what good sons are. When told to go the vineyard he immediately said "Yes," because that is what a good son would say. But then he forgot all about it. He didn't feel any need to subject his self-image to the test of practical behavior. His judgment of himself as son was based on the title itself, on his recognition as son by others, on the way he was treated in the house, and on the respect he thought he had for his father because of the way he expressed it in words and in ritualistic or "proper" gestures. For him, being a good son meant minding his manners towards his father; it didn't get down to the nitty-gritty of actually doing his father's will. It never crossed his mind to be concerned about this, because he just took for granted that he was everything he should be.

This might sound far-fetched. Could any son really have an image of himself so divorced from reality?

Perhaps not. But Jesus wasn't actually talking about a son here; he was talking to the "chief priests and elders" of his time about themselves. And what we have said above is a fair description of those members of the Church in our time who are caught up in what Bishop De Smedt called "triumphalism."

Triumphalism is the attitude which assumes that one is a good Christian because one is a Catholic; that is, a member of "the one true Church." This attitude focuses on what the Catholic Church has that other churches do not have, and scores fidelity to Christ on this basis. The triumphalist does not compare the churches on the basis of what we all have in common, such as deep, personal faith, prayer, disciple-ship, love of neighbor, and sincere efforts to respond to Christ and his grace, because Catholics, both individually and in groups don't always get the highest marks in this. The triumphalist just focuses on the gifts of God that are found exclusively in the Church: the full range of sacra-ments, infallibility, the legitimacy of unbroken descent from the Apostles, the two-thousand-year-old treasure of tradition, the "first-string" lineup of the saints, and — in relation to most other churches — Eucharist. Triumphalists draw assurance from the fact they are in the Church that possesses these riches. And they see the spiritual riches or the Church embodied in the pomp and splendor of Vatican City: the magnificence of its art and architecture, the hier-archical pageants parading the pope in his sedan chair, the cardinals in their red robes, and the mitered ranks of bish-ops from all over the world. All of this is so dazzling, and appears so dependable, established and complete, that it becomes the foundation of their security. Its impressiveness lulls the triumphalists into thinking that to belong to all this is to belong to Christ, and there is nothing more one needs to be concerned about. Jesus confronted this attitude in thoseJews who thought it was enough to be members of the Chosen Race (see Mt. 3:9; 8:11-12; John 8:31-58). [3]

In practice, this comes down to the assumption that we are pleasing to God just by belonging to the Church and by doing and saying those things which identify one as a Catholic in good standing rather than by living in the true spirit of the Gospel. The real focus is not on growing in union with Christ, but on conforming to a cultural image of Catholicism approved by custom and Church authorities. Triumphalism fosters the "good boy" and "good girl" mentality which looks to the power structure of the Church for affirmation of one's way of life rather than to the Gospel.

The triumphalists among the clergy assume that if they are accepted for ordination by a bishop they must be good Christians; that if they are chosen by the pope to be bishops they must be a good priests; and that if they are "promoted" to be archbishops or cardinals they must have been good bishops.

The triumphalists among the laity assume that membership in organizations favored by the pope makes them good Catholics, and that selection for an honorary ecclesiastical title — such as "Papal Countess" — is proof that they are exemplary Catholics. It is important to them to receive the pope's blessing, or to be honored by the bishop, because they take for granted that those public figures who speak for the Catholic Church are always speaking for Christ or at least as Christians. This is contrary to theology, common sense and experience.

The spirit of triumphalism holds that everything is the best that can be in the best of all possible churches, provided things look the way the public authorities in the Church say they ought to look. They identify the religion of Jesus with its external embodiment in approved policies and practices. Emotionally their devotion is inseparably intertwined with the splendor of the Church's buildings and decorations, with the grandeur of her regal robes and titles and ceremonies, with the power apparent in her protocol, with the order and dignity of her hierarchical structure, and with the promise of security pulsing from her centralized control.

This is blindness, and it blocks the experience of God. To experience the reality of the Church and of God's grace acting in the Church, we have to measure our lives constantly by the standards of the Gospel. That should be obvious, but to triumphalists it isn't.

Triumphalism is self-delusion. Fr. Richard McBrien calls it "a misinterpretation of divine election. We assume that we are God's favored ones, that we have privileged status in the world, that we are better than the rest of humankind. It is a form of deafness and blindness. We do not see the games of power and domination at work, nor do we appreciate how alienating these games are to those outside the Church."[4]

All this makes us ask whether the pomp, ceremony and protocol which give such cosmetic splendor to Church officials are not like the make-up on a corpse: an outer layer of elegance which distracts both them and us from the reality underneath.

Triumphalism also leads to the devastating destructiveness of Catholics who are present at Mass every Sunday, and who identify themselves as practicing Catholics and Christians, but whose lived-out values in business and politics, even in family and social life, are inspired more by the culture than by the Gospel. The problem is not that Christians are involved in bad business practices, political cover-ups, the indiscriminate bombing of civilians in war, the revenge-killing of criminals by capital punishment, and the simultaneous exploitation of the poor and corruption of the rich through selfishness in business and politics. The problem is that Christians do these things without any admission, even to themselves, that what they are doing is serious, devastating sin.[5]

The problem is not with those criminals, whether on the streets or in conservative office buildings, who frankly admit that they are choosing to sin. The problem is with those who believe they are saying, "Yes, Lord!" to God because they perform all the rituals which identify them as religious Christians, while in their family and social life, business and politics, there are no visible "fruits of repentance," no evidence at all of a Christian *metanoia* or radical change of course in response to the preaching of the Gospel. Their true religion is the "cultural Catholicism" of their day, in which "being a good Catholic" is defined by the practices and standards of ecclesiastical conformity. To the Lord they say "Yes" in church; but in their actions outside of church they say "Yes" to whatever is acceptable in their particular social and professional milieu.[6]

On the importance of being honest

This is where the "tax collectors and prostitutes" Jesus spoke about had an advantage. They were breaking the law of God, but they were honest about it. They took responsibility for the decisions they were making; they knew they were choosing to sin. When John came announcing the good news of the Kingdom and calling for a change of heart, they were able to take another look at themselves and reevaluate their position; they knew where they stood.

But the chief priests and elders, the establishment of Israel, along with the Pharisees and Sadducees, could not rethink their stance toward God, because they didn't know what it was! They could not repent, because they would not admit they had anything to repent of. They could not change course in response to John's preaching, because they refused to examine the course they were on! They were the establishment in Israel, and Israel was the Chosen People. Since everyone identified Judaism with them, they took for granted that what they were was the essence of the Judaism that was precious to God. They would not look to see what was underneath their facade of fidelity to the Covenant. Because they said, "Yes, sir!" to all the external observances, and performed all the rituals which expressed a willingness to do God's will, they were blind to the fact that they were not actually living what they professed and did not have true love for God at all. (Now go back and substitute "the Church" for "Israel" and "Catholicism" for "Judaism" in the sentences above).

This same set of assumptions characterizes the attitude of triumphalism in the Church. Because God founded the Church, triumphalists assume the Church is perfect the way they found it. Because they do things that identify them with the true Church, they assume that the truth of the Church is identified with the things they do. They look at the abstract image of the Church in all her glory and assume that the reality of the Church today is the embodiment of this glory. Triumphalists assume that the Church is actually being whatever God intended it to be, regardless of what its leaders and members have made of it. They don't really experience God in the Church because they have made the Church as they experience it their god.[7]

Triumphalists do not "hunger and thirst" for more. They are content with what they have; therefore they will never be "satisfied" through that experience of God which the Beatitude promises: the experience of intimate union with Jesus Christ found only by those who hunger to give and to receive passionate love.

Triumphalists do not belong to the "poor in spirit" — to that group of people who are deeply conscious of the sinful, searching condition of the "pilgrim Church." They identify, rather, with those who deck themselves in the doctrines of the Church's ultimate infallibility and indefectibility as if these were dress for daily wear and parade around in them like a preview of the Parousia.[8]

To experience the action of the Holy Spirit in the Church we need to convert to the more Scriptural notion of the "pilgrim Church," adopted by Vatican II, and see the Church as it is: the true Church Jesus founded, yes; but also "a weak, suffering Church... sinful in its members, at times ignorant, imprudent, ineffectual in its leadership," a Church guided by the Spirit but never complacent in its response, always seeking its way, a human Church in which Jesus again has "emptied himself, taking the form of a slave, being born in human likeness" (Philippians 2:7).[9]

A "pilgrim" Church is a Church on the move, a Church of change, a Church committed to continual conversion. This is the essential condition for being a prophetic Church.

The opposite of triumphalism is the state of the poor in spirit, of those who know they "haven't got it made." They know they are needy, and so they are looking for more. They know the Church is forever losing and rediscovering her way. And so they keep looking for the guiding star, listening for the Spirit, searching the Scriptures for clarification. Theirs is the kingdom of heaven; theirs is the experience of God.

The parable of the tenants
Matthew 21:33-46

Jesus continues with a second parable. He tells about a landowner who leased his vineyard out to tenant farmers before going on a journey. While away, he sent servants to collect the rent, but the tenants turned on them with violence. Finally the owner sent his own son, thinking, "They will respect my son." But the tenants said to each other, "This is the heir to everything; if we kill him, we will have his inheritance!" So they seized him, dragged him outside the vineyard, and killed him.

"When the owner comes back," Jesus asks, "What do you think he will do to those tenants?"

"He will trash that trash," they answer, "and lease his vineyard out to others who will make sure he gets his share when it is due."[10]

Jesus warns them, "Didn't you ever read in the Scriptures, 'The stone which the builders rejected has become the keystone of the arch?' Let me tell you something: the Kingdom of God will be taken away from you and given to a people who will bear fruit."

The meaning of clericalism

Even if the Gospel did not specifically identify the tenants with the "chief priests and Pharisees" (see verse 45), we could hardly comment on this parable without taking up the issue of *clericalism*. The vineyard, which in the parable refers to the "house of Israel" (see Isaiah 5:7), would in our day refer to the Church, and we spontaneously think of the "tenants" as being those in charge of the Church; that is, the hierarchy with the rest of the clergy. This is clericalism.

A true understanding of the Church viewed in the light of Vatican II would see all the members of the Church as the "tenants," since the authority of the hierarchy does not extend to everything the Church does. The authentic teaching of the Church is that the apostolate of the Church includes both the "apostolate of the hierarchy" — those functions and activities performed officially in the name of the Church, for which the hierarchy must answer, and over which, therefore, the hierarchy have authority — and the "apostolate of the laity": those actions performed by lay Catholics (that is, the Church) acting on their own initiative as Christian witnesses, but not officially in the name of the Church. Both clergy and laity are equally stewards of the kingship of Christ.

Over the apostolate of the laity the hierarchy declare that they have no authority. The laity have their own role and their own responsibility, for which they alone must answer. The bishop does not have to answer for what lay people do in his diocese as Christians acting on their own initiative, and so he has no authority over what they do as laity. Nor does a pastor have authority over what people in his parish do as lay Catholics, so long as neither Church property nor the name of the parish is involved. It is characteristic of clericalism, however, to ignore this theological fact and to speak and act as if everything done in the Church should be directed by the clergy under the authority of the bishops.

To quote Dulles again, clericalism "views the clergy, especially the higher clergy, as the source of all power and initiative. Bishop De Smedt spoke of the pyramidal pattern in which all power is conceived as descending from the pope through the bishops and priests, while at the base the faithful people play a passive role and seem to have a lower position in the Church... Clericalism tends to reduce the laity to a condition of passivity, and to make their apostolate a mere appendage of the apostolate of the hierarchy..."[11]

Dulles says there is an historical explanation for this way of thinking. "Catholicism has always attached great importance to the priestly hierarchy, often in such a way as to give the impression that the laity were somehow inferior or of small account...." But the mistake has been recognized. In an effort to counteract this, "Vatican II... unequivocally taught that all the faithful have a common priesthood, which is a participation in the one priesthood of Christ... Generally speaking, the Council sought to clarify the rights and freedom of the laity. Far from restricting the workings of the Spirit to priests and bishops, it spoke of the graces and charismatic gifts which the Holy Spirit freely distributes among the faithful of every rank."[12]

Catholic teaching is that the laity and the clergy are equally consecrated by God to exercise their own apostolates. When it comes to bearing fruit in the vineyard of the Lord, they are both equally "tenants," equally responsible and empowered by God for their own particular function in the Church and for establishing the reign of God on earth. The apostolate of the laity is as much the apostolate "of the Church" as is the apostolate of the hierarchy, because the laity are as much "the Church" as the clergy and hierarchy are.

Teaching vs. commanding

Obviously, bishops and pastors are responsible for teaching and proclaiming the general moral principles which must be respected in any human activity; but this is a teaching function, not a governing one, and it applies to the formation of conscience, not directly to the conclusion one comes to in conscience about the particular response one should or should not make to a concrete complicated problem.

A vote, f or example, is an exercise of the lay apostolate. For their judgments of conscience in this area the laity must answer to God alone, because "through their baptism and confirmation, all are commissioned to that apostolate by the Lord himself" — not by the hierarchy.[13]

The clergy do not have the authority to impose decisions in the areas of the lay apostolate. But they do have the obligation to judge these areas in the light of the Gospel and to express their opinion in preaching and teaching. They are responsible, together with the laity, for being a prophetic voice summoning people to Gospel values, not only in their private, personal lives, but in every area of human activity: social and family life, business and politics. The clergy and the laity are equally responsible for this. Clericalism, however, attempts to silence the voice of prophetic challenge in clergy and laity alike. How does it do this?

The restriction of leadership to authority

Clericalism encourages passive obedience to those who have authority in the Church. But this authority is restricted to the area of "religion," understood as "churchy" things and traditional, private morality. The fact is that clericalism gives the clergy no voice, either as preachers or as teachers, in the "practical" areas of temporal affairs, such as business and politics and, especially, social justice. It is understood that the clergy will not presume to interfere in these areas.

But because clericalism has restricted "religion" to just doing what the clergy says, the laity don't recognize it as their
religious responsibility to give moral leadership in these
areas either. The pay-off for the laity who take refuge in
clericalism is that they can consider themselves good, even
fervent Catholics if they simply do everything Church
authorities command in the area of private morality — and
ignore everything else.

The heart of the problem lies in the identification of leadership with authority. Only those in authority — the clergy
— are expected to exercise religious leadership. This dispenses the laity from giving the kind of religious leadership
in business and politics, family and social life that they are
most capable of giving. And because the clergy have no
authority in these areas, the restriction of leadership to
authority excludes them from these areas also.

In reality, leadership and authority are two distinct and different functions, even though they might sometimes be
combined in the same person. Authorities are those who
have the right and duty to command, and those subject to
them follow out of commitment. Leaders are those whom
others follow voluntarily because they agree with them or
have trust in their judgment. Authority is restricted to those
who are elected, appointed, or otherwise invested with the
right to command. But leadership can and should be exercised by anyone in a group who happens to see what needs
to be done. There is no such thing as a "natural leader."
Everyone is or should be a leader when the situation calls
for his or her particular expertise. In any organization or
community there is ultimately only one authority or
authoritative, decision-making body. But all the members
of the group should exercise leadership by pointing out
what their particular vantage point enables them to see.

For example, on a ship only the captain is in command. But
in some situations the real leader is the sailor at the radar
screen who alone is able to see what lies ahead. If the per-

son who can see fails to cry out, or if the person in command refuses to listen, then authority is blind. Clericalism,
by restricting leadership to authority, would make the
whole Church an example of the blind leading the blind. [14]

The problem of remote leadership

Some of the current problems in the Church stem from the
fact that those who make its rules and give approval to its
official moral teaching are quite commonly people who
have little or no pastoral contact with the laity whose lives
they are presuming to direct. They are not pastors, and
many never have been. They seldom hear confessions or
deal directly with the spiritual problems about which they
are legislating. They are administrators and professors who,
understandably, are more familiar with the writings and de-
crees of other professors and administrators than they are
with the needs, anguish and lived spiritual experiences of
the Catholics in the pews. There is a tendency to lose contact with reality and to live in an abstract, even legalistic
world. How else, for example, can we explain the fact that
before Vatican II all the bishops and moral theologians together continued to promulgate the absurdity that it was a
mortal sin — "grave matter" — to eat a hamburger on Friday or to miss Mass on a single Sunday? And because this
was the unanimous teaching of the authorities, at least in
American culture, it didn't enter the minds of pastors or
parishioners to question it. Everyone was so accustomed to
accepting blindly what was handed down from above that it
never occurred to the people on ground level to look around
them with the eyes of common sense.

It is significant that the same professors and legislators who
taught that people could go to hell for missing Mass on a
Sunday were unable to see serious evil in slavery, the state-
inflicted tortures of the Inquisition, exploitation of the poor,
racial segregation or the death penalty. Bishops and theologians alike ignored or justified these practices. Most still

justify war. None of these teachings was accepted as infallible, of course, but a practical status of infallibility was conferred upon them all by the rank-and-file's unchallenging assent.

Notice the pattern in the examples above. The laity obediently accepted without question the clergy's teaching about the "churchy" (and relatively unimportant) matters of Sunday Mass and Friday abstinence. And the clergy obligingly refrained from questioning what the laity were doing as slave owners, government torturers, executioners, soldiers and exploiters of the poor. The laity did not challenge the clergy about "religious" issues, and the clergy did not challenge the laity about secular issues. This is clericalism.

Clericalism leaves all religious leadership to the clergy, but they are excluded from business and politics. The laity, who are involved in business and politics, are dispensed from religious leadership. As a result, the role of prophetic challenge in the arena of public life is not in anyone's job description. The fruit of this is silence in the marketplace.

Fostering a tame clergy

Usually as an adjunct to their clericalism, the laity make sure the priests and bishops enjoy a fairly gratifying level of comfort and prestige. This ensures that it will not be in the clergy's best interest to disturb the *status quo*. The laity can rest assured that a clergy with gold cuff links, fancy cars and guest privileges in the country club will ask nothing more of them than continuance in the kind of decent behavior that society approves. The laity will find moral security in doing only what "Father says," and the comfort and prestige "Father" enjoys will assure that he says nothing the laity do not want to hear. This leads to a pathetic, rather than to a prophetic Church.

Clericalism also silences leadership within the Church itself. In ecclesiastical as well as in secular matters the spirit of clericalism makes the people listen passively to the priests, the priests listen passively to the bishops, and the bishops listen passively to the pope. This gives us a Church in which the bishops do not challenge the pope, the priests do not challenge the bishops, and the laity comfortably leave all church policies in the hands of the clergy, as if the good of the church or diocese were their responsibility alone.

One wonders where clericalism began. Did the clergy invent it and impose it on the laity for the sake of status and power? Or were the laity astute enough to see that if they could keep the clergy comfortable with affluence, prestige and ecclesiastical authority, they could keep them from being prophetic — and so keep them out of their hair in the areas that really matter to them: the secular areas of business and politics? Those who give the clergy the most exalted place in the Church are also the most insistent that the clergy should "stay in their place." Clericalism is a pedestal with a chain on it.

The core of clericalism is the failure to recognize that the laity are just as responsible for exercising leadership in the work of the Church as the clergy are. And for this failure the laity are just as much to blame as the clergy. The rewards of clericalism are equally tempting to both: what the clergy get out of clericalism is status and power; what the laity get from it is freedom from responsibility. Both in church activities and in the secular areas of business, politics, family and social life, clericalism keeps the clergy from seeing what is to be done and the laity from saying what is to be done. This is a rejection and refusal of leadership. [15]

Clericalism blocks the experience of *faithful stewardship* in the Church because it discourages the clergy from taking responsibility for what happens in business and politics; and it relieves the laity from taking religious responsibility for anything about which the clergy is silent. For both clergy and laity this is an obstacle to the ongoing process of conversion that obscures the experience of God.

The strategy of the devil

St. Ignatius of Loyola taught that the basic strategy of the devil is to tempt people, "first with a longing for riches... so that they might more easily become caught up in the empty status symbols of this world, and so fall into pride." He summarizes: "the first step is *riches*, the second is *prestige*, and the third is *pride*."[16]

The effect of clericalism in the Church is proof that this strategy works. We see it most clearly in those "Catholic" countries where there is the greatest separation between the rich and the poor, and where the clergy are traditionally identified with the rich (or were, until things changed drastically after Vatican II and the famous "option for the poor" taken by the Latin American hierarchy meeting at Medellín and Puebla). The strategy works in the United States as well. The pattern is not as obvious in every place and time, but it is still identifiable.

First the rich, established class among the laity give "*riches*" to the clergy in the form of a secure lifestyle that is somewhere between comfortable and affluent. In many places what they are actually doing is sharing with the clergy the fruits of their own oppression of the poor.

Secondly, the rich share their own *status* with the clergy by treating them as social equals. They invite the priests into their homes and seat them at table with themselves. There a pastor might find himself waited on by a parishioner (perhaps the head of his pastoral council!) who, being a servant, is treated as an inferior and a member of a lower class. This identifies the clergy with the rich, established class and separates them psychologically from the poor, both in the clergy's mind and in the eyes of everyone else.

The third step follows naturally, or is the work of the devil himself. The clergy, like the rich, slip into the *pride* of seeing their clerical caste and the social class with which they are identified as the standard of truth and falsehood, the criterion of good and evil.

When external signs of wealth and prestige keep telling individuals or an established social class that they are the "right" kind of people, and that their lifestyle is the "right" way to live, it is a short step into the conviction that their way of thinking must be the "right" way to think, and their way of acting must be the "right" way to act — and by contrast, that the poor are an unenlightened, ignorant lot whose best chance in life is to live in subjection to the paternalistic rule of the established class and the clergy — sustained, if necessary, even by a military dictatorship!

It is merely conceit, not pride, to think oneself better than one is. But we fall into pride when we make ourselves the *criterion*. To make oneself, or one's social class, the standard of good and evil is to make oneself God. This is the definition of pride. It is the sin of all sins. It is the devil's greatest victory.

"He sent his servants to the tenants..."

The alternative to clericalism is a collaborative Church, a Church of *koinonia* and community, a Church in which clergy and laity alike listen for the voice of the Holy Spirit speaking in every member of the body of Christ.

In particular, those who are subjected to the blinding influence of affluence and prestige should take pains to listen to the poor. These are often the "servants" whom the owner sends to ask those in charge of the vineyard to deliver the fruit expected of them. If the bishops, priests and laity who are established in wealth and power do not listen to the poor, and do not give them a voice, they will answer to the owner of the vineyard.

It was to a bishop that Jesus said:

> For you say, 'I am rich, I have prospered, and I need nothing.' You do not realize that you are wretched, pitiable, poor, blind, and naked (Revelation 3:17).

Repeatedly throughout the history of the Church the clergy have allied themselves with the established class against the poor. They have rejected the messengers God sent them and done them violence — if not personally, then through oppressive governments and economic practices against which they failed to cry out. Repeatedly their blind pride has brought devastation to the Church. In their refusal to "respect the Son" in the person of all his members they have handed over the Body of Christ himself to be torn asunder. The Protestant Reformation and the French Revolution are only two obvious examples of the way a clergy and hierarchy deaf to the voice of the people can provoke the Body of Christ into tearing itself apart. They are not the only examples.

The same abuse is evident when pastors and bishops refuse to listen to the laity crying out to be fed, or when the pope refuses to listen to the bishops of the world crying out for freedom to respond to the needs of their flock. Under a regime of clericalism, these messengers too are often treated with violence.

But the spirit of clerical control can be replaced by the servant spirit of Christ. The Latin American bishops took a significant step toward this when at Medellín and Puebla they made their "option for the poor."[17] If Church leaders begin to listen to the voices of their people, taking responsibility for the vineyard as *faithful stewards* in a spirit of true collaborative communion with all of Christ's members, the vineyard can flourish again. The clergy who do this will be recognized for what they are: stewards of the King who entered his city in unassuming lowliness, mounted on a donkey, the foal of a beast of burden. Then the poor will approach their priests and bishops as the blind and the lame approached Jesus in the temple, and even hearts silent as stones will cry out with the enthusiasm of little children, "Blessed is he who comes in the name of the Lord!"

This is the kind of conversion that will fill the Church with experience of God.

The wedding banquet (Matthew 22:1-14)

The parables of the two sons and of the self-serving tenants show us how we can be blinded to conversion and blocked from the experience of the Kingdom by the twin attitudes of triumphalism and clericalism.

Jesus now adds a third parable — the parable of the wedding feast — which goes to the heart of the third great obstacle to the experience of grace: *legalism*. Legalism, as we have said above, is a focus on law-observance which actually makes law-observance ineffective, because it dispenses those who observe the law from achieving the goal of the law.

Jesus tells of a king who gives a wedding banquet for his son. But the guests he invites refuse to come. They obviously feel neither hunger nor need. They are established property owners: some have farms; others have businesses. They are also arrogant: some just ignore the invitation; some go so far as to insult or even kill the servants the king sends as messengers.

The king is furious, of course. He sends his army to wipe out the murderers and burn their city. Then he says to his servants, "Those I invited were unfit to celebrate with me. So now I want you to go out into the streets and invite everybody you find."

The servants do as they are told and bring in everyone they meet, "bad as well as good." They fill the banquet hall.

When the king comes in to greet the guests, however, he sees a man who isn't dressed in the white garment which is considered proper for a wedding banquet. When he challenges him on it, the man has nothing to say. So the king tells his guards, "Bind him hand and foot, and throw him out into the darkness."

And just to make sure we know that he is talking about what is going to happen at the end of the world, in the eschatological or "end times," Matthew adds here his clue phrase, "where there will be wailing and grinding of teeth."[18]

The spirit of legalism

What is wrong with the people who refuse the king's invitation? Why would they exclude themselves from the experience of the wedding feast? The answer is, they don't have any desire to celebrate with their king. Their relationship with him is one of contract and obligation; love and celebration don't enter into it. They will do what they are obliged to do by the terms of their contract. If he insists on more they can turn ugly to his messengers.

This is the spirit of legalism, which is described by Fr. Richard McBrien as "a religious attitude that makes [law] observance the end of religion. Obedience to law is [for legalists] the ultimate sign of religious faith and the principal means to holiness." Another name for this is "Phariseeism." Although Jesus characterized the Pharisees so vehemently as "hypocrites" that the two words have become synonymous for us, the Pharisees were essentially legalists. For them the whole of religion consisted in observing the laws.[19]

In a legalistic Church the Christian faithful are urged to nothing more than ritualistic observances and the moral conformism of "keeping the Ten Commandments" — which in practice gets reduced to humanly decent behavior as understood by their culture. Legalism walks hand in hand with *clericalism* because the clergy are seen as the official interpreters of the law. Both clericalism and legalism are reinforced in a Church which has gone on the defensive in the face of real or imagined threats to its security.

Thus historically, according to Avery Dulles, "Catholics in the Counter Reformation period became overly concerned with fulfilling ecclesiastical obligations and insufficiently attentive, at times, to fulfilling the law of charity. Concerned with maintaining the right relationship with pope and bishops, they attended less than they should to God, to Christ, and to the Holy Spirit." We experience the same phenomenon in our own day in reactionary groups whose main focus is on defending the Church against aberration. [20]

One of the first victims of legalism is the sense of proportion. While I was writing this book I gave a mission on an air force base overseas. The Catholics on base had just been terribly upset by a legalistic priest who told them he would have to deny them absolution if they were practicing artificial birth control. The same priest apparently had no problem with the fact that every Catholic on base was committed to assist, directly or indirectly, in raining nuclear bombs on foreign cities should they (or their spouses) be commanded by our government to do so. Yet such bombing was condemned by the entire episcopacy of the Catholic Church in the strongest denunciation pronounced by Vatican Council II:

Any act of war aimed indiscriminately at the destruction of entire cities or of extensive areas along with their population is a crime against God and humanity itself. It merits unequivocal and unhesitating condemnation. [21]

How can we explain the fact that Catholics and non-Catholics alike are much more aware of the Church's official stance against birth control than they are of her official stance in favor of weapons control? The whole American hierarchy, echoing Vatican II, has spoken out much more emphatically against war and the arms race than any pope or bishops' conference has ever spoken out against birth control, but the general Catholic conscience doesn't seem to be affected by this. In *Challenge of Peace... A Pastoral Letter on War and Peace*, the United States Conference of Catholic Bishops declared:

> We need a 'moral about-face.' The whole world must summon the moral courage and technical means to say no to nuclear conflict; no to weapons of mass destruction; no to the arms race which robs the poor and the vulnerable; and no to the moral danger of a nuclear age which places before humankind indefensible choices of constant terror or surrender. Peacemaking is *not an optional commitment. It is a requirement of our faith.* We are called to be peacemakers, not by some movement of the moment, but by our Lord Jesus. The content and context of our peacemaking is set, not by some political agenda or ideological program, but by the teaching of his Church.[22]

The most obvious reason why birth control gets more recognition than arms control as a moral issue among Catholics is that the prohibition of contraception is perceived as a *law* while all the prohibitions concerning war are perceived as general teaching to be interpreted and applied by each individual as best one can. Legalists take laws seriously; they do not take seriously the obligation to think, decide and act on general moral principles.[23]

Also, birth control is something individuals do, while war is a communal action for which people who were brought up in the individualistic morality of legalism tend to take no personal responsibility.

In an example closer to daily life, one mother on the same air base told me of a child in her religious education class who abstained from Communion at Mass because she had forgotten to stop eating an hour before Communion time. Granted that the Church has made a rule about fasting before Mass; and granted that Catholics should enter into the spirit of this reverential practice; how much importance do the lawgivers intend us to attach to it? Is it not a total loss of proportion to assume that this devotional gesture is so important in the eyes of God, or even of Church lawgivers, that it should be seen as a *condtion* for receiving Communion? Did the lawgivers ever dream that this devotional gesture would be thought so important that if a little child forgot to observe it she should give up the sacred opportunity to receive the Body and Blood of Jesus Christ? Jesus would say to whoever taught the rules to this little child without teaching her to put them into perspective, "You blind guides! You strain out a gnat but swallow a camel!" (Mt. 23:24). Unfortunately, almost all of us in the pre-Vatican II generation were taught to think that way.

Perhaps Church administrators found it easier in the past — as administrators do in every day — to simply declare particular obligations in the form of laws than to insist on the more general and fundamental obligation to think. This would explain, for example, why Catholics in Germany before World War II who would never, under any circumstances, have joined the Masonic Order, enthusiastically joined the Nazi Party in support of Hitler. At that time, to be a Mason was forbidden by Church law; to be a Nazi wasn't. And it would explain why some Catholics follow scandalous political, economic and social customs in the United States today: it is because the spirit of legalism dispenses them from using their consciences on issues that Church authority has not made specific laws about. This is both clericalism and legalism. It explains how people who consider themselves good Christians can tell racist jokes, pay unequal wages to women, drive after drinking, refuse to communicate deeply with their spouses, pollute the environment, ignore causes of poverty, shop without social consciousness, support the death penalty, or join the military to fight indiscriminately in any operation to which the President chooses to send them — without any of this ever being mentioned in Confession!

It also explains why Catholics who would not dream of missing Mass on Sunday have no scruple at all about not reading the Bible prayerfully every day. Some never read it at all. They justify this by the fact that the Church has made no law obliging them to read the Bible. But what does it say about the attitude of the Catholic population when the mere absence of an ecclesiastical law is considered sufficient justification for ignoring the word of God?

The characteristics of legalism are:

• To focus on law observance rather than on growing into deeper relationship with God and with others through ever-expanding knowledge and love.

• To think one is only obliged to obey laws; not to take personal responsibility for thinking, deciding and acting according to general principles being preached or taught in the Church, so long as these have not been concretized in specific laws.

• In particular, to take seriously personal, private sins, while participating without scruple in more serious, communal sins against love and justice in business, politics and social life.

• To look only at the letter of the law without examining its purpose, and to think one is obeying the law by doing what the law says, whether or not one is achieving its purpose.

• To refuse the responsibility of judging whether it will achieve or frustrate the purpose of the law to do what the law says in a particular set of circumstances.

• To obey all laws as if they were equally important; to lose the sense of proportion.

Voices from the past

Legalism is a recurring temptation in any religion, including Christianity. But the Catholic tradition against legalism is ancient and clear, and one of the most beautiful expressions of it was given in the 1930's by Amleto Giovanni Cicognani, who was later to become Cardinal Secretary of State under Pope Pius XI. Some selections (italics added):

> Because human actions which are the subject of laws are individual and innumerable, it is not possible to establish any law that may not sometimes work out unjustly. Legislators, however, in passing laws, attend to what commonly happens, although to apply the common rule will sometimes work injustice and defeat the intention of the law itself. *In such cases it is bad to follow the law; it is good to set aside its letter and follow the dictates of justice and the common good* .

Cicognani points out that the ability to do this well is a virtue that has been taught in the Church for centuries under the name of *epieikeia*. This virtue

> does not interpret law (at most it can be called practical interpretation of law), but rather the intent of the lawgiver. Nor is it implied dispensation, but rather the application of law in a particular case. Briefly, it is law tempered with the principles of natural justice. Such application of law is *legal*, that is, *lawful*, although it disagree with the strict letter of the law and deflect from legal justice. *For what is equitable and good is the law of laws.*

Catholic tradition also recognizes that a law can cease to exist before the machinery of repeal can function:

> It is proper and fitting that a law should be stable and firm. However, every law has its element of uncertainty, since the reasons and the purpose for which the law was made can change. Consequently, since a law is an ordinance in according with reason, it ought to be revoked if it becomes useless, harmful, or unreasonable. And if it has not actually been revoked, it is to be reasonably presumed to be revoked. *For its purpose is the soul of law, and a law without a soul lapses, ceases to exist, dies.*

To attempt to impose obedience to laws that are unreasonable because they have lost their purpose is tyranny:

> Persecutors often appeal to written laws, as did the Roman Emperors in their attack upon the Christians.... *It is not justice that is wrought by laws, but laws themselves should be formulated ac-*

cording to justice. Justice should not be measured by laws, but laws themselves should be adapted to justice and right.

This is the Catholic theology of law! [24]

Not dressed for a wedding

In his parable of the wedding feast Jesus makes it clear that just being "in the Church" with official approval is not enough. When the king comes in to meet the guests, he sees a man who was legitimately present — who had been invited and admitted by the king's own servants, and who had not misbehaved in any way. But he "had no wedding garment." He was not properly dressed for what was actually going on. He was not dressed for a wedding. He wasn't really asking what the goal, the purpose of the celebration was; he was there but not there; present, but not to celebrate what everyone else was celebrating.

According to the imagery used by Jesus in the Gospels and by St. Paul in his letters, to be "in the Church" is to be in a relationship of spousal love with Jesus Christ. Jesus is the Bridegroom; the Church is his Bride. The wedding feast in the parable is given by the "king" for his "son" — an obvious reference to Jesus and his Father. All who are truly "present" at the wedding feast — present, that is, in heart and soul as well as in body — must be there to celebrate a wedding: and the wedding is their own!

In every Mass the Rite of Communion alludes to the text of Revelation: "Blessed are those who are invited to the marriage supper of the Lamb." This is what we are celebrating in anticipation when we receive Communion. We are accepting the invitation to the wedding feast. [25]

But we cannot take part in the wedding banquet — in the "wedding feast of the Lamb" — unless we are there to surrender ourselves to him as bride. Because Baptism makes us members of the Church, the Bride of Christ, it makes us "brides in the Bride," committed to him in a covenant of spousal love. The white robe of Baptism is a sign, not just of new life, but of purity: that is, of unmixed, undivided love; it is a symbol of the unreserved, passionate surrender of the bride to the Bridegroom.[26]

A wedding dress is also a pledge of nakedness; it is a dress the bride puts on as a promise to take it off. And when we celebrate the wedding feast to which we are called by Jesus Christ, we must come clothed in a pledge of nakedness: ready and willing to strip ourselves passionately of all things which stand between us and total union with the Bridegroom.

In the measure we are inclined to wrap ourselves up in the complacency of our law observance instead of in the wedding garment, we would do well to ponder again God's warning to the bishop of Laodicea:

> I know your works; you are neither cold nor hot. I wish that you were either cold or hot. So, because you are lukewarm, and neither cold nor hot, I am about to spit you out of my mouth.
>
> For you say, 'I am rich, I have prospered, and I need nothing.' You do not realize that you are wretched, pitiable, poor, blind, and naked. (Revelation 3:14-19)

What is so scary about the parable of the wedding feast is that the man "without a wedding garment" did not know he was "wretched, pitiable, poor, blind, and naked." He may have been dressed quite elegantly — just not for a wedding. But in fact he was naked; not with that nakedness which is the prelude to passion, but with that nakedness which, because it is not a pledge of anything, is just an experience of shame. And nobody had told him. So far as he knew, he fitted right in. In his own eyes he may even have outshone everyone else. But when he encountered the king face-to-face he was excluded and thrown out into the darkness his heart had already embraced.

Legalists are neither cold nor hot: not openly sinful enough to recognize their rejection of Christ and repent; not fervent enough to experience their union with him in passionate love. They do what they have to do. They respond to God out of obligation, not passion. That is why they are out of place at a wedding banquet.

Legalism is the mind set which makes it possible for "good Christians" to do horrible things without losing sleep at night. Because legalism reduces all religion to the observance of laws, those who are blinded by it can fool themselves into believing that they are saying "Yes" to the wedding feast when in fact they don't know what the party is all about. They are in the Church without being of the Church. For this reason they have reason to fear that when they can no longer avoid encounter with the living God they will find themselves excluded from a celebration they have never in fact been a part of.

In the Gospels, the call to conversion is an invitation to the experience of God. When the Spirit calls the Church to turn away from legalism, this is an invitation to experience the passion of grace. It is an invitation to the wedding feast. "Listen! I am standing at the door, knocking; if you hear my voice and open the door, I will come in to you and eat with you, and you with me." (Revelation 3:20).

It is not enough just to accept the invitation and "show up." We must be clothed in the wedding garment of passionate desire; clothed in a lifestyle that expresses our desire to be stripped totally and surrendered to the Beloved in the unreserved union and embrace of passionate love.

Conclusion: Choice, Conversion and Experience

As a Church we can refuse to give up our *triumphalism* and our complacency, and continue to deceive ourselves into thinking we are saying "Yes" to God when in reality we are saying "No." If we do this, we will give up at the same time the experience we could have of ourselves as a Church responding to the living voice of God. We will abandon our baptismal call to be *prophets* by refusing to look at the reality of the Church in our times in the light of the Gospel. Triumphalism is the corruption of a prophetic Church. By just taking for granted that we are the obedient children of God, whether or not we are reflecting the mind of our Father in action, we silence the voice that Jesus heard at the Jordan and lose the experience of the Father saying to us, "This is my Son, the Beloved, with whom I am well pleased."

We can cling to *clericalism,* and insist (both as laity and clergy) that the true "tenants" in charge of the Church are the clergy and hierarchy alone. We can refuse to listen to our own hearts and to all the members of the Church — especially to the poor — as fellow stewards and messengers sent by the Father. We can refuse to recognize the Son in ourselves and in all the members of his Body consecrated by baptism to share in his mission. But if we do, we will not experience ourselves as *faithful stewards* of the kingship of Christ who look after the interests of God with undivided hearts. We will be giving up the experience we could have both of the fruits and of the reward of stewardship. Clericalism is the corruption of stewardship. The vineyard will be taken away from us and others will bring in the harvest.

And we can continue to clothe ourselves in *legalism* and parade about in our pretense of being present for a wedding when everything in our lifestyle denies all intention of passionate love. If we do this, we will never experience passionate union with Jesus who "emptied himself... accepting even death, death on a cross." Legalism is the corruption of our baptismal *priesthood* because it is the refusal of passionate love. Jesus consummated his priesthood when he offered his body naked on the cross as Bridegroom abandoned in love to the Bride. If we clothe ourselves in anything else but his passionate love — expressed in constant, dedicated ministry to others: at home, at work, in our social lives — we will find ourselves excluded from the wedding feast.

But if we convert, we will enter into the experience of God.

CHAPTER NINE:
RESPONSE AND EXPERIENCE
"The Experience of God" — *Matthew 21:28 to 21:14*

Summary

Three parables of Jesus help us understand three attitudes prevalent in the Church which distort our perception of what Christianity is all about. Because they are ways to avoid personal interaction with God through choices and conversion, they block our experience of God. The three attitudes are *triumphalism, clericalism* and *legalism,*

1. Triumphalism appears in the *self-deluding son* who sees himself as a good son because he declares his allegiance to his father in words and gestures of respect that distinguish him from the rebellious. But his obedience is more conformity to the cultural image of a good son than true union of mind and will with his father.

Triumphalism is the attitude which assumes one is a good Christian because of one's visible conformity to "the one true Church." Its focus is not on growing in union with Christ, but on conforming to a cultural image of Catholicism fostered by custom and Church authorities. Triumphalists look to the power structure of the Church rather than to the Gospel for affirmation of their way of life. They draw assurance from the ecclesiastical pomp and splendor that portray the Church as stable, established and complete.

To experience the action of the Holy Spirit in the Church we need to convert to the more Scriptural notion of the "pilgrim Church," adopted by Vatican II, a Church guided by the Spirit but never complacent in its response, a Church committed to continual conversion. This is the essential condition for being a *prophetic* Church.

2. Clericalism is exposed in the parable of *the unfaithful tenants* who withhold rents from a landowner, do violence to his messengers, kill his son, and try to seize his vineyard for themselves.

Clericalism ignores the theological fact that the true "tenants" of God's vineyard are all the members of the Church. Clericalists speak and act as if everything done in the Church should be directed by the clergy.

Clericalism tends to reduce the laity to a condition of passivity, and to make their apostolate a mere appendage of the apostolate of the hierarchy.

The authentic teaching of the Church is that both clergy and laity are equally stewards of the kingship of Christ. The apostolate of the Church includes both the "apostolate of the hierarchy" — those actions performed officially in the name of the Church, over which the hierarchy have authority — and the "apostolate of the laity" — those actions performed by Catholics acting on their own initiative as Christian witnesses, but not officially in the name of the Church. Over the apostolate of the laity the hierarchy have no authority.

The clergy do not have the authority to impose decisions in the areas of the lay apostolate. But they do have the obligation to judge these areas in the light of the Gospel and to express their opinion in preaching and teaching.

Clericalism identifies leadership with authority. But by restricting all leadership to clerical authorities, it silences the voice of prophetic challenge in clergy and laity alike. The clergy are only allowed to exercise leadership in the narrow area of their religious authority. The laity, having no authority, are not expected to exercise religious leadership at all. This leaves the proper field of the lay apostolate, the secular arena of "temporal affairs" — business and politics, family and social life — without any religious leadership.

For authority to function well, it must encourage all members of a group to exercise leadership by pointing out what their particular vantage point enables them to see. Without leadership from its subjects, authority is blind.

Clericalism blocks the experience of *faithful stewardship* in the Church because it discourages the clergy from taking responsibility for what happens in business and politics; and it relieves the laity from taking religious responsibility for anything about which the clergy is silent. For both clergy and laity this is an obstacle to the ongoing process of conversion that obscures the experience of God.

The alternative to clericalism is a collaborative Church, a Church in which clergy and laity alike listen for the voice of the Holy Spirit speaking in every member of the body of Christ.

3. Legalism is revealed in the parable of the people who do not appreciate the invitation to the wedding feast. Their relationship with the king who invites them is one of contract and obligation; they keep the king's laws. Love and celebration don't enter into it.

Legalism is a religious attitude that makes law observance the focus of religion. And the focus of legalists is on observing the laws, not on understanding them. Legalists do not take personal responsibility for thinking, deciding and acting according to general principles being preached or taught in the Church, so long as these have not been concretized in specific laws.

In the Gospels, the call to conversion is an invitation to experience the passion of grace. It is an invitation to the wedding feast. Because legalism reduces all religion to the observance of laws, those who are blinded by it can fool themselves into believing that they are saying, "Yes" to the wedding feast when in fact they don't know what the party is all about.

Have you understood?

What is triumphalism? What does it have in common with the parable of the self-deluding son? What image of the Church must we adopt if we want to fulfill our baptismal consecration as prophets?

What is clericalism? What mistake is at the core of clericalism? How does it keep us from fulfilling our baptismal consecration as stewards of Christ's kingship?

What is legalism? What do legalists have in common with the people who refused the invitation to the wedding feast? Why is legalism the corruption of our baptismal consecration as priests?

What is the challenge of this chapter? To our faith? To our hope? To our love?

Making it your own

What are the key thoughts in this chapter? (Jot them down and give the page number where each is found).

What questions do I have about this chapter? (Bring them up in discussion or ask someone who should know the answers).

What struck me the most in this chapter? After reading this chapter, what do I understand better than I did before? What do I appreciate more?

What do I think is the point of the whole chapter? What response does

Matthew want to evoke from those who read or hear this part of his Gospel?

What can I use as a visible reminder (a symbol) to keep me aware of the challenge of this chapter? Where will I put it?

Questions for prayer

How do I feel about the pomp and pageantry, the impressive robes and titles of the clergy and hierarchy? Why?

How do I exercise religious leadership in my parish? My home? My work? My social and civic life?

How have I experienced union with the Holy Spirit in the way I have interpreted or applied Church laws? Which ones?

How can I apply to my life what I have come to see by reflecting on this chapter? What concrete action do I choose to perform to express my belief in what I have seen?

FOOTNOTES

[1] See Mt. 3:13-17 as explained in my book *A Change Within* (previously published as *Blessed Are They*, 1994), His Way Inc., chapter 2.

[2] See Avery Dulles, *Models of the Church - Expanded Edition*, Image-Doubleday, 1987, chapter two, "The Church as Institution," pp. 39-46. In 2001 John Paul II made Fr. Dulles a cardinal. To be made a cardinal is to receive a purely political or administrative title and position (or in some cases a purely honorary one), not a religious one. But it indicates that the recipient is approved by the Vatican.

[3] See Triumphalism" in the *Catholic Encyclopedia* published by Our Sunday Visitor Press in 1991. The *New Catholic Encyclopedia* edited by the Catholic University of America and published by McGraw-Hill in 1967 defines triumphalism as describing "a tendency to think of the Church as irresistibly conquering throughout the centuries, always receiving universal admiration for the words and deeds of its heads, and seemingly more interested in upholding its own rights and privileges than in promoting the salvation of all." See also Richard P. McBrien, *Catholicism* (Study Edition), Harper-SanFrancisco, 1981, Part V, chapter 26, under "The Virtue of Religion," pp. 978-9.

[4] Richard P. McBrien, *ibid.*

[5] To give just one example of this: In 1980 the Salvadoran National Guard raped and murdered Maryknoll Sisters Ita Ford and Maura Clarke, Ursuline Sister Dorothy Kazel, and a lay volunteer working with them, Jean Donovan. But President Reagan's Secretary of State, Alexander Haig, who was presented in the media as an exemplary Catholic (his brother was a Jesuit), tried to make people believe that the nuns were the ones at fault. According to a *National Catholic Reporter* article (Oct. 27, 2000, p. 4):

> Alexander Haig spoke before Congress on March 17, 1982, and painted the women as pistol-packing guerrillas who ran a security blockade while trading shots with Salvadoran military. It's a memory that sparks Bill Ford's anger [Ita Ford's brother, who was suing the Salvadoran generals accused of ordering the murders].
>
> "Al Haig was willing to smear my sister and the other women, even though he knew what he was saying wasn't true," Ford said. "Haig was a bad man working for a bad policy."
>
> Haig later said that he was only repeating what the Salvadoran government had told him at the time of his testimony, a claim Ford dismisses.
>
> "The FBI and the U.S. government knew the truth," he said.

The *NCR* article quotes another prominent Catholic:

> In what was surely the most reckless calumny of the time, Jeane Kirkpatrick implied that the women got what they deserved for meddling in politics and not being real nuns. It was a remark former ambassador Robert White described as "an incitement to murder."

[6] For a development of what "cultural Catholicism" or "civil religion" is, see my book *His Way*, chapter one. For the deadening effect this has on the Catholic education of youth, see William J. O'Malley, S.J., "Plow Before You Plant," *America* magazine, Sept. 16, 2000, p. 15 ff.

[7] Richard McBrien (*op. cit.*, pp. 978-9.) identifies triumphalism with *idolatry*, which is "the worship of something less than the Absolute — e.g. money, personal gain, political power," and continues, "We can make an idol even of the Church or of institutional elements within the Church."

[8] See the Beatitudes in Mt. 5:3-12. See also Vatican II's "Decree on Ecumenism," chapter 2, parag. 6: "Christ summons the Church, as she goes her pilgrim way, to that continual reformation of which she always has need, insofar as she is an institution of men here on earth. Therefore, if the influence of events or of the times has led to deficiencies in conduct, in Church discipline, or even in the formulation of doctrine (which must be carefully distinguished from the deposit itself of faith), these should be appropriately rectified at the proper moment."

[9] See the *New Catholic Encyclopedia* , under "Triumphalism." And see again McBrien, *op. cit.*, p. 827.

[10] "He will trash that trash" is an attempt to capture the force of Matthew's *Kakous kakos apolesei* — "He will destroy the bad badly." It was a fun try, but probably the chief priests and Pharisees were too stiff to speak in the contemporary language of the people!

[11] Avery Dulles, *op. cit.*, pages 39, 43.

[12] Avery Dulles, *The Catholicity of the Church*, Clarendon Press - Oxford, 1987 (paperback edition), p. 161-2, referring to Vatican II's *Constitution on the Church*, paragraph 12.

[13] Vatican II, *The Church*, no. 33. See also no. 31 and "Decree on the Apostolate of the Laity," no. 7: "The laity must take on the renewal of the temporal order as their own special obligation. Led by the light of the Gospel and the mind of the Church, and motivated by Christian love, let them act directly and definitively in the temporal sphere. As citizens they must cooperate with other citizens, using their own particular skills and acting on their own responsibility."

[14] For the distinction of leadership and authority, see the contribution of John Sheets, S.J., to the series *Studies in the Spirituality of Jesuits*, Vol. IV, no. 2 (March, 1972), "Two Discussions: (1) Spiritual Direction. (2) Leadership and Authority." Fr. Sheets was later made auxiliary bishop of Fort Wayne, Indiana.

[15] We listen to Avery Dulles again: "The dominant temptations of Catholicism are, on the one hand, clericalism, and on the other, by way of reaction, anti-clericalism. Both these deformations derive from a failure to appreciate the mutual complementarity of the many states of life within the Church, which serve on occasion as checks and balances." (*The Catholicity of the Church*, Clarendon Press - Oxford, 1987 (paperback), p. 124.

[16] See St. Ignatius of Loyola's *Spiritual Exercises*, the "Meditation on the Two Standards." I have translated freely but faithfully.

[17] See *The Church in the Present-Day Transformation of Latin America in the Light of the Council* (Second General Conference of Latin American Bishops, Medellin, Colombia, 1968). And see the famous Puebla document: *La Evanglización en el Presente y en el Futuro de América Latina, III CONFERENCIA GENERAL DEL EPISCOPADO LATINOAMERICANO, 1979,* Segunda Parte, Capitulo II, Cuarta Parte, Capitulo I.

[18] See McKenzie, *The Jerome Biblical Commentary*, 43:149, on Mt. 22:1-14. "Matthew by the use of his tag line (see 8:12; 13:42, 50) introduces an eschatological note that changes the image from the Church to the eschatological Messianic banquet."

[19] See Richard P. McBrien, *Catholicism*, Study Edition, Harper San Francisco, Part V, chapter 26, under "The Virtue of Religion," pp. 978-9.

[20] See Avery Dulles, *Models of the Church - Expanded Edition*, Image-Doubleday, 1987, chapter two, "The Church as Institution," pp. 39-40.

[21] The Vatican II doctrine is from "The Church in the Modern World," paragraph 80. For more information about the conflict between the Church's moral teaching and our country's political policy, see chapter six, footnote six, of my book *No Power but Love*, His Way Communications, 1999. In fairness to the Holy Spirit and the Christian conscience, we should acknowledge that even in the military it is not certain that every individual can be counted on to obey an immoral order. Those who press the buttons to launch nuclear missiles are frequently tested by being commanded to do so without knowing whether the order is part of a drill or the "real thing." Some refuse to press the button. The number of beautiful Catholics one meets in the military is also proof that subjectively, in their consciences, they do not see that all killing is forbidden to Christians. This is the fruit of an insufficiently prophetic Church. In previous centuries there were also devout Catholics who owned slaves.

[22] *The Challenge of Peace:...A Pastoral Letter on War and Peace*, United States Catholic Conference, 1983; Summary, p. vii. In this context the bishops wrote: "The decisions about nuclear weapons are among the most *pressing moral questions* of our age;" and "A *serious*

moral obligation exists to develop non-nuclear defensive strategies as rapidly as possible" (pp. v and vii). Given the destructive power of even non-nuclear weapons today and the devastating effects of modern war on whole populations, I think it is obvious that the bishops are saying that every Christian has a "serious moral obligation" to "undertake a completely fresh reappraisal of war," as Vatican II declared ("The Church in the Modern World," #80, cited by the bishops, parag. 23). The very fact the bishops chose to write a pastoral on peace is evidence that they are summoning us to examine this question with serious moral concern.

[23] We should note here that, in spite of common perception, the Church has made no law against contraception. Her official position is presented as a conclusion about God's law based on a philosophical interpretation of natural law. When Pope Paul VI condemned contraception in his famous encyclical *Humanae Vitae*, his personal theologian, Carlo Colombo, was quoted by the *Washington Post* as saying in a press conference, "This teaching is not irreformable." "Not irreformable" means the doctrine can be changed. The use of this technical theological term is evidence that the reporter probably quoted Colombo correctly. William O'Malley, S.J., *art. cit.*, p. 16, gives us a perspective in which to place legalism: "Harvard's Lawrence Kohlberg discovered six step-by-step stages of moral motivation: 1) fear of the cost, 2) hope of reward, 3) small-group loyalty, 4) law-and-order, 5) reasoned principle, 6) personal integrity — moral integrity expanding further outward from the self. But, his researchers found, anyone at a lower stage just cannot comprehend the motivation of anyone two stages above...." This may explain why the legalists simply cannot understand the prophets, whose motivation is based on faith-experience that goes beyond even reasoned principles.

[24] I am quoting from pages 12-21 and 608-628 of the Second Revised Edition of Cicognani's book *Canon Law*. (translated by Joseph M. O'Hara and Msgr. Francis J. Brennan, Newman Press, 1934). In this book Cicognani is giving the teaching of St. Thomas Acquinas, Summa Theologica, Part II-II, Question 120, article 1. For more on legalism, see chapter eight above, pages 186-187.

[25] Revelation 19:9. The official Latin text for the Communion Rite of the Mass is identical, except for one word, to the Latin translation of this verse in the 1592 Sexto-Clementine edition of the Vulgate found in

Augustinus Merk, S.J., *NOVUM TESTAMENTUM GRAECE ET LATINE*, Pontifical Biblical Institute, Rome, 1957. The Biblical text is "Beati qui ad cenam nuptiarum Agni vocati sunt." The liturgical text is "Beati qui ad cenam Agni vocati sunt," omitting only the word "nuptiarum," which specifies the feast as a wedding. For some reason the vernacular translations of the liturgical text in all the Western hemisphere languages I have been able to check also omit all reference to the Lamb, changing the text to read, "his supper" or "supper of the Lord." This obscures the full eschatological focus of the text. To receive Communion is to affirm one's faith in and acceptance of the transcendent blessedness and glory of dying. I have been told that the Chinese and Vietnamese translations do not make this mistake.

[26] See Mt. 9:15 and 25:1-13; John 3:29; Ephesians 5:25-32; Revelation 19:7-9; 21:2-9; 22:17. Just as Jesus is the only Son of the Father and all who are "in Christ" are "sons in the Son," *filii in Filio*, so the Church is the Bride of Christ, and all who are in the Church are "brides in the Bride."

Chapter Ten
How We Lose The Way
The Temptations — Matthew 22:15-40

The chief priests and Pharisees would not answer Jesus' question about John the Baptizer, because they feared the reaction of the crowd. And so Jesus in his turn left them without an answer to their question about the source of his authority. And he went further: he told three parables to warn them that if they did not "wake up and smell the coffee" they would never experience the Kingdom of God. They were cutting themselves off from reality, and therefore from conversion, by their shortsighted focus on all the pomp and ceremony which they mistook for the real "glory of Israel"; on their own status as religious guides; and on law observance as the be-all and end-all of religion.

We have seen how the experience of God and of personal relationship with God in the Church today can be obscured by these same three ecclesiastical defense mechanisms, identified during Vatican Council II as *triumphalism, clericalism* and *legalism.*

It was only to be expected that the Pharisees would regroup and strike back. And sure enough, the next thing Matthew tells us is, "Then the Pharisees went off and began to plot how they might trap Jesus in his speech."

The First Temptation (Matthew 22:15-22)

They don't approach Jesus directly. They send their disciples to him "accompanied by herodian sympathizers," people who would be recognized as favoring collaboration with the Roman government. The Pharisees themselves agreed with the Zealot party that Jews should not acknowledge Rome's authority (although, unlike the Zealots, the Pharisees were not in favor of violent revolution). But Herod was committed to collaboration, and the fortunes of

his supporters were built on submissive loyalty to Rome.
So the Pharisees send some Herodians with their disciples
to make it appear that the question they are posing to Jesus
is a sincere effort to resolve an argument between the
Herodians and the Pharisees about paying taxes.[1]

"Rabbi," they begin, "we know that you are an honest man
and that when you teach the way of God you tell it the way
it is. You aren't concerned about what people think, and it
makes no difference to you who they are."

Jesus is being set up to take a stand which, while confirm-
ing the fact that he isn't afraid, either of the Romans or of
the Zealots, will put him on the side of one political faction
while alienating him from the other.

"So give us your opinion on this: Is it according to the law
of God to pay the census tax to Caesar or not?"

Jesus recognizes the setup. He answers, "You hypocrites,
why are you testing me? Show me the coin you use to pay
the census tax."

They hand him a Roman coin.

Then he says, "Whose image is this? Whose inscription is
on the coin?"

They answer, "Caesar's." At that he says to them, "Then
give back to Caesar what belongs to Caesar and to God
what belongs to God."

The temptation to change the goal

There is more here than just a clever trick to get Jesus to
say something which could discredit him. Underlying the
Pharisees' question is the same temptation we have already
seen Jesus face and overcome three times: the temptation to
change the goal of his mission.

In the desert he was tempted to make "feeding the hungry"
the goal which would identify him as Messiah. This was

the temptation to aim at establishing a kingdom of earthly prosperity, which was what his people really expected of the Messiah. Jesus refused; his goal was to teach people to *know God through faith*. If he taught them that, they would feed the hungry, but it would be a *consequence*, and not the goal, of their religion (see Mt. 4:1-4).

Later he faced the same temptation under a form that constantly confronts the *Church*. The Pharisees saw his disciples feeding themselves when they were hungry by pulling heads of grain off the stalks while walking through a field on the Sabbath. For the legalistic Pharisees this was the same as harvesting the field! They complained to Jesus that his disciples should keep the law and rest on the Sabbath instead of working to satisfy their hunger. After all, Jesus had said in the desert that feeding the hungry was not the goal of his mission.

But Jesus saw this was the same temptation the devil offered him in the desert: they wanted him to reduce the goal of his mission to something merely human — in this case, not material prosperity, but the human satisfaction and sense of security which can be found in a religion that focuses on keeping rules. They wanted Jesus to make, not feeding the hungry, but *law-observance* the goal of his religion. Jesus refused, saying again that the goal was to understand the mind and heart of God through faith (see Mt. 12:1-8).

After he announced his way of saving the world through the *cross*, he faced the same temptation, this time in the form of a difficulty felt by his own disciples. Their faith was shaken because they could not cast a demon out of a little boy. In reality, they were confusing the goal of Jesus' mission and theirs with *success* on this earth — in this case the power to relieve suffering. They too were making the goal of Christianity something visible and tangible on this earth, something which, like feeding the hungry and drawing security out of law-observance, was the satisfaction of a felt human need: the need for healing. Jesus' answer was to urge them to have more faith (see Mt. 17:19-20).

Now the same temptation comes up in the form of an urging by the Pharisees to give the Church credibility by endorsing some popular movement that aims at achieving some particular human value on earth. The problem here is not with supporting a human goal. The Church can and should support any human values that are good. The problem lies in trying to win acceptance for the Church (or for oneself or one's institution within the Church) by giving the impression that what Christianity is all about, at least in this particular moment of history, is achieving some particular popular value.

This temptation can take the form of enthusiastically subordinating the Church's mission — in practice, though not in theory — to that of some seductively appealing political movement or some other popular movement perceived to be serving urgent human needs. This could be anything from violent revolution to ecology. The delusion does not consist in working for a cause that is good, but in making all of one's religious fervor and devotion focus on this cause, even to the extent of identifying one's religion, for all practical purposes, with support for the group that espouses it. The Pharisees and Herodians wanted Jesus to identify true religion with acceptance or rejection of the Roman government and to place himself as Messiah within the camp of those he agreed with. Our temptation is to identify authentic Christianity with some "cause" in such a way that the Church becomes a subdivision of the party that is working for it.

In the measure people do this — whether clergy or laity — they are in fact changing the goal and identity of the Church, but they are not conscious of it. They think they are serving the Church and making her more authentic or popular by putting religion at the service of a movement which seems to answer the current need of the world.

The banner of the bandwagon

This is very much like the first temptation Jesus himself faced in the desert. The difference between them lies in the fact of *identifying* the Church with some existing group and in the *motive* behind this identification. Instead of just focusing the Church on feeding the hungry or achieving some other humanly beneficial goal on earth (which was the temptation Jesus faced in the desert), those who succumb to this temptation try to tie the Church as such to the coattails of some other group or movement they believe in. And the motive for doing this is the seductive expectation of imminent success. The group they espouse shows promise of achieving results; if not immediately, then in the foreseeable future. The future that Jesus promises, on the other hand, is not foreseeable. It is certain, but never in sight. Those who fall into this temptation are in fact jumping on a bandwagon, and they are doing it because the bandwagon is moving faster than the Parousia: at least, the bandwagon appears to be going faster than Jesus is coming. It is more humanly satisfying to get somewhere, to achieve any visible result at all, than to keep working and waiting indefinitely for the kingdom of God to appear.

This is the temptation to *subordinate the goal of the Church to the goal of a political party.* If we just said "to make the goal of politics the Church's goal," this would be the same as Jesus' first temptation in the desert, the temptation to make the realization of the common good, the well-being of society on this earth, the goal of his religion. That is the goal of politics as such. But this temptation is a little different; it is the temptation to ride the coattails of a current movement, leader or party in order to experience the satisfaction of achieving some popular objective, without realizing that in fact the goal of the Church as such is being obscured.

At different times in history elements in the Church have

allied themselves with the rich and powerful of the established right, or with the poor and persecuted seeking power as the revolutionary left. When people do this in such a way that they are not just proclaiming values and goals, or directions in which society should move, but are actually identifying the Church with a particular political party or movement, they are leading the Church into this temptation.

The Church's mission is to call people to a response of faith by proclaiming and living the truth. She must do this even when it is unpopular, as it was when Pope Leo XIII wrote the first of the great "social encyclicals" and supported the right of workers to form unions; or when the Latin American bishops met in Medellín and Puebla and articulated the famous "option for the poor" which brought bloody persecution down on the heads of laity, priests and bishops alike. The Church need not and should not try so hard to keep her skirts so clear of all contact with economics and politics that she keeps herself on the margin of life. But it is one thing for the Church to enter the lists as a free agent and fight for justice with her own weapons, which are truth and love, with total abstinence from violence. It is another thing to identify herself with a specific political party or movement and to participate in the struggle under someone else's banner. To do that is to accept solidarity with a particular group of people and to become co-responsible with them for everything they identify as their goal and for all the means they use to achieve it. In reality, it is to make the Church the servant of a political party and to subordinate the Church's mission to the aims and intentions of that party.[2]

The appeal of the visible

Why is this a temptation? The answer is quite clear: visible goals are more appealing than invisible goals, especially if the visible goals seem achievable and the invisible ones do not. The visible, measurable achievement of some human value on earth is more humanly satisfying than working for the spiritual conversion of the world and hoping, in spite of appearances, that it is taking place. To offer food to those who are clearly hungry for it is more gratifying than to offer the word of God to an apathetic congregation. And to join forces with the established class in an effort to preserve simple law and order in society is more gratifying than to urge people to embrace and live the impossibly high ideals of Jesus Christ or to apply them prophetically to the complex reality of modern life. The achievement of direct results through violence or any other use of power that "works" is a seductive goal — more alluring than Christ's way of renewing society through the free conversion of free human hearts. And for that reason the Church — meaning the people who are the Church, both clergy and laity — will always be tempted to jump on any bandwagon which seems to be rolling. "Nothing succeeds like success," the saying goes, and nothing seduces like the promise of success.

Bishop Victor-Hugo Martinez of Guatemala — himself a defender of the poor, and a staunch opponent of government oppression — once observed, in answer to a question about "activist priests," that the clergy are always tempted to "lose their identity" by identifying themselves with some movement which is popular in their time. The temptation is to seek status, or image, or a sense of value and fulfillment, through identification with some group, whether on the left or on the right, which is being hailed as the savior of the people. In this the clergy are no different from the laity, except that when the bishops and priests make this mistake, their visibility as representatives of the Church makes the Church as such appear to be losing her identity as well.

Jesus refused to do this. He refused to identify himself either with the Herodians or the Zealots. He refused to identify himself with defenders or opponents of the state.[3]

Subordination through alliance

This temptation can also take a form that has elements in
common with Jesus' third temptation in the desert: the
temptation to "make a deal" with the devil. Church leaders
can be tempted to identify themselves with some powerful
group — the rich, for example, or powerful members of
government — for the sake of using that group's power to
achieve objectives which they see as conducive to the
Church's goal or mission.[4]

Sometimes the temptation originates in an effort on the part
of the rich and powerful to make the Church appear as their
ally through what is in reality bribery. The bribery is never
clear and overt. The power group does not hold up before
the eyes of Church leaders all the resources, riches and influence that are at their disposal and say as the devil said to
Jesus in the desert, "All these I will give you, if you will
fall down and worship me." On the contrary, those who
have these resources are lavish in the reverence they show
to "the gentlemen of the cloth," even to the point of hum-
bling themselves before them. Kings kneel before the pope,
and the heads of multi-national corporations kiss the bishop's ring; not vice-versa. But underneath the sham of protocol everyone (except, perhaps, the Church leaders who
are the mark of the scam) knows where the real power lies,
and who is becoming subordinate to whom. All that the
rich and powerful ask is that Church leaders express toward
them — toward their government, their party or their lifestyle — some kind of general acceptance, without going
into details. Once under that umbrella those in power will
know how to profit from it. No need for Church leaders to
"fall down and adore" them; they have received all the ap-
probation they need.

For example, the government will do everything it can to
promote Church ministry to members of the armed forces.
The government will bestow on chaplains rank, pay and all

the privileges of the officer class, with generous retirement benefits. All the Church has to do is cover the military as a whole with her approval by allowing her priests to become uniformed members of the armed services (although without carrying arms themselves) and so identify the Church with the goals and lifestyle of the warrior class. There is an unwritten understanding, of course, that no chaplain will ever proclaim from a military pulpit that war in itself is evil or condemn any particular war which the government chooses to engage in. It is a trade-off: the Church receives the right to minister; the government receives the right to subordinate that ministry to the overall aims and policies of the state.

When the government urges the Church to put priests into uniform as members of the armed services, we can hear the voice of the tempter repeating, "So give us your opinion on this: Is it according to the law of God to...." To what? To support Caesar in Caesar's wars against the enemies of the state. Every priest in uniform proclaims that the Church has taken her stand alongside of Caesar on the battlefield. After that, whether or not the priest personally engages in killing is a relatively minor issue.

It is not cooperation with the state as such which is the temptation; there are many projects or endeavors in which the objectives of Church and state coincide. The temptation comes when the Church is asked to make those gestures which, overtly or subtly, cause the Church to appear as an ally of the state, or of any other group or movement. Chaplains, for example, could minister as civilians without actually being members of the armed services, wearing the uniform, receiving a government salary or accepting military rank and privileges. One does not have to be a soldier to minister to soldiers, or become a member of the country club in order to minister to the affluent. The problem lies, not in ministry, but in the manipulation to which identification with the rich and powerful inevitably exposes the minister.[5]

Jesus did, in fact, identify himself with a particular group of people. He became visibly one with the poor and powerless. He did this to teach us how to act against the seduction of affluence and prestige.

Almost inevitably, when members of the hierarchy accept to sit on the same platform with the rich and powerful for the sake of achieving some particular objective, the Church winds up compromising the goal of her mission, sacrificing the whole for the part, which is idolatry. When the reign of God is complete, all things will be "brought together into unity under Christ's headship" (see Eph. 1:10). Until that time, if the lion lies down with the lamb it is the lion, not the lamb, who is most likely to get up again.

The Second Temptation (Matthew 22:23-33)

The Pharisees and Herodians didn't know what to say after Jesus told them to "give to Caesar what is Caesar's and to God what is God's." So they just turned around and left. But the Sadducees stepped up to take their place in the lists. "That same day," Matthew tells us, "some Sadducees, who claim that there is no resurrection of the body, came to him with a question."

Their question parallels Jesus' second temptation in the desert. When the devil urged Jesus to jump off the pinnacle of the temple in order to prove he was the Messiah, the reasoning behind the devil's temptation was that if Jesus was the Messiah, God had to preserve him from death. This was based on the assumption that the Messiah was going to be a powerful conqueror who would establish an earthly kingdom by invincible force. If God allowed Jesus to die, therefore, he could not be the Messiah. If he was the Messiah, God would not allow him to die. The devil says, "Put it to the test."

Actually, in reporting this temptation Matthew is address-

ing the problem Jesus' first followers had with the crucifixion. Because they had assumed, like everyone else, that
the Messiah would be an earthly king, Jesus' death on the
cross said to his followers as well as to his foes that he
must not have been, could not have been, the Messiah in
whom they "had hoped" (Luke 24:21). Matthew counters
this way of thinking by showing that Jesus himself was
tempted to reject the cross as God's way of saving the
world. But by refusing to force the Father to proclaim his
invincibility by saving his life, Jesus accepted the Father's
way of overcoming evil through vulnerability and love:
through crucifixion.

At the core of this temptation is the assumption that death
has no value in itself; that it is the final termination, not
only of our lives, but of any good we might hope to accomplish on earth. That is where the Sadducees come in: the
Sadducees, by denying the resurrection of the body, which
in the contemporary Jewish context denied any fullness of
life after death, are likewise denying that there is any value
in dying. This strikes at the heart of belief in Jesus as the
"Suffering Savior," the "Lamb of God" who "takes away
the sin of the world" by offering up his life on the cross. If
there is no resurrection, Christ's death was in vain. So was
his life. And so do our lives ultimately count for nothing. If
there is no life after death, there is no value in dying. If
there is no value in dying there is no real value in living.
All is passing, a "fleeting shadow," illusion, doing something for nothing, getting something that ultimately is
nothing. This demolishes human hope. In a very particular
way it demolishes Christian hope, which can accept suffering and apparent defeat in this world because of belief in
the ultimate triumph of Christ and the ultimate reward of
life everlasting.

Seven brothers, one wife

The Sadducees begin their attack on Jesus by recalling that, in the Law, if a man dies without children, his brother is obliged to marry his widow. The first-born son from this union is then to be accepted as the deceased brother's son so that his line will continue and "his name may not be blotted out from Israel" (Deuteronomy 25:5-6; and see Genesis 38:8).

Anyone who has ever argued religion with sophisticated cynics can see the smirk on the Sadducee's face and hear the mocking tone in his voice as he continues:

"Well, you see, once there were seven brothers. The oldest died after marrying, and since he had no children, he left his wife to his brother, see?"

"The same thing happened to the second, see? And to the third; and so on, down to the seventh, you see?"

"Finally the woman died. Now then, at the resurrection, whose wife will she be? All seven of them married her, you see?"

Jesus looks at this would-be intellectual and simply sweeps the ground out from under his feet.

"You are speaking nonsense," he tells him, "because you don't understand anything about the Scriptures or the power of God."

The Sadducee is trying to argue from the word of God without having the slightest understanding either of God or of his word, because that is an understanding only faith can give. The Sadducee's basic mistake is to think that all truth is on the plane of his own petty reasoning, and that all reality is on the plane of the reality he has experienced. The truth is, Jesus tells him (quoting Shakespeare!), "There are more things in heaven and on earth than are dreamt of in your philosophy!" The reality of life in heaven is totally different from the reality of life on earth.

"When people rise from the dead," Jesus explains, with exasperated patience in his voice, "they neither marry nor are given in marriage but live like angels in heaven."

The "crux" of the Sadducees' question: the cross

The Sadducees' question about the seven brothers who
married the same wife was just a skirmish. What the Sadducees were really at war against was the whole idea that
there is any fulfillment to be found in life after death. This
naturally strikes at the heart of everything we believe, and
everything the Apostles preached, about the value of
Christ's death on the cross and the victory revealed in his
resurrection. If Jesus did not rise, then his way of saving
the world through dying was an illusion. And his call to us
to continue saving the world by "taking up the cross" and
"loving back" in response to all the suffering imposed on us
by others' sins is absurdity. If Jesus did not rise, he was a
false messiah, and the only hope of the world is to find and
embrace another messiah who will match the description of
the one the Jews expected in the first place: a temporal king
and conqueror who will impose order on society by power
and force.

The Sadducees' question is a temptation very much alive in
the Church and in the world today, because the Sadducees
speak for all those people who, now as well as then, base
their hopes, plans and choices on the practical assumption
that this life is "where it's really at." Christians are not
likely to deny the afterlife in theory, but for many the fulfillment God promises in heaven is hardly the guiding principle which directs their day-to-day choices in practice.

People do not always do business solely for the Kingdom
of God. Social life and entertainment are not always focused primarily on fostering that "life to the full" which
Jesus came to teach. Even families do not always see and
structure themselves before everything else as "Christian
communities" united in and by their communal expression
of faith and worship in their homes. Many families focus

most consistently, to all appearances at least, on the values
of this world, not on eternal values. Many do not gather together regularly at home to share their faith through prayer
and discussion. Not all families are consciously and explicitly united in a common desire to work at making their lifestyle bear witness to hope in the promises of Christ. And
while every family that is not completely non-functional
tries to base itself on love, not all are striving systematically to do everything they can to "comprehend the breadth
and length and height and depth, and know the love of
Christ that surpasses knowledge," so that they may be
"filled with all the fullness of God" (Ephesians 3:16-19).
Families don't always work at the kind of love Jesus
taught.[6]

In practice many people, whether in family or social life,
business or politics, are just trying to survive in this world
with as little pain as possible and as much comfort (psychological as well as physical) as they can manage, without
fixing too much practical hope on any satisfaction to be
found after death. We believe in life after death, just as we
believe there will be a Christmas ten years from now. But
for practical purposes it does not enter into our day-to-day
choices.

Killing for life in this world

Perhaps the most glaring practical denial of belief in life
after death is found in our almost unreflective willingness
to kill others in order to save our own lives. In spite of the
fact that Jesus insists on love of enemies and proclaims in
the most solemn way that those who choose to save their
lives on this earth will lose their souls, our whole nation
(and every nation) responds to aggression with knee-jerk
predictability: we go to war. We have demonstrated again
and again that, not just when attacked, but to avoid being
put into a position where we might be attacked, we are
willing to cause the death of thousands or hundreds of thou-

sands of people, including women, children, the aged and the sick. Our record is clear on this point.[7]

And all of the violence we use against others is motivated by only one thing, ultimately: the *desire to save our lives, or our way of life, in this world.* It is a more practical, and more real, denial of the resurrection than anything the Sadducees could have dreamed of. In spite of our professed belief in life after death, and in heaven as the goal of earthly existence, for practical purposes we live as if preserving our lives and property on this earth were the highest value there is. That is in direct contradiction to the Gospel, just as the Gospel is in direct contradiction to the "common sense" of human culture. To those who think it is "obvious" that people should defend their lives by violence and that nations should go to war, Jesus' answer is the same he gave the Sadducees: "You are wrong, because you don't understand either the Scriptures or the power of God."

Anyone who does not accept to judge reality by the light of faith, and to be guided by a "guidance system" which is not of this earth — by the Spirit of God, in fact — has no other alternative than to reject Jesus' way of saving the world as foolishness. Without belief that true fulfillment and happiness are found in the afterlife, the teaching of Jesus — "whoever would save his life will lose it, and whoever loses his life for my sake will find it" — is simply ridiculous.

> Those who are unspiritual do not receive the gifts of God's Spirit, for they are foolishness to them, and they are unable to understand them because they are spiritually discerned. Those who are spiritual discern all things, and they are themselves subject to no one else's scrutiny. For who has known the mind of the Lord so as to instruct him?" But we have the mind of Christ (see 1Cor. 2:1-16).

A recurring temptation

The "mind of Christ" — that is what Peter had so much trouble accepting when he objected to Jesus' way of saving the world and was told he was a "satan" (adversary, destroyer) and an "obstacle" in Jesus' path (see Mt. 16:22-23). The "mind of Christ" is what the Sadducees were ignorant of when they mocked the very concept of resurrection. And the "mind of Christ" is what we must grow into if we are to accept his way of saving the world.

Jesus himself was tempted in the desert to reject the "mind of the Father," the way of saving the world the Father had determined for him, when the devil urged him to "throw himself down" from the temple in a presumptuous act of insistence that the Father save his life in this world (see Mt. 4:5-7).

He was tempted again by the Pharisees (see Mt. 12:9-21), when they brought him a man with a shriveled hand and asked him if it was lawful to heal on the Sabbath. Behind their question was the threat that if he did not agree to make rigid observance of the Law the supreme rule of his religion they would kill him. This was a logical follow-up to the second temptation in the desert, when Jesus refused to "put God to the test" by throwing himself down from the temple. Jesus' answer to the devil at that time indicated that he did not believe in "tempting fate" by risking death unnecessarily. So why, they argued now, should he risk their hostility — which would be deadly — by refusing to go along with their request to give first priority in religion to observance of the Law?

Jesus responded to the Pharisees, "Suppose one of you has a sheep that falls into a pit on the Sabbath: won't you go down into the pit yourself to lift it out?"

When Jesus says "the pit" here, he really means the grave. And the word translated as "lift out" (*egerei*) is the same word Jesus uses later when he says that he is going to be "put to death and *raised up* on the third day" (Mt. 16:21). Jesus is talking about death and resurrection. He is saying that, although he would not throw himself off the temple to test God's faithfulness when the devil tempted him to do it, he will throw himself into the grave to save, to "raise up" his people when the time for that comes.

He is countering here the Church's constant temptation to back away from "going down into the pit" when faced with opposition and the threat of persecution. His way of saving the world is not to align himself with the power-structures of society for the sake of saving his life in this world, but to "bear witness to the truth" by laying down his life for his sheep in testimony to the reality of eternal life (see John 10:11; 18:37).

This same temptation appears a third time (Mt. 17:22-23) in the form of non-comprehension on the part of his own disciples, when Jesus repeats to them that he is going to be delivered over to his enemies and put to death — and rise again on the third day. They hear the first part of what he says, but the promise of resurrection passes them by; it just isn't real to them. At Jesus' words, the Gospel tells us, his disciples are "overwhelmed with grief." In spite of his efforts to explain it to them, they just cannot accept God's way of saving the world by "enduring evil with love." They still echo in their hearts the cry of Psalm 30:10: "What gain would there be from my lifeblood, from my going down into the grave? Would dust give you thanks or proclaim your faithfulness?" They have not put on the "mind of Christ."

And so it is, even two thousand years after his resurrection: it still is not real to us. We are still tempted to act, on a day-to-day basis, as if life after death were not a practical consideration. Our constant temptation is to manage our time and our resources; to choose schools and jobs and lifestyle; to acquire property and defend it, as if there were nothing beyond the grave significant enough to give real direction to our choices in this life.

We don't speak like the Sadducees, but our natural tendency is to think like them. We need to work at putting on the "mind of Christ."

According to the mind of Christ, what appears to be success in this world is often the greatest failure; and what appears to be failure is often the only real means to success. Jesus demonstrated this the day he entered Jerusalem in mock triumph on a donkey to let himself be put to death. We believe that through the apparent defeat of all his hopes and plans on the cross Jesus established his Kingdom and redeemed the world. And we believe that if Christian efforts to transform society are carried out in the same loving, sacrificial spirit Jesus showed on the cross, then even through the apparent failure of those efforts he is doing it still. The resurrection of Jesus is the source and foundation of all Christian hope for "success" in this world and the next. If life after death is a vain hope, there is no hope at all.

The Sadduceees would restrict success and personal fulfillment to the time-frame of this life, and all hope to the dimensions of this world. This is pure myopia.

The Third Temptation (Matthew 22:34-40)

Even though the Pharisees were natural enemies of the Sadducees, they followed with interest the Sadducees' effort to make Jesus look bad. Their own previous effort to "trap him in his speech" in alliance with the Herodians failed when he sidestepped their question about the payment of taxes. And now, when they hear that he has also silenced the Sadducees, they gather together for one more try.

One of the group, who is a scribe specialized in the study of the Law, asks the question designed to "trip him up": "Teacher, which commandment in the law is the greatest?"

Jesus answers, "You shall love the Lord, your God, with all your heart, with all your soul, and with all your mind. This is the greatest and the first commandment."

Then he adds, "The second is like it: You shall love your

neighbor as yourself."

And he concludes, "On these two commandments the whole law is based, and the prophets as well"

The idolatry of divided response

What the Pharisees are doing here is trying to "make a deal" with God. They have already assumed that what religion is all about is keeping laws, and they have boiled down all the obligations in the Old Testament to 613 laws: 248 positive commands and 365 prohibitions. They have further categorized these as "light" or "heavy," according to the seriousness of the behavior they deal with.[8]

Now the Pharisees are assuming that to keep all the laws all the time is not possible, or perhaps too much to ask, and they are asking which law is the most important. Then, if some people do not want to be perfect, they will at least know what they have to do to "pass."

This is idolatry. First it is idolatry to make the goal of religion consist in observing laws, because then those laws (and the human satisfaction which comes from observing them) become the focus of our devotion, and not the person of God.

Secondly, to ask which law is the greatest is idolatry because in recognizing many laws as the supreme reality of religion the Pharisees are recognizing many gods. (Idolatry is by definition polytheistic: since no one creature or created good contains all goodness in itself, those who direct their lives toward created values must accept a number of goods as their gods). To ask which law is highest among the laws is like asking which god is highest among the gods. And this implies that we will be rationing out our response to each god according to its merit. We will observe each law according to its rank in the hierarchy of laws. This is idolatry.

What Jesus' answer does is show that the refusal of total love is idolatry. There is only one God and one response that is worthy of him: the response of total love. Measured love is not perfect love. One might question whether, as God understands love, a rationed love is love at all. Certainly a divided love of God is a contradiction in terms: love that is divided between God and any creature is not love of God as God, because God can only be known and loved authentically as the All.

Love divided between God and anything or anyone else is idolatry. That is why those who divide their love between God and other goods cannot really know God. Only the "pure of heart" can "see God." Only those who love him with an unmixed love understand and appreciate God as the All he really is.

And in the same way, those who are not pure and undivided in their response of love to God cannot understand what Jesus teaches. Jesus teaches love for God. The only love that can truly be given to God as God is undivided love. Those who refuse to surrender their whole hearts, their whole minds, their whole beings to God in love are by this fact blocking themselves both from knowing God and from understanding the teaching of Jesus.

Jesus is not really answering the Pharisees' question. As he did with the question about taxes, he is sidestepping it. He answers by proclaiming, not the "greatest commandment," but the *only* commandment: the only one which makes the observance of any commandment authentic worship of God.

"You must love the Lord, your God, with your whole heart, soul and mind. Any observance of the Law which does not come from the desire to do this is inauthentic worship of God."

In his response to the question Jesus is condensing into one concept the whole of his New Law as presented in the Sermon on the Mount. To those who find his teaching there unrealistic, or literally "too hard" to understand — that is, unintelligible simply because it appears to be too hard to carry out into action — he responds with one idea. If we can accept it, everything else will be clear and intelligible to us. And the one idea is simply a call to perfect love.[9]

This is what the religion of Jesus Christ is all about: perfect love of God and perfect love of others. Growing to perfect love. If this is not what we are aiming at and working towards, we have not embraced the Christian way of life.

This is a "hard saying." For centuries it was commonplace in the Church to teach that there are two ways to follow Jesus Christ: the "way of the commandments" and the "way of the counsels." The "way of the commandments" was for the laity, who aimed at nothing more than keeping out of sin by observing the Ten Commandments and the laws of the Church. The "way of the counsels" was for those who took religious vows of poverty, celibacy and obedience. The vowed life was called the "way of perfection."

This split-level description of Christianity was based on Jesus' answer to the young man who asked him, "Teacher, what must I do to possess everlasting life?"

Jesus told him to keep the commandments. The young man answered that he had done this all his life. "What more do I need to do?"

Jesus said to him, "*If you want to be perfect*, go sell your possessions and give to the poor. Then you will have treasure in heaven. After that, come back and follow me" (see Mt. 19:16-22).

The interpretation given to this story comes out of a mindset which looks at the teaching of Jesus in terms of obligation. The first question people with this mentality ask about any teaching is, "Is this something we have to do or do not have to do?" From this point of view, Jesus' answer, "Go, sell everything you have" can only be one of two things: either a command or an exhortation. And since it has never been considered obligatory in the Christian community to literally sell all of one's possessions and give the proceeds to the poor, the conclusion is that Jesus is simply giving some advice here. To those who desire to follow him perfectly Jesus says, "Embrace a life of poverty; give everything away and live the way I did on earth." But to people who just want to "save their souls," he says it is enough to keep the Commandments and stay out of sin.

The same reasoning has been applied to another statement of Jesus: "There are some who have voluntarily renounced sex for the sake of the Kingdom of God. Let anyone who can accept this teaching do it!" This was identified as the voluntary commitment to celibacy. It was lumped together with the exhortation to "sell everything" and presented as the second counsel of Jesus to those who would be "perfect" (see Mt. 19:3-12).

Out of this way of interpreting the Gospel came the Scriptural justification for the eremitical or "hermit" life — the lifestyle of those who choose to "seek perfection" by living alone in voluntary poverty, celibacy and prayer. Later, as the hermits began to live in community and to form monasteries — and later religious congregations — the commitments to poverty and celibacy were formalized in religious vows, and the vow of obedience to a religious rule was added (or made to embrace the other two). The lifestyle based on these three commitments — the vows of poverty, celibacy and obedience — came to be known in the Church as "religious life" or the way of the "evangelical counsels" — the way Jesus counsels every Christian to live who would be "perfect," but which he imposes on no one.

There is no doubt that the life of religious vows is in fact a "way of perfection." This has been proven again and again by its fruits in those who have given themselves to a life of prayer lived in real and voluntary poverty; in celibacy understood as a way of living out the baptismal commitment every Christian makes to seek perfect union of mind and heart and will with Jesus Christ in love; and in obedience to a religious rule that has passed the test of time and received Church approval.

The lifestyle of religious orders does not depend for its Christian authenticity on the faulty interpretation that was given to these texts from the Gospel. It is probably more true to say that the interpretation came out of those committed to this lifestyle than to say that the lifestyle came out of this interpretation. Scripture scholars today say there is no justification in the Gospels for a theory of "two-track Christianity" — a "way of the counsels" for those who would be perfect and a "way of the commandments" for those who just want to do what they "have to do" to get to heaven. When Jesus said to the young man, "If you want to be perfect..." he meant, "If you want to follow the perfect way of life, the way of life I teach, the way that leads to life in its fullness...." In other words, he was talking about the *Christian* life, and he was saying that this is what everyone needs to do in order to be his follower.

The mistaken interpretation of Jesus' words did no damage to those who accepted poverty, celibacy and obedience as a "way of perfection," because this way of life is in fact a way of perfection. But damage was done by those who concluded that every other lifestyle was *not* a "way of perfection" and preached this to the laity. Out of this mind-frame came the perception of the lay life — by clergy and laity alike — as "second-string Christianity," with a complacent abandonment of the "life of perfection" to those who were called to it by special vocation from God, such as the religious Brothers, priests and Sisters.

Out of this mindframe came all the Sunday sermons which aimed at nothing more than keeping the flock from committing "mortal sin." Out of this came the "hell and damnation" approach in retreats and parish missions, which aimed at nothing more than getting people to go to confes-

sion and resolve in fear and trembling to "sin no more."
And out of this came the assumption — unarticulated but
still active today — that some behavior which would be
clearly inappropriate for priests and nuns, who are called to
be "holy," can be taken for granted in the laity, who are
not. The behavior judged acceptable for the laity ranges
from the molehill to the mountain: from using bad language
to killing human beings in battle. Even St. Thomas Aqui-
nas, saint and genius that he was, fell into this error.

Thomas taught that the clergy could not engage in war *because it does not fit in with their character or role [their
'persona'] as clerics.* Priests, says St. Thomas, are *ordained for service at the altar,* upon which, under the sacramental sign, the passion of Christ is made present. Therefore it is not appropriate for those in holy orders to kill or
shed blood; instead they should be prepared to shed their
own blood for Christ, *so as to imitate in deed what they
portray in their ministry.*[10]

St. Thomas may be focusing on a particular question of his
day concerning the clergy. But he appears to be taking for
granted here that the laity do not have the *persona*, the role
of being the Body of Christ on earth; that they are not as
actively engaged in offering the Mass as the ordained priest
is; and that what is enacted in the liturgy is not something
the laity are called to live out in action. This amounts to
saying that, not only "real" Christianity, but full participation in the Mass itself is reserved for those who are called
by a special grace and "vocation," over and above Baptism,
to live the Gospel in its entirety.

No one would teach this today, although it is still generally
taken for granted in practice. Many of the laity still accept
in themselves and in other lay persons behavior which they
would find shocking in a priest. And many still think of the
ordained priest as "offering" the Mass and of themselves as
spectators. But at least the Church has officially and force-
fully declared in explicit language that "two-track Chris-

tianity" is an error to be vigorously abandoned.

The most powerful modern expression of this truth was given in Vatican Council II, when the bishops of the world proclaimed that the "perfection of love" is the goal of every Christian way of life. More recently, Pope John Paul II has urged every Christian to live "evangelical poverty" as a means to overcome the unequal distribution of goods which is an obstacle to peace in the world. He extended the call of voluntary poverty to the laity by saying that the choice "not to accumulate the goods of this passing world" is "a duty intrinsic to the Christian vocation, no less than the duty of working to overcome poverty." In other words, we are not talking anymore about a "counsel," but about a necessary ingredient of Christian living.[11]

What, then, about the question of obligation? Does everyone literally have to "sell everything" in order to be a Christian?

In a sense, yes. Jesus compared entrance into the Kingdom of God to a merchant who sold everything he had for the "pearl of great price." He said the Kingdom was like a treasure hidden in a field, and that we have to sell everything we have in order to buy that field. This is not surprising when we recall his teaching that all those who choose to "save their lives" on this earth will lose them, and that those who want to follow him must be willing to "take up the cross" and offer their lives as he did for the life of the world (see Mt. 13:44-46 and 16:24-26).

But the example of "selling everything" is just that: an example. It is neither a rule nor an exhortation; it is simply an example of the kind of gesture which would express some understanding of what following Jesus is all about. To become a disciple of Jesus, to enroll in his school of perfection, one has to pass an "entrance exam." Basically, this consists in showing, through some voluntary choice, through some credible gesture, that one understands what one is signing up for. The dramatic gesture of giving everything away to the poor would do it. So would the dramatic gesture of "becoming a eunuch for the Kingdom of God." Both of these sacrifices express an understanding that to follow Jesus one has to be willing to give all for All. It is only on the basis of that understanding that one will be able to understand anything else Jesus teaches. But these are just examples; there are other gestures that express the same radical understanding.

As a matter of fact, every Christian makes such a dramatic gesture at the moment of Baptism, although it is not certain that all understand what they are doing. It has become our custom, legitimate but unfortunate, to baptize by a gesture which is a symbol of washing rather than by one which is a symbol of dying and rising. We pour water on the head instead of immersing the whole body as was customary in the early Church. This has obscured the basic meaning of Baptism for us. The gesture of pouring suggests that what Baptism is essentially all about is *washing*. This symbol makes us think of Baptism as a sacrament which "washes away Original Sin."

In reality, what Baptism is essentially all about is *dying and rising*. Baptism is the act of accepting to "die" here and now to everything life on this earth has to offer, in order to live entirely and exclusively for Jesus Christ and his Kingdom. In Baptism by immersion this is clear: those baptized go down into the water as into the grave, and they emerge like Jesus from the tomb to live a new life, the divine life of grace, as his risen Body on earth.

What Baptism really expresses is the giving-up of the life we received at birth in exchange for the eternal life offered by Jesus. Implicit in this gesture is the renunciation of anything and everything which stands in the way, or might come to stand in the way, of living the life of grace "to the full." Those who accept the dying and rising of Baptism have already "sold everything," in the sense that they have renounced all claims on the kind of life in this world that money can provide. They have renounced all desire for riches as opposed to poverty, asking only for that style of life which will best enable them to show their love for Jesus Christ on earth and to grow in that love. And the same is true for everything else that is part of life on this earth: at Baptism Christians give up all accepted and ratified attachment of the will to money, marriage, family ties, career, and even physical survival — not to mention status and "success" on earth — in order to dedicate themselves with pure, undivided hearts to loving and serving God perfectly according to the teaching and example of Jesus Christ.[12]

If we look at our Baptismal commitment in terms of obligation, this explanation makes it a crushing burden. But if we look at it in terms of a commitment to perfect love, nothing less than what we have said above makes any sense at all.

Unless we accept perfect love, total love, passionate love for God as the "first and greatest commandment" — as the root and basis for every other commandment — nothing that Jesus teaches makes any sense. Either we want to surrender in love everything we are and have, and abandon ourselves entirely to God's every will and desire, or we do not want to follow the way of Jesus.

Why is this temptation a temptation?

Why would anyone be tempted to restricted love for God? Why would anyone refuse God's invitation to enter into a relationship of total, passionate love?

I think the answer is: despair. Perhaps "discouragement" would be the word we relate to more immediately. Or we could call it just a lack of sufficient faith and hope. Down deep, we just don't believe that this relationship is possible for us: not with God, not with Jesus Christ. We don't believe we can love him enough to experience on earth the fruits of total abandonment to God.

Like a couple whose marriage has lost its soul, we turn our relationship with God into a contract. We make an implicit "deal" with God: "I will do such-and-such for you if you will do such-and-such for me." We draw lines and map out territory. We agree to keep on our side of the bed if God will keep on his. We agree on rules for interaction which legitimize reserve on both sides — in fact, impose it. We agree to do certain things for God, and to do them faithfully. But we will not abandon ourselves totally to him in love, and we do not want him to abandon himself totally to us. In our hearts we have decided that total love won't work; that it might be a possibility for some couples, but not for us; not for ourselves and God. And so we settle for less.

We ask God, "What do you expect of me? What do I have to do to keep you happy?" — which is a way of acknowledging that true happiness is no longer even in focus; that nothing more is being aimed at than co-existence in peace, and even with pleasantness, both parties having renounced all claim to total love because they have mutually given up all hope of it.

We ask God, "What is the greatest commandment — or what are the really important commandments — of the Law? What will you settle for? What do you require of me under pain of 'mortal sin'? Tell me, and I will do that. And on your side, you must agree to let me into heaven when I die. That is all I ask — and the answer to a few prayers now and then." And we settle down to co-existence with God in a religion of unrewarding mediocrity.

This is the greatest temptation of all.

CHAPTER TEN:
HOW WE LOSE THE WAY
"The Temptations" — Matthew 22:15-40

Summary

In the three questions of the Pharisees and Sadducees we see a recurrence, under a different form, of the same three temptations Jesus experienced in the desert at the beginning of his ministry.

The First Temptation (Matthew 22:15-22): "Is it according to the law of God to pay the census tax to Caesar or not?" This is the temptation to *change the goal of Christ's mission.* It comes in the form of an invitation to seek credibility by putting religion at the service of some popular movement which seems to answer the current need of the world; that is, to subordinate the Church's goal to that of a political party.

Cooperation with the state or with secular movements as such is not wrong; the temptation comes when the Church is asked to make gestures which, overtly or subtly, cause the Church to appear as an ally of the state, or of any other group or movement.

The motive for doing this is the seductive expectation of imminent success. Those who fall into this temptation are jumping on a bandwagon because it seems to be moving faster than the Parousia. It is more humanly satisfying to get somewhere, to achieve any visible result at all, than to keep working and waiting indefinitely for the kingdom of God to appear.

The Second Temptation (Matthew 22:23-33): The Sadducees come to Jesus with a problem about the resurrection of the body. "Jesus tells them they are speaking nonsense because they don't understand anything about the Scriptures, the power of God, or about what the risen life was really like.

The Sadducees ar attacking the very idea that there is fulfillment to be found in life after death. This strikes at the heart of everything we believe about the value of Christ's death on the cross. Without the resurrection, his way of saving the world through dying is an illusion. And his call to us to continue saving the world by "taking up the cross" is absurdity. Without the resurrection, there is nothing to live for but the "pursuit of happiness" on this earth. And if this is the highest good available to us, we will naturally fight and kill to acquire or preserve whatever we think makes it possible.

The Sadducees speak for all of us who base our plans and choices on the practical assumption that this life is "where it's really at." Our constant temptation is to manage our time and resources as if there were nothing beyond the grave significant enough to give real direction to our choices in this life.

The resurrection of Jesus is the source and foundation of all Christian belief in the value of living and dying. The Sadducees would restrict success and personal fulfillment to the time-frame of this life, and all hope to the dimensions of this world. This is a temptation to myopia.

The Third Temptation (Matthew 22:34-40): The Pharisees ask which commandment in the law is the greatest. Jesus answers, "You shall love the Lord with all your heart."

The temptation here is *to "make a deal" with God*. Assuming that to keep all the laws all the time is too much, we ask which law is the most important. Then, if we do not want to be "perfect," we will at least know what we have to do to "pass."

This is idolatry. If we make the goal of religion consist in observing laws, then those laws become the focus of our devotion, not the person of God. And to ask which law is highest among the laws is like asking which god is highest among the gods. It implies that we will be rationing out our response to each god according to its merit.

Jesus' answer is that there is only one God and one response that is worthy of him: the response of total love. A divided love of God is not love of God as God, because God can only be known and loved authentically as the All. Love divided between God and anything or anyone else is idolatry.

The heart of this temptation is discouragement: down deep, we just don't believe that this relationship of total love is possible for us or that we can love God enough to experience on earth the fruits of total abandonment to God. So we make an implicit "deal" with God, a "contract": "I will do this much for you if you will do this much for me." We settle down to co-existence with God in a religion of unrewarding mediocrity.

This is the greatest temptation of all.

Have you understood?

What is the danger in making gestures which cause the Church to appear as an ally of the state, or of any other group or movement? Why are we tempted to do this?

How do Christians who believe in resurrection nevertheless live as if this world were really "where it's at"? In particular, what ultimately motivates all the violence we use against others?

Give two reasons why it is idolatry to ask which commandment of the law is the greatest? Why is it idolatry to love anything else in addition to God?

What is at the heart of our refusal to try to love God with our whole heart, mind and soul? What do we do instead?

What is the challenge of this chapter? To our faith? To our hope? To our love?

Making it your own

What are the key thoughts in this chapter? (Jot them down and give the page number where each is found).

What questions do I have about this chapter? (Bring them up in discussion or ask someone who should know the answers).

What struck me the most in this chapter? After reading this chapter, what do I understand better than I did before? What do I appreciate more?

What do I think is the point of the whole chapter? What response does Matthew want to evoke from those who read or hear this part of his Gospel?

What can I use as a visible reminder (a symbol) to keep me aware of the challenge of this chapter? Where will I put it?

Questions for prayer

Does it make me feel good to see my Church involved in any secular, idealistic or political movement? Why? How do I feel about flying the American flag on church property? Why? What are the good and bad, true and false messages this gives?

How much does the hope of rising from the dead influence the deci-

sions I make from day to day? Has my belief in the resurrection changed the direction of my life in any way?

What do I do, not just because I am obliged to do it, but because I want to grow in love for God? What do I value for itself alone, without any reference to God? Is this idolatry?

How can I apply to my life what I have come to see by reflecting on this chapter? What concrete action do I choose to perform to express my belief in what I have seen?

FOOTNOTES

[1] See John L. McKenzie in the *Jerome Biblical Commentary*, 43:150, on Mt. 22:15-22. Other quotes from McKenzie in this chapter are from *Did I Say That?*, Thomas More Press, 1973, ch. 1, pp. 9-22; and from *The Power and the Wisdom*, Bruce, 1965, ch. 12. pp. 244-245, 251.

[2] For details and statistics of the persecution in Latin America up to 1978, and of United States collaboration in it, see Penny Lernoux, *Cry of the People*, Garden City, N.Y., Doubleday, 1980; reprinted by Penguin Books, 1982. This book received the Sidney Hillman Foundation book award for 1981 and was cited by *The New York Times Book Review* as one of the most notable nonfiction books of 1980. See also the official report of the Guatemalan bishops' Recovery of Historical Memory Project (REMHI), on human rights abuses in Guatemala. The report "is based on the testimonies of 65,000 people interviewed in their communities by some 600 pastoral agents. It documents 55,000 victims of a total of 150,000, and 440 massacres in 36 years of war and genocide" (*Maryknoll* magazine, April, 2000, p. 21). The bishop in charge of the project, Juan Gerardi, was beaten to death at his home two days after he presented the report to the press for publication. Two Guatemalan army officers, Col. Disrael Lima Estrada and his son, Capt. Byron Lima Oliva, were convicted of the murder along with a military bodyguard and a priest-accomplice. An abridged version of the report in English has been published by Orbis Books, 1999, under the title *Guatemala, Never Again!* See *National Catholic Reporter*, June 29, 2001, p. 14.

[3] In an interview conducted by Evelyn Blanck for the Guatemalan magazine *Crónica*, Bishop Martinez was asked whether the Church takes part in politics. He answered that in a general sense, every citizen

is obliged to participate in furthering the common good. But when it comes to partisan politics, he said, a bishop would be very stupid if, in order to dedicate himself to that, he were to lose "the treasure entrusted to his hands, the word of God." He went on to say, "On more than one occasion Bishop Gerardi made it known to me that they wanted to compromise him as being on the side of the left and he said, '*No. I am a bishop of the Catholic Church.*'"

[4] See the example previously cited in chapter ten of *No Power But Love*, footnote 8, p. 200: When Eugenio Pacelli, future Pope Pius XII, was Pius XI's Vatican Secretary of State, he

> helped to smooth Mussolini's way to power by withdrawing Vatican support from the Catholic Popular Party and causing the resignation of its leader, the priest Don Sturzo. The Pope reaped his reward when Mussolini signed the Lateran Concordat and Treaty with the Vatican in 1929... The treaty granted the Pope a munificent sum of money [the Vatican was approaching bankruptcy] and complete sovereignty over Vatican City..., accorded to the Catholic religion a privileged status in Italy and imposed Catholic teaching as the norm for religion courses in the state school system." (Father Thomas Bokenkotter, *A Concise History of the Catholic Church*, Doubleday, 1977, p 368).

[5] It is significant in this context that although Church authorities are insistent about the value of clerical garb for priests, they not only allow priests serving the military to put aside clerical dress, but also allow them to wear a uniform that positively identifies them with the military profession. The normal dress for chaplains on military bases, even in peacetime, is the camouflaged "battle dress uniform" with combat boots.

[6] On the other hand, 71% of American married couples pray together: 34% "a lot" and 27% "sometimes." Andrew Greeley, *The Faithful Attraction*, TOR, N.Y., 1991, pp. 24, 38, citing the Gallup surveys, *Love and Marriage I and II*, done for *Psychology Today* in the winter of 1989-90.

[7] In addition to the nuclear devastation of Hiroshima and Nagasaki, some outstanding examples of American willingness to sacrifice the innocent in order to further our war aims are the fire-bombing of Dresden and Tokyo in World War II, the economic sanctions applied against the whole population of Iraq after the Gulf War, and the pro-

motion of terrorism, assassination and torture against the native populations of Latin America through soldiers trained at the School of the Americas located at Fort Benning, Georgia. See Jack Nelson-Pallmeyer, *School of Assassins*, Orbis Books, 1997.

[8] See the *Jerome Biblical Commentary*, 43:152, on Mt. 22:36.

[9] Actually, this isn't new. Jesus taught it in the Sermon on the Mount when He said, "You must be made perfect as your heavenly Father is perfect;" and again, "Seek first [that is, only] the reign of God and its way of holiness." He also taught it when He laid down the conditions for entering into the Kingdom: selling all for the "pearl of great price" and the "treasure hidden in the field" (Mt. 13:44-46); and the conditions for being His disciple: being willing to have "nowhere to lay one's head" and to "let the dead bury their dead" (Mt. 8:19-22); to "sell everything and give it to the poor" (Mt. 19:21); and to "take up one's cross" and not seek to save one's life in this world (Mt. 16:24-26).

[10] *Summa Theologiae*, Question 40, article 2.

[11] See the Constitution on the Church, paragraph 11: "All the faithful, whatever their condition or state, are called by the Lord, each in his own way, to that perfect holiness whereby the Father Himself is perfect." And paragraph 40: "All the faithful of Christ of whatever rank or status are called to the fullness of the Christian life and to the perfection of charity." And in the Decree on Ecumenism, chapter one: "Every Catholic must therefore aim at Christian perfection." The text refers us to James 1:4 and Romans 12:1-2. (In Abbott, page 348). Pope John Paul's teaching about perfection and poverty was given in his message for the World Day of Peace, January 1, 1993, entitled, "If You Want Peace, Reach Out to the Poor" (in *Origens*, Vol. 22, No. 28 [Dec. 29, 1992], pp. 476-479). For a commentary on this see David M. Knight, "Adjusting the Focus of Formation: Poverty, Peace and the Pope," in *Journal of Spiritual Formation*, Duquesne University, Vol. XV, No. 1, Feb., 1994, pp. 47-63.

[12] St. Ignatius of Loyola presents this attitude as the "first principle and foundation" of the Christian life:

> People are created to praise, reverence, and serve God our Lord, and by this means to save their souls. And all other things on the face of the earth are created for people, in order to help them achieve the end for which they are created.

It follows from this that we need to use things in the measure they help us achieve our end, and rid ourselves of them in the measure they hinder us in that.

For this reason we have to make ourselves indifferent with regard to all created things, insofar as this is left to our free choice and is not forbidden; so that we do not desire, from our side, health rather than sickness, affluence rather than poverty, respect rather than disrespect, a long life rather than a short one, and so for everything else. We only desire and choose that which leads us to the end for which we are created (*Spiritual Exercises*, no. 23).

Chapter Eleven
The Once And Future King
Revelation of Identity — Matthew 22:41-46

Chapters twenty-one and twenty-two of Matthew's Gospel show Jesus repeatedly raising a question and refusing to give a direct answer to it. Instead, he answers in such a way that he is in reality answering another question which was a major stumbling-block to the early Church — and still is to us today, even if we are not always explicitly aware of it.

The question he refuses to answer directly is always the same: "Who is Jesus? Is he the promised Messiah, the 'Son of David'?"

The question he answers is: "How can Jesus be — or how could he have been — the Messiah, since God let him be defeated and killed?"

A series of side-steps

Jesus is already avoiding the question when he tells his disciples how to answer anyone who challenges them when they go into Bethphage to appropriate a donkey for him. He tells them just to say, "The Master (or "owner" or "Lord") has need of it." Nothing more.

When he rides into Jerusalem on the donkey, with the crowds shouting, "Hosanna to the Son of David!" the "whole city" starts asking, "Who is this?" The only answer they get is, "the prophet Jesus, from Nazareth in Galilee."

Then the chief priests and scribes reproach him for letting the children shout "Hosanna to the Son of David!" In answer, Jesus quotes Psalm 8 to them: "Out of the mouth of infants and nursing babies you have called forth praise." Psalm 8 is clearly talking about praise of God himself. But Jesus draws no conclusions.

After that the chief priests and elders ask him directly, "On what authority are you doing these things? Who has given you this power?" And Jesus responds by asking them a question in turn: "What authority did John the Baptizer have? Who authorized him?" When they refuse to answer his question, he refuses to answer theirs — except to warn them in three parables about the consequences of their refusal to convert: first, by their failure to repent in response to John's preaching; secondly, by their rejection of himself as "son and heir" and "keystone of the structure"; and thirdly, by their indifference to God's invitation to the "wedding feast" of his Son.

Then he dismisses as trivial the Pharisees' and Herodians' question about paying taxes to Caesar; he tells the Sadducees their question about the resurrection of the dead is nonsense; and he answers the Pharisees' question about the "greatest commandment of the Law" by showing that the question itself is idolatry. All three of these questions are attempts to discredit his authority and to silence the crowd's acclaim by leading him into a response which will misrepresent his mission.

Jesus refuses to answer any questions about his identity which are raised because of the power or *authority* he is exercising, or because of the *acclaim* he is receiving. Jesus doesn't accept either one of these as the starting-point for questions about his identity

In the way he answers — or refuses to answer — all these questions, Jesus is teaching us how to find the answer to another one: a question which has been a problem to believers from the earliest times until now: "How could Jesus have been the Messiah, since God let him be defeated and killed?" Today we ask, "How can the Church be the continuation of Christ's saving presence on earth when the Church's pastoral efforts appear so frequently to be failing or frustrated?"

How can we, the Church (the "assembly") of his followers, be right in believing in him when everything seems to be going so wrong? Where is all this promised power of God which is supposed to work such wonders on earth? Why isn't the whole world flocking in to be converted? Why are we ourselves so torn by factions and divisions? Why is there still so much violence, poverty and exploitation; so much sin in us and power of sin all around us? How can we say the "reign of God" has begun while ruin is still on a rampage?

By refusing to give to the people who questioned him the kind of answers they were expecting, Jesus was teaching us not to expect our questions to be answered in the obvious, simplistic way we would like. Yes, Jesus is Savior and Messiah, the promised King and "Son of David." But no, he is not going to be the kind of Savior our culture leads us to expect and desire. Yes, the reign of God has begun. But, no, Jesus is not going to reign on earth with power in the manner of earthly kings. Yes, Jesus has overcome sin and death; but no, he is not going to abolish all sin and suffering instantly, either in individuals or in society, by a dramatic use of divine power. The reign of God has begun, but it will be extended slowly, by divine grace working through human efforts, like the leaven which causes the whole mass of dough to rise, like the mustard seed which slowly grows from its tiny beginning to become the "largest of plants." It will triumph through the invisible power of God working in the only-too-visible powerlessness of human instruments.

If power and prestige are the starting point of our search for signs of the reign of God present among us, we will never find them. The reign of God is marked by powerlessness and unpopularity.

In his answers to the questions presented to him Jesus does proclaim his divine authority and power — but in a way which says that his followers will have to wait if they want to know him as he really is. If they want to see him in all of his glory they will have to persevere in faith and fidelity, believing and working and enduring in spite of all appearances until he comes again.

The answer to the question, "How can Jesus be a loser Messiah?" is that Jesus is not losing but winning. His victory, however, will not be made evident until the end of time. So enduring faith in Jesus is impossible without enduring hope. And to express faith and hope through persevering efforts to establish the reign of God on earth is enduring love.

A final fly-over: seeing the map

In Matthew's chapters twenty-one and twenty-two we see again the same cycle of seven themes which we find recurring four times in Matthew as he asks the questions that can be taken as the thematic structure of his Gospel: I. "Can you accept *Jesus* as Savior and Teacher of Life?" II. "Can you accept the *Church* as the continuing presence of Jesus on earth?" III. "Can you accept the way of the *cross*, the rejection of power and violence, as God's way of saving the world?" IV. Can you accept to *persevere* in faith and fidelity until Christ comes again?" .[1]

As these themes recur in this final part of Matthew's Gospel, the underlying message behind them all is that we are being called to *active waiting*; that is, to *persevere* in *faith* and *fidelity*. We are called to keep believing in Jesus as victor and Lord, and to express this faith by undiscouraged labor in the vineyard until Christ comes again.

The first theme: *Mission*: First, by the way he enters Jerusalem as king Jesus alerts us to change our expectations about the nature of his mission. He lets himself be proclaimed "Son of David" and Messiah, but his triumphal procession is a procession of poverty and powerlessness on a borrowed donkey, symbol of peace. This is the only triumphal entry of the Son of David into "David's city" that his followers will ever see. What he is going to do in Jerusalem will not fulfill his people's expectations of the Messiah. But it will surpass their wildest hopes and dreams. Jesus' mission is to inaugurate the reign of God, but not to bring it to immediate perfection. Jesus will indeed save the world by conquering sin and death on the cross, but the work of extending his salvation to every member and to every activity of the human race will continue until the end of time. It will be carried on by Jesus risen and working in his Church; that is, through the weakness and sinfulness of his human body on earth. And as Jesus comes to "full stature" in his body on earth, he and the whole human race will come into the unimaginable glory of undiminished likeness to God.

The second theme: *Conflict*: Jesus' entry into Jerusalem causes an "earthquake" of excitement, as friends and enemies alike are called into "crisis" by the question, "Who is this?" In answer to the question Jesus makes the dramatic, prophetic and ambiguous gesture of driving the money-makers out of the temple. He shows his authority — one time, to make his point — but he doesn't rally his supporters to occupy the temple and reclaim it by force; he leaves the chief priests and their allies still entrenched and in control. Then his followers gather around him, but they are the "blind and the lame" who come to him for healing and the children who shout his praises. These are the only "power structure" he chooses to have. And this decision to exercise his divine power through powerlessness will be a continuing source of conflict, of "crisis," to believers and non-believers alike until he comes in glory.

The third theme: *Triumph*: Jesus withers up a fig tree as a sign of what is going to happen to the power-structure of Israel which rejects him. But that is all he uses his divine power to do: to give a symbol, a sign, a preview of his triumph. His enemies remain in power, and Jesus himself is delivered into their hands to be visibly defeated and destroyed. In the darkness of faith he perseveres in believing — and asks his followers to persevere in believing — in the

invisible redemption of the world which he is ac-
complishing through his death. The only triumph we can
count on being visible today is the triumph of grace enabling Jesus' followers to keep believing when everything is
dark, to keep hoping when everything seems hopeless, to
keep loving when love feels like an empty gesture, and to
keep praying when our prayers seem like echo-less emis-
sions lost in a silent sky. For his triumph as the world understands "triumph," the human race will have to wait until
he comes to full stature in his body totally redeemed.

The fourth theme: *Call to conversion*: When the chief
priests and elders challenge his authority to do what he is
doing, Jesus summons them to conversion. He urges them
to take a stance toward him, to declare themselves, to accept and use their human powers of intellect and will to cooperate with the grace offered them and enter into life. But
they refuse to choose. And in response, Jesus refuses to answer their question until they answer his. He is teaching us
that the answer to our question about his identity can only
be given in the answer we make ourselves, in the act of our
response. The gift of adult faith can only be received in the
act of choosing to believe. And it is only by persevering in
faith until Jesus comes to fullness that we will grow to the
experience of faith in its fullness. The fullness of faith and
of understanding can only be given to those who are willing
to persevere in the faith they already have.

The fifth theme: *Experience of God*: When the Pharisees,
chief priests and elders refuse the act of conversion by refusing to answer his question about John's baptism, Jesus
warns them in three parables that they are cutting themselves off from experiencing God in his Kingdom. By focusing all their attention on the appearances of religion they
are blinding themselves to the absence of real religion in
their lives. As long as they refuse to see they are empty
they can never be filled. Conversion to God — or away
from God — is accompanied by an experience of related-

ness (or of non-relatedness) to God. But if we "stonewall" God by refusing to respond at all, our silence will carry as its consequence the experience of the silence of God.

The sixth theme: *Temptations*: Jesus resists the three basic temptations to falsify his mission:

• By sidestepping the question about taxes to Caesar, he refuses to subordinate his mission to any political goal. He will not make himself a more acceptable Messiah and lose his own identity by joining forces with the powers of this earth to work for any merely human fulfillment, no matter how popular. The fulfillment he offers is not limited to the time and space of this world. And it is recognized only by faith.

• In refuting the Sadducees' argument against resurrection he refuses to limit his vision or his hopes to what he can accomplish by staying alive. The very thing which seems to be the defeat of his mission — his crucifixion — will be, in fact, the means for its accomplishment. And the apparent defeat of his Church down the ages will likewise be the formula for her victory. The means God has chosen for establishing his Kingdom are not intelligible to a perspective enclosed within the horizons of this world, limited to this life only. They are the "absurdity" of the cross, of overcoming evil by "enduring evil with love." But to those who understand the true meaning and value of time as the prelude to eternity they are "the power of God and the wisdom of God" (1Cor. 1:18-31). Our mission is to persevere in hope.

• Finally, in response to the Pharisees Jesus exposes the temptation we have to "make a deal" with God by negotiating for observance of the "essentials only" of our religion, the "important" laws, or those which bind under penalty of "mortal sin." Jesus identifies the "greatest commandment" as something which is not a specific law at all, but the unreserved commitment to total love which gives life to all lawobservance and to everything else we do. By declaring as the "greatest commandment" something which is not a particular, concrete action, but the total response of the ever-expandable capacity of our hearts to the infinite reality of God — Jesus abolishes forever the identification of religion with "religious observance." The religion of Jesus is very simple: it is to "be perfect" as our Father in heaven is perfect. Either we are aiming at this or we have not embraced the religion of Jesus. The only religion he preaches is a relationship of total, passionate love for God expressed in the unreserved surrender of ourselves. For this reason it follows that we can never say we have "arrived" at living our religion perfectly on this earth. Our response to God can never claim to be perfect until he comes to call forth from us the total abandonment of ourselves to him in death. Our religion is a summons to accept the reign of God over us and to help establish it throughout the world. God's reign will not be perfect until Jesus comes into his glory in every member of the human race. And therefore it is an essential element of our religion to work and to wait for the "blessed hope" which is the coming "to full stature" of our Savior, Jesus Christ, in every human heart. Our labor and constant wish for every person must be the prayer of Paul: "that you may know the love of Christ that surpasses knowledge, so that you may be filled with all the fullness of God" (Eph. 3:19). Our vocation as Christians is to strive for the perfection of love.

The seventh theme: *Further revelation of identity*: Now after all this, Jesus himself raises the question of his identity. It is Jesus who takes the initiative.

Since the Pharisees have all gathered together to ask him the question about the "greatest commandment," Jesus is able to pose his question to them as a body. What he wants is the answer of the Pharisees as such, their best shot as a group, not just the opinion of some particular one of them.

"Tell me," he says to them, "What is your opinion about the Messiah? Whose son is he?"

They answer, "David's. He is the son of David."

"Then how is it," Jesus asks, "that David by the Spirit calls him Lord, saying, 'The Lord said to my Lord, "Sit at my right hand, until I put your enemies under your feet"'? If David thus calls him Lord, how can he be his son?" (See Psalm 110:1).

The Pharisees can't answer this. And Matthew concludes: "From that day on, no one dared to ask Jesus any more questions."

In the *Jerome Biblical Commentary* (on Mt. 22:41-46) Fr. John McKenzie explains that the Jews in Jesus' time did not pronounce the actual name of God, *Yahweh*, but substituted for it the title *Adonay*, "Lord," which was used only for God. The form *adoni*, meaning "my lord," was the usual Old Testament address for a king. So in the text that Jesus is quoting, what the people would have heard David saying was, "*Adonay* said to *adoni*..." or "Yahweh said to my lord, the king..." And Jesus asks, "Why would David have addressed his own son as 'my lord, the king'?"

According to McKenzie, if we just take this passage alone, without putting it into the context of the rest of Matthew's Gospel or using other texts to interpret it, all Jesus is doing here is demonstrating that the Pharisees are not competent to teach religion. They can't interpret a text from Scripture which talks about the Messiah, so why should anyone trust their opinion about the Messiah's identity? Who are they to judge? Whether they accept Jesus as the Messiah or not is unimportant, since they can't even explain the Scriptures which refer to him.

All Jesus actually does in this passage is raise a question without answering it. But in the context of the whole Gospel he is doing much more than that.

Matthew's goal from the beginning of his Gospel has been to present Jesus as the promised "Son of David." His theme has been that Jesus is the fulfillment of God's promises, the long-awaited Messiah, the object of Israel's hope and expectation. He has shown Jesus being addressed as "Son of David" three times: twice by men who were blind, and once by a Canaanite woman, a Gentile. He showed the confusion of the crowds when Jesus asked his disciples, "Who do people say that the Son of Man is?" and they answered, "Some say John the Baptist, but others Elijah, and still others Jeremiah or one of the prophets." Finally he shows Jesus being acclaimed as "Son of David" by the crowd and by little children as he enters Jerusalem in apparent triumph. And when Jesus is challenged by the chief priests and Pharisees for accepting the title, he refuses to disclaim it. But Jesus knows his people have no idea what the title really means or how the fulfillment of God's promises is going to come about. It is still a mystery.

That is why, in a final confrontation with the Pharisees, he asks them as a body, "What do you think of the Messiah? Whose son is he?"

When they answer, "The son of David," he shows them that they don't have enough understanding of Scripture to even begin to explain who he is. He is making his point very clearly: he is the "Son of David" in a way that is beyond their understanding. Anyone who accepts him as Son of David is going to have to be open to mystery. It is the mystery of his own identity and of the kingdom he is going to establish. That is the message behind his question to the Pharisees.

How can we, with the benefit of hindsight, answer Jesus' question? What does it mean that David should call his son "my lord"?

We know that Jesus did claim to be the Messiah, and all throughout his Gospel Matthew has presented him as the promised "Son of David." So Jesus is in fact speaking of himself when he asks why David calls the Messiah "my lord."

Who, then, is Jesus, that King David should address him as

"my lord, the king"?

We know that Jesus rejected the common assumption that the Messiah was to be a king as his people understood kingship on this earth. But in this text he accepts the term *adoni*, which was used in addressing kings. If, then, Jesus accepted this title from his father David while insisting he was not the kind of king that David was, what kind of kingship did he have? And where did it come from? He didn't just inherit it by being born as the son of David, because it wasn't David's kind of kingship. Then from whom did he receive it? And when did his kingship begin? Does "Son of David" just mean a biological descendant of David? Should we understand the Messiah to be a man like any other except for the fact of being chosen by God to fulfill the destiny of saving Israel? Or is there more to Jesus' reality than the merely human? Is there something about his origin, his being, his life, which transcends the ordinary limits of life on this earth? And is his kingship, therefore, something more than just a political reality? In the "kingdom" he came to establish is there something more than the benefits good government can provide?

Jesus is not just posing a question here which the Pharisees can't answer. He is posing a question which reminds us that we in fact do have the answer: Jesus is not just David's son by human genealogy; he is also the only Son of the Father by eternal generation. His existence did not begin with his birth on earth, and it did not end with his death. Nor did his kingship begin with his birth and end with his death. His kingship is not circumscribed by time. When God says, therefore, "Sit at my right hand, till I make your enemies your footstool," this does not have to take place within the span of the years Jesus lived and worked before he was put to death. The crucifixion, which seemed to cut short Jesus' ministry and dash all hopes in him as the Messiah who would "liberate Israel (see Luke 24:13-35) did not, in fact, forestall his reign on earth. By rising from the dead, Jesus became able to continue working on earth for the establishment of his kingdom until the end of time. He rose to continue his mission in us his risen body. Through us he will establish his reign. Jesus is the fulfillment of God's promises, and the promises are still being fulfilled.

"Awaiting the blessed hope and coming..."

In the Communion Rite of the Eucharistic celebration we describe the Church as a people who "wait in joyful hope for the coming of our Savior, Jesus Christ." This is not a precisely accurate translation of the official Latin text, which describes the Church as *expectantes beatam spem et adventum Salvatoris nostri Jesu Christi* — "awaiting the blessed hope and coming of our Savior, Jesus Christ." According to the Latin text, what we are looking forward to (*expectantes*) is the realization of the "blessed hope" we have in what the "coming of our Savior" is actually going to be. And what is this "blessed hope"?

It is the manifestation of Christ in his glory, the Jesus who is yet to come. This is not just the return to earth of the historical Jesus who was born of Mary, as if Jesus were going to come down from the sky in the body he received from his mother and land somewhere on this planet. A simple attempt to visualize the scene establishes that. Where would he land? Who would see him? Where would he go from there? Besides, Jesus tells us explicitly that if someone reports he has returned and can be seen in some particular place, "Do not believe it. For as the lightning comes from the east and flashes as far as the west, so will be the coming of the Son of Man" (Mt. 24:26-27). When Jesus appears in his glory, it will be an instant manifestation to everyone, and the body we see will be the whole body of Christ, Jesus head and members, visible, glorified and perfect.

His glory will be the glory of "the church, which is his

body, the fullness of him who fills all in all" (Ephesians 1:22-23). The Christ who comes in glory will be Christ brought to "full stature" in all the members of his body. It will be Christ appearing in the beauty and glory of every diverse member of the human race who has entered into the fullness of redemption, totally freed and purified from all sin, totally surrendered to the Spirit in mind and will and heart. In those who are members of his body in unreserved, unrestricted conformity to their head the beauty of God will appear as human and embodied in every conceivable realization of human nature brought to perfection in grace. Like the one light of the sun shining through the multiple shapes and colors of a stained glass window, the beauty of Jesus will shine through those who have lived his life on earth as men and women, old and young, healthy and sick, geniuses and retarded, wounded and innocent. And the beauty of all will be perfect. It will be the beauty of God shining through their humanity; the beauty of their human natures giving particular shape and color to the divine beauty of Christ.

This is what we mean when we say his glory will be the glory of "the church, which is his body, the fullness of him who fills all in all." It is to bring this about that God the Son took flesh to live, die and continue to live in us, his body. It is for this that he joined us to himself, espoused us to himself, became "one flesh" with us. And until he comes again, the work of Christ on earth is to form his bride to perfect union with himself, to "make her holy by cleansing her with the washing of water by the word, so as to present the church to himself in splendor, without a spot or wrinkle or anything of the kind — yes, so that she may be holy and without blemish" (Eph. 5:25-27).

This is the ministry of Christ in the Church. "He who descended" in the Incarnation, being born of a human woman, ascended into heaven again "so that he might fill all things" through the growth and ministry of the Church. He ascended so that he might send the Spirit into the Church, his "first gift to those who believe," and through the gifts of the Spirit bring the whole human race to perfection as his body.

> The gifts he gave were that some would be apostles, some prophets, some evangelists, some pastors and teachers, to equip the saints for the work of ministry, for building up the body of Christ, until all of us come to the unity of the faith and of the knowledge of the Son of God, to maturity, to the measure of the full stature of Christ" (Eph. 4:11-13).

This is "the blessed hope and coming of our Savior, Jesus Christ" for which the Church is waiting. And while she waits she is working as a *faithful steward* of the kingship of Christ to bring it about. St. Paul spoke to and for all of us when he addressed the Galatians as "my little children, for whom I am again in the pain of childbirth until Christ is formed in you" (Galatians 4:19). What motivates and guides our ministry is the "blessed hope" for the world for which Jesus prayed at the Last Supper:

> I ask not only on behalf of these, but also on behalf of those who will believe in me through their word, that they may all be one. As you, Father, are in me and I am in you, may they also be in us, so that the world may believe that you have sent me. The glory that you have given me I have given them, so that they may be one, as we are one, I in them and you in me, that they may become completely one, so that the world may know that you have sent me and have loved them even as you have loved me.
>
> Father, I desire that those also, whom you have given me, may be with me where I am, to see my glory, which you have given me because you loved me before the foundation of the world (John 17:20-24).

Every time the Church meets to celebrate the Lord's Supper she prays again for this with "joyful hope," consciously looking forward to "the blessed hope and coming of our Savior, Jesus Christ."

The "once and future king"

In his dialogue with the Pharisees Jesus leaves his identity
an open question. But it is not just an unanswered question;
it is a question opened in a particular direction which points
us toward the answer. Jesus won't "close the books" on the
question of his identity, because the final revelation of who
he is and what he came to do has not been given yet. The
core of it will be given in his death on the cross and resurrection from the tomb. But we will not really know him as
he is until he comes again in glory. Until then Jesus calls on
his followers to wait, persevering in believing what we already know, recognizing him in those who are his body on
earth today, and keeping our minds open to what is yet to
be revealed.

We know Jesus and we do not know him. We know him,
and we have seen him, as Messiah and "Suffering Servant."
We know him, but we have not seen him, as Messiah and
Lord.

We have "seen" Jesus in his weakness and defeat upon the
cross, because that event, although we learned of it through
witnesses who reported it to us, is something our human
minds and senses can absorb. It was an historical event as
clear and stark as any other human being's death. We know
what it is for a human body to be tortured to death and die.
We have seen Jesus as "Suffering Servant."

We have both "seen" and not "seen" Jesus in the mysterious glory of his resurrection. That event was also reported
to us reliably by witnesses. But it escapes our understanding. The reality of the redemption accomplished by Jesus'
death and resurrection remains a mystery to be celebrated
in liturgy and pondered in our hearts until the end of time.
We know there was more to the physical reality of Jesus'
resurrection than just the fact that Jesus' body came alive
again. There was more to his risen body than even those
who saw him with their eyes and touched him with their
hands were able to perceive. That is why Jesus the risen

Lord has not been "seen" in the same way Jesus the "Suffering Servant" was seen defeated on the cross. Jesus was speaking about his resurrection (not about his death) when he said, "Blessed are they who have not seen, but have believed." And he meant this for us all. He even meant it for Thomas, who believed after he saw the risen Jesus with his eyes (see John 20:29). There is more to the risen Jesus than is visible to the eye; more to his risen body than is visible to the senses. Day after day, year after year, century after century, we grow in understanding of the resurrection as we see the risen Jesus living and acting and revealing himself in his Body, the Church.

And we do see him. We all see the risen Jesus. We see him every day in those who are the members of his Body on earth. And yet we do not see him. Jesus told his apostles that they had already "seen" the Father: "Whoever has seen me has seen the Father. How can you say, 'Show us the Father'? Do you not believe that I am in the Father and the Father is in me?" (see John 14:7-10). In a parallel way, every one of us has "seen" the risen Jesus in his Body on earth. And we have not seen him.

Even more obviously we have not seen Jesus in his glory: in the glory which he had with the Father before the world began; in the glory the disciples saw in preview when he was transfigured on the mountain top; in the glory he claimed before the Sanhedrin from the very depths of his abandonment and defeat when he promised they would see "the Son of Man seated at the right hand of the Power" and "coming on the clouds of heaven." We know that Jesus is the promised "Son of David." But we will not fully know him as Son of David or comprehend "whose Son he is" until the "Son of Man comes in his glory, and all the angels with him," and he "sits upon his glorious throne" to judge the nations in triumph. (See John 17:5; Mt. 25:31; 26:64).

In the meantime, "Blessed are they who have not seen, but have believed." In the meantime, we know Jesus as "Son of

David," as Messiah and Lord, not just as the realities of this earth are known, by the natural light of senses and intellect, but as the deep things of God are known: by the "dark light of faith," which is the clearest, most certain light of all.

We know Jesus as "Son of David" through what we have "seen with our eyes, and heard with our ears, and touched with our hands of the word of life" by reading the Scriptures, the recorded memory of history and faith. We know him as the Son of David who was truly born in the flesh of Mary the virgin, born in time to live in time and die in time. We know him as the Jesus who was.

But Matthew, the theme of whose Gospel is that Jesus is the promised "Son of David," alerts us in this chapter to the truth that he is much more than "Son of David" as the Jews understood that term. He is also "Lord," and in his reality as Lord his glory is something "eye has not seen, and ear has not heard"; a glory which "God has prepared for those who love him," and which it "has not entered the human heart" to imagine (see 1 Corinthians 2:9). We know Jesus through faith and expectation as the "Son of David" who came, who is still with us, and who is to come.

In every celebration of the Eucharist we proclaim during the reading of the Gospels the historical fact of the Jesus who was; who breathed the air and ate the food of our earth; who walked the roads of Israel, touring towns and villages, speaking and touching, proclaiming the good news of the Kingdom, teaching in the synagogues and healing every variety of sickness and disease (see Mt. 4:23; 9:35).

And in every liturgy we also proclaim the Jesus who is: we celebrate his active presence on earth today: Jesus speaking now through his words proclaimed in Scripture; Jesus offering himself now in the bread and wine which have become his body and blood; Jesus "lifted up" now as the Lamb of God who takes away the sins of the world; Jesus giving himself to us now in Communion as the Bread of Life; Jesus sending us now to go out as his real body and bring his peace to the world; Jesus living and revealing himself now in all the members of his body on earth.

And finally, in every liturgy we proclaim the Jesus who is to come; the Jesus who is yet to be revealed. In every liturgy we declare that we are *waiting* "in joyful hope for the coming of our Savior, Jesus Christ"— until he comes.

Jesus was, he is, and he will be, the "once and future king": *rex olim, rexque futurus*, "Jesus Christ, "yesterday, today and the same forever." And so in every Eucharist the Church proclaims and will proclaim until the end of time, "Christ has died, Christ is risen, Christ will come again!" And in every action and effort to establish on earth the reign of Christ the King the Church continues, in faith and fidelity, to give "glory to the Father, and to the Son, and to the Holy Spirit, as it was in the beginning, is now, and will be forever." Amen.

CHAPTER ELEVEN:
THE ONCE AND FUTURE KING
"Revelation of Identity" — Matthew 22:41-46

Summary

Throughout his Gospel, Matthew has presented Jesus as the promised "Son of David." But Jesus has never explicitly given himself the title. After he is challenged, however, for not disclaiming the title when the crowd and little children give it to him as he enters Jerusalem, Jesus himself raises the question of his identity. He asks the Pharisees: "What is your opinion about the Messiah? Whose son is he?"

When they answer, "The son of David," he asks them another question, the purpose of which is just to show that they don't have enough understanding of Scripture to explain what the title "Son of David" means or whether or not Jesus should claim it.

Jesus' purpose here is to make the point that he is the Messiah in a way that is beyond people's understanding. Anyone who accepts Jesus as "Son of David" is going to have to be open to mystery: the mystery of his own identity and of the kingdom he is going to establish.

By not direct answering the question of his identity, Jesus is in reality answering another question which was a major stumbling-block to the early Church — and still is to us today: "How can Jesus have been the Messiah, since God let him be defeated and killed?"

By refusing to answer any questions about his identity which are raised because of the *power* he is exercising or the *acclaim* he is receiving, Jesus is answering another question which was a major stumbling-block to the early Church — and still is to us today: "How can Jesus have been the Messiah, since God let him be defeated and killed? How can the true Messiah (or the true Church) be so weak and so unrecognized?"

Jesus is a Messiah who is not going to reign on earth with power in the manner of earthly kings. The reign of God has begun, but it will triumph very slowly through the invisible power of God working in the only-too-visible powerlessness of human instruments. He comes to us as a king "humble, and mounted on a donkey." If his followers want to know him as he really is they will have to *wait*, persevering in faith and fidelity, believing and working and enduring in spite of all appearances until he comes again.

Jesus is winning. But his victory will not be made evident until the end of time. So enduring faith in Jesus is impossible without steadfast hope. To keep expressing faith and hope through persevering efforts to establish the reign of God on earth is enduring love.

Jesus won't "close the books" on the question of his identity, because the final revelation of who he is and what he came to do has not been given yet.

From Scripture and historical testimony we know Jesus as *the Jesus who was* —the Son of David who was truly born in the flesh of Mary the virgin, born in time to live in time and die in time.

We also know him as *the Jesus who is*. In every liturgy we celebrate his active presence on earth today: Jesus speaking to us now through his words proclaimed in Scripture; Jesus offering himself now in the Mass; Jesus giving himself to us now in Communion and sending us out as his real body to bring his peace to the world; Jesus living and revealing himself now in all the members of his body on earth.

And in every liturgy we proclaim *the Jesus who is to come*; the Jesus who is yet to be revealed. We declare that we are *waiting* "in joyful hope for the coming of our Savior, Jesus Christ." We will not really know him as he is until he comes again in glory.

Christ brought to "full stature" in all the members of his body, appearing in the beauty and glory of every diverse member of the human race who has entered into the fullness of redemption, this is "the blessed hope and coming of our Savior, Jesus Christ" for which the Church is waiting. Jesus calls on his followers to work and to wait, as faithful stewards of his kingship, to bring it about.

Have you understood?

In what ways was Jesus the same as the Messiah his people expected? In what ways was he different?

Specifically, how was Jesus as "Son of David" greater than the Son of David the people expected? What was the mystery of his being?

What do we know about the Jesus who was, the historical Jesus born of Mary? How do we know him?

What do we know of the Jesus who is: the Jesus who has a human presence on earth today? How do we know him?

What do we know of the Jesus who is to come? How do we know it? What should this knowledge motivate us to do?

What is the challenge of this chapter? To our faith? To our hope? To our love?

Making it your own

What are the key thoughts in this chapter? (Jot them down and give the page number where each is found).

What questions do I have about this chapter? (Bring them up in discussion or ask someone who should know the answers).

What struck me the most in this chapter? After reading this chapter, what do I understand better than I did before? What do I appreciate more?

What do I think is the point of the whole chapter? What response does Matthew want to evoke from those who read or hear this part of his Gospel?

What can I use as a visible reminder (a symbol) to keep me aware of the challenge of this chapter? Where will I put it?

Questions for prayer

What am I doing to know more about the Jesus who was? How can I get to know him better?

What can I do to grow in awareness of the Jesus who is interacting with me now through his words and sacraments, through his Spirit in others and in my heart?

How consciously am I "awaiting the blessed hope and coming of our Savior, Jesus Christ?" What do these words mean to me? How do they motivate me?

How can I apply to my life what I have come to see by reflecting on this chapter? What concrete action do I choose to perform to express my belief in what I have seen?

FOOTNOTES

¹ These themes are developed in sequence in the other books in this series: *Why Jesus?* (on Matthew, chapters 1-2 and 8-9); *A Change Within*, (previously *Blessed Are They*: on Matthew, chapters 3-4 and 5:1-12); *Make Me a Sabbath of Your Heart* (on the rest of the Sermon on the Mount, Matthew 5-7); *Saving Presence* (on Matthew, chapters 10-12); *No Power but Love* (on Matthew, chapters 16-17). The last theme is developed in this present book, *Until He Comes* (on Matthew, chapters 21-22). These books are all available through His Way Communications, located at the Monastery of St. Clare, 1310 Dellwood Ave., Memphis TN 38127 (901 357-6662; *www.hisway.com*).